REBOOTING INEQUALITY

CRITICAL CULTURAL COMMUNICATION

General Editors: Jonathan Gray, Aswin Punathambekar, Adrienne Shaw
Founding Editors: Sarah Banet-Weiser and Kent A. Ono

Dangerous Curves: Latina Bodies in the Media
Isabel Molina-Guzmán

The Net Effect: Romanticism, Capitalism, and the Internet
Thomas Streeter

Our Biometric Future: Facial Recognition Technology and the Culture of Surveillance
Kelly A. Gates

Critical Rhetorics of Race
Edited by Michael G. Lacy and Kent A. Ono

Circuits of Visibility: Gender and Transnational Media Cultures
Edited by Radha S. Hegde

Commodity Activism: Cultural Resistance in Neoliberal Times
Edited by Roopali Mukherjee and Sarah Banet-Weiser

Arabs and Muslims in the Media: Race and Representation after 9/11
Evelyn Alsultany

Visualizing Atrocity: Arendt, Evil, and the Optics of Thoughtlessness
Valerie Hartouni

Authentic™: The Politics of Ambivalence in a Brand Culture
Sarah Banet-Weiser

The Makeover: Reality Television and Reflexive Audiences
Katherine Sender

Love and Money: Queers, Class, and Cultural Production
Lisa Henderson

Cached: Decoding the Internet in Global Popular Culture
Stephanie Ricker Schulte

Black Television Travels: African American Media around the Globe
Timothy Havens

Citizenship Excess: Latino/as, Media, and the Nation
Hector Amaya

Feeling Mediated: A History of Media Technology and Emotion in America
Brenton J. Malin

The Post-Racial Mystique: Media and Race in the Twenty-First Century
Catherine R. Squires

Making Media Work: Cultures of Management in the Entertainment Industries
Edited by Derek Johnson, Derek Kompare, and Avi Santo

Sounds of Belonging: U.S. Spanish-language Radio and Public Advocacy
Dolores Inés Casillas

Technomobility in China: Young Migrant Women and Mobile Phones
Cara Wallis

Orienting Hollywood: A Century of Film Culture between Los Angeles and Bombay
Nitin Govil

Asian American Media Activism: Fighting for Cultural Citizenship
Lori Kido Lopez

Struggling For Ordinary: Media and Transgender Belonging in Everyday Life
Andre Cavalcante

Homegrown: Identity and Difference in the American War on Terror
Piotr M. Szpunar

Dot-Com Design: The Rise of a Usable, Social, Commercial Web
Megan Sapnar Ankerson

Postracial Resistance: Black Women, Media, and the Uses of Strategic Ambiguity
Ralina L. Joseph

Netflix Nations: The Geography of Digital Distribution
Ramon Lobato

Celebrity: A History of Fame
Susan J. Douglas and Andrea McDonnell

Fake Geek Girls: Fandom, Gender, and the Convergence Culture Industry
Suzanne Scott

Locked Out: Regional Restrictions in Digital Entertainment Culture
Evan Elkins

Beyond Hashtags: Racial Politics and Black Digital Networks
Sarah Florini

The Digital City: Media and the Social Production of Place
Germaine R. Halegoua

Distributed Blackness: African American Cybercultures
André Brock, Jr.

Wife, Inc.: The Business of Marriage in the Twenty-First Century
Suzanne Leonard

Race and Media: Critical Approaches
Edited by Lori Kido Lopez

Border Optics: Surveillance Cultures on the US-Mexico Border
Camilla Fojas

Dislike-Minded: Media, Audiences, and the Dynamics of Taste
Jonathan Gray

Digital Media Distribution: Portals, Platforms, Pipelines
Edited by Paul McDonald, Courtney Brannon Donoghue and Tim Havens

Digital Black Feminism
Catherine Knight Steele

The Identity Trade: Selling Privacy and Reputation Online
Nora A. Draper

Latino TV: A History
Mary Beltrán

The Digital Border: Migration, Technology, Power
Lilie Chouliaraki and Myria Georgiou

Digital Unsettling: Decoloniality and Dispossession in the Age of Social Media
Sahana Udupa and Ethiraj Gabriel Dattatreyan

Streaming Video: Storytelling Across Borders
Amanda D. Lotz and Ramon Lobato

Chinese Creator Economies: Labor and Bilateral Creative Workers
Jian Lin

Fandom Is Ugly: Affective Attachments and Networked Harassment in Participatory Culture
Mel Stanfill

Projecting Desire: Media Architectures and Moviegoing in Urban India
Tupur Chatterjee

After Mass Media: Storytelling for Microaudiences in the Twenty-First Century
Amanda D. Lotz

Social Media and Ordinary Life: Affect, Ethics, and Aspiration in Contemporary China
Cara Wallis

Targeted: Corporations and the Police Surveillance Economy
Kelly A. Gates

Rebooting Inequality: Critical Takes on Film and Television Remakes
Edited by Isabel Molina-Guzmán and Angharad N. Valdivia

Rebooting Inequality

Critical Takes on Film and Television Remakes

Edited by
Isabel Molina-Guzmán *and* Angharad N. Valdivia

New York University Press
New York

NEW YORK UNIVERSITY PRESS
New York
www.nyupress.org

Library of Congress Cataloging-in-Publication Data
Names: Molina-Guzmán, Isabel editor | Valdivia, Angharad N. editor
Title: Rebooting inequality : critical takes on film and television remakes / edited by Isabel Molina-Guzmán and Angharad N. Valdivia.
Description: New York : New York University Press, 2026. |
Series: Critical cultural communication | Includes bibliographical references and index.
Identifiers: LCCN 2025028427 (print) | LCCN 2025028428 (ebook) |
ISBN 9781479821891 hardback | ISBN 9781479821914 paperback |
ISBN 9781479821921 ebook other | ISBN 9781479821938 ebook
Subjects: LCSH: Film remakes—United States | Television remakes—United States |
Minorities in motion pictures | Minorities on television | Nostalgia in motion pictures |
Nostalgia on television | LCGFT: Film criticism | Television criticism and reviews | Essays
Classification: LCC PN1995.9.R45 R38 2026 (print) | LCC PN1995.9.R45 (ebook) |
DDC 791.436—dc23/eng/20250616
LC record available at https://lccn.loc.gov/2025028427
LC ebook record available at https://lccn.loc.gov/2025028428

This book is printed on acid-free paper, and its binding materials are chosen for strength and durability. We strive to use environmentally responsible suppliers and materials to the greatest extent possible in publishing our books.

The manufacturer's authorized representative in the EU for product safety is Mare Nostrum Group B.V., Mauritskade 21D, 1091 GC Amsterdam, The Netherlands.
Email: gpsr@mare-nostrum.co.uk.

Manufactured in the United States of America

10 9 8 7 6 5 4 3 2 1

Also available as an ebook

To the authors in this collection and their insightful analyses, my favorite binge buddy Ian T. Sprandel, and my much-loved gen alpha media critic Luciano H. Molina-Sprandel.

—Isabel Molina-Guzmán

To the contributors in this volume, who patiently waited for this project to come together; to ICR nation for the intellectual inspiration; and to my family,
whose love undergirds everything.

—Angharad N. Valdivia

CONTENTS

Introduction

The Nostalgic Rebooting of Ethnicity, Gender, Race, and Sexuality

ISABEL MOLINA-GUZMÁN AND ANGHARAD N. VALDIVIA

> Viewers have earned the right to be picky—and even disdainful—when it comes to the steady excess of TV reboots, resurrections and revivals. Not only do such shows feed a troubling nostalgia addiction in our popular culture, they also prevent progress and true innovation. For every reboot that crowds the schedule, an original idea is lost at sea.
> —Hank Stuever, "A New 'Party of Five' Capably Tells the Story of a Family Facing the Immigration Crackdown," *Washington Post*

The shadows of a global pandemic, the most consequential elections in the history of the United States, the global (re)emergence of nationalist political parties across the world, the mainstreaming of the #BlackLives-Matter (BLM) movement against racialized state-sanctioned violence, and the #MeToo movement against gender-based violence might raise questions about the importance of yet another collection on entertainment television and film. However, as Netflix executives signaled to their subscribers with their start-up banner during the 2020 pandemic #BLM protests, "Representation Matters." We and the authors of this collection on media reboots, revivals, and remakes agree.

Representation matters because the news we watch influences how we think about crime, urban cities, and Black, Latino, and Muslim communities.[1] It matters because who tells our cultural stories, how we tell those stories, and what those stories tell shape who we give value to and how we give meaning to marginalized lives.[2] It matters because film and television productions are informed by an ideology of neoliberal multiculturalism that celebrates diversity while maintaining the broader unequal economic structures of racism, sexism, and heteronormativity in place.[3] It matters because, at a basic material level, employment in the entertainment industries is highly segregated, impinging on the livelihood of creators of color, from the producers of intellectual property[4] to the actors and behind-the-scenes workers. Finally, it matters because the urgency for change advocated globally by women and marginalized Black and Brown communities to see the complexity of their lives politically and culturally represented has deepened while a sense of white resentment and disenfranchisement grounded in nostalgia becomes entrenched. This book engages representational analysis to study film and television reboots by foregrounding issues of production and the experiences of audiences within the contemporary social, political, and cultural context.

A Media and Communication Studies Framework

Our collection of essays about contemporary reboots, revivals, and remakes as mediated cultural artifacts creates a space for studying white nostalgia and ethnic, racial, gender, and sexual inequality in representations, productions, and audience responses, what we term as "rebooting inequality." *Rebooting Inequality* brings into conversation critical ethnic studies scholars and critical communication scholars with queer-of-color and Black and Latina feminist theories. Together the collection of essays creates a framework for studying the production of inequality in rebooted film and television and its relationship to the contemporary US politics of white heteronormative nostalgia, as well as ethnic, racial, gender, and sexual resentment and inequality. While the essays focus on rebooted media texts, the framework is applicable across a range of mediated texts and forms of communication. In this introduction, we lay out three key conceptual elements. First, we establish how the political economies of reboots or recycled texts in film and television allow for the reproduction of inequality. Second, we discuss the industry demographics and history of gender, ethnicity, and race in the productions of film and television. Doing so links the political economies of recycled texts to the continuation of production and representational inequalities in the contemporary moment. Finally, we bring in the concepts of *racial capitalism* and *white nostalgia* to explore the relationships between the inequalities in rebooted media productions and ongoing national and global conservative cultural politics.

A Note on Terminology

We use *reboot* as a simplified umbrella term housing three genres of film and television recycling: reboots, remakes, and revivals. Film and television reboots are defined by a loose connection to a previous fictional storyline but with different actors, characters, and themes (*Charmed*, *Ghostbusters*, *Party of Five*, *One Day at a Time*). Film and television remakes are characterized by an updated retelling of the original story that may include different actors and characters or narrative themes (*Aladdin*, *Charlie's Angels*, *Jurassic Park*, *She-Ra*). Finally, revivals of television shows feature an update of a fictional storyline with the same actors playing the same characters and often produced and/or written by the same creators (*And Just Like That . . .* , *Gilmore Girls*, *Roseanne*, *Will and Grace*). From 2015 to 2024, there have been more than fifty US film and television reboots, and counting. The collection focuses on some of the most relevant reboots produced in the continuing wake of Trumpism.

Ethnic, Racial, Sexual, and Gender Terminology

Because we recognize that identity labels are highly personal and highly politicized, each author uses the labels that most make sense to their intellectual and personal politics. Thus, if an author prefers to use the term *African American* and another author prefers to use the adjective *Black*, we the editors accommodate them. Similarly, if an author prefers to use the terms *Latine*, *Latinx*, or *Latina/o*, we also accommodate them. However, to limit confusion and help readers focus on the important observations of the essays, we will provide a simplified primer regarding identity terms.

Within the United States, the adjectival use of *African American* or *Black* modifying a noun such as *men* or *audiences* arose in response to the use of terms such as *Negroes* or *Colored people* increasingly being viewed as pejorative during the 1970s and now largely passing out of everyday social and political use. According to a 2024 Pew Research Center report, the number of US residents who identify as Black has grown by 32 percent since 2000 to 47.9 million, or 14.4 percent of the population.[5] This population is defined by its growing ethnic diversity due to immigration flows from Africa and the Caribbean, and thus includes people who identify as Black only and other ethnic groups such Haitians, Ethiopians, Latinos, or Asians who also identify as Black. Although the majority who identify as Black speak only English at home, 11 percent speak Spanish, French, Haitian, Amharic, or other African languages. Because of changing identity politics and growing ethnic diversity within the community, the use of *Black*, *African American*, or specific ethnic identities such as Haitian may be interchangeable.

Similarly, the use of ethnic umbrella terms *Latina*, *Latino*, *Latina/o*, *Latinx*, and *Latine* have arisen as grassroot responses to various conditions, such as the US government–imposed term *Hispanic*, or what some grassroots communities perceive as sexist or gender-binary terms, such as *Latina*, *Latino*, or *Latina/o*. According to a 2020 Pew Research Center report, 23% of the Latina/o population had heard of the term *Latinx* but less than 3% used it to identify.[6] *Latine* is an even newer identity term and has yet to be surveyed. Because the terms *Latine* and *Latinx* have not gained common usage except in academic and journalistic writing, we use the term *Latina/o* in the introduction. Continuing their demographic increase, the Latina/Latino population grew at a rate of 12 percent in 2023, and they maintain their status as the largest US ethnic and racial minority group, at 63.7 million or 19 percent of the US population.[7] For geopolitical reasons, the dominant Latina/o ethnicity is Mexican, followed by Puerto Rican and Cuban, with populations from Colombia, Venezuela, El Salvador, and others quickly gaining ground. As a result, *Latine* has grown in academic popularity, as a term that foregrounds the diverse Latin American origins of US communities. The terms *Latine* and *Latinx* position themselves as more inclusive by recognizing ethnic, sexual, and gender diversity and disrupting the gender-norming terms *Latina* and *Latino*. Similar to critiques of *Latina/Latino*, *Latine* and *Latinx* are also called out for their erasure of indigeneity and race and the reduction of gender or sexual differences to an *x* or *e*. Within the past ten years, the use of the terms *Afro* and *Black* has gained visibility among communities who are of mixed racial identity or African ancestry. From 2010 to 2020 the share of the Latina/o population identifying as Black has increased from 2 percent to 11 percent.

Finally, the terms *queer*, *gay*, and *LGBTQI+* (lesbian, gay, bisexual, transgender/transsexual, questioning, intersex, + additional non-heteronormative and non-gender-normative identities) also arose as grassroot community responses during the 1970s and 1980s to what became perceived as the increasingly pejorative use of *queer* and *homosexual*. The term *queer* in particular gained popularity as a celebratory and politically oppositional identity that positioned itself as against the sex-negative, heteronormative, conservative Christian politics of the 1980s. In the context of social and political invisibility and increasing homophobia during the AIDS crisis that disproportionately impacted gay men in the community, some communities also chose to identify politically as queer and thus as non-hetero- or homo-normative. It was also during this time that *LGBT* arose as a non-pejorative less politicized term to self-identify as or describe sexual minorities. Today the political term *queer* and umbrella term *LGBTQI+* are often used by allies of and people who define themselves as outside of normative or conventional gender, sexual, and sexual identities.

The Political Economy of Reboots

From reboots to revivals, film and television texts are meant to be recycled, always "meant to return from the dead."[8] Indeed, media reboots are part of a long-standing industry practice that offers executives and producers an economic advantage. Media reboots are an effective and necessary economic practice to extend the life and profit of copyrighted intellectual property.[9] Extending the life of copyrighted film and television content maximizes the profits of texts, many of which are successful because they reinforce culturally conservative representations.[10] This media strategy dates back at least to the 1900s and the birth of US film and radio, when black voices and cultural forms in live performances were recycled as forms of entertainment for white audiences. In this sense, the contemporary reboots, revivals, and remakes studied in this collection are a "new" take on an old media commercial and economic strategy.

Drawing on work by political economist of communication Eileen Meehan,[11] the perpetual recirculation of film and television franchises is driven by the capitalist practice of synergy. Economic synergy motivates transnational media corporations to acquire original content, produce original content, and distribute that content across its platforms and networks. According to *Forbes*, the Comcast Corporation, Walt Disney Company, Charter Communications, Warner Brothers, and Fox Corporation globally own approximately 90 percent of all media companies.[12] Comcast, the largest transnational media conglomerate, owns multiple international production and distribution networks, including NBC Universal Media Group, NBC, NBC News, CNBC, NBC Sports, Telemundo, Bravo, USA Network, and Peacock, and many others. By owning the production, the distribution, and the content, these companies maximize profits by recycling content and disseminating it through their vast international networks.

Meehan provides five common synergistic practices used by major media conglomerates to maximize ownership of production, content, and distribution networks: content recirculation, content repackaging, content re-versioning, content recycling, and deployment of intellectual property through its various networks and platforms.[13] In Diana Leon-Boys's research about Disney's contemporary efforts to leverage original Latinx content across its platforms, she adds repromotion to the typology to account for the synergistic labor that ethnic actors and their characters perform across communication platforms in relation to content such as *Elena of Avalor* and *Coco*.[14] Walt Disney presents one of the most lucrative case studies of synergy. The company bought both Marvel Comics and Marvel Studios in 2009 for US$4 billion, making it one of the most astute and profitable acquisitions. Doing so enabled executives to reboot Marvel stories and characters across its film, television, and general marketing licensing agreements; its live-entertainment platforms (parks, cruises, etc.); and their film, television, and streaming studios, thereby maximizing profits.

Transnational reboots follow complicated licensing paths along with an incentive to bypass intellectual property agreements, which potentially result in legal skirmishes. International media studies scholar Michelle Hilmes documents the global recirculation of original film or television programs through four formats: imported texts (e.g., telenovelas on Netflix), genres adapted to a specific culture (e.g., Hollywood musicals and Bollywood), texts that are rebooted to another format (e.g., *Percy Jackson* novels to films to streaming television), and the global adaptation of reality show formulas (e.g., the global *Survivor* franchise).[15] Other scholars, such as Jeremy Tunstall, nuance the schema for the exportation and global recirculation of film and television programs by adding the ability of original texts to be sold as is, through linguistic translation (subtitling or dubbing), re-versioning by adding culturally specific elements or casting local talent, or acquiring foreign financing to completely redo a version of the original.[16]

The production of a cultural property beyond its country of origin shifts financial control and regulation from the original owner and location to a company in another country seeking to produce local programming versions that follow proprietary formula guidelines, or a company that sells script for local production. By optioning the foreign script or formula, such as that of reality television shows, as an intellectual property (IP), the producer in another country may copy the formula or genre without payment, which potentially leads to IP lawsuits.[17] The impetus for rebooting mediated texts to enhance the value of the original's intellectual property is a financially and creatively risk-averse maneuver, and thus is a pervasive strategy used by media companies. Accordingly, transnational media executives perpetually seek to develop innovative and heterogeneous ways to reuse their original content, which may have been derived from a previous version of that story or form. The hugely successful *High School Musical* was rebooted through local Latin American, Indian, and Japanese versions, in addition to all the US versions of the franchise.

The closer the remake to the original media text, the more IP control and increased profit-making the owner of the original property has. To return to Walt Disney, the company's vast archive of characters, films, and television programs increases its ability to leverage IP franchise acquisitions to infinitely expand content through the art of reimagining old and new materials through remakes, revivals, and reboots on its streaming platform. Moreover, technological advances such as CGI enable Disney to turn its hugely profitable archive of global animated hits into pseudo-live-action reboots, such as *Mulan* (2020), *Aladdin* (2019), and *The Lion King* (2019) (see also Zhui Ning Chang and Shyamala

Parthasarathy in this volume). Streaming services, with their seemingly endless on-demand programming, are in a perpetual quest for content, a quest that must inevitably draw on old media material to meet audience demands.

In relation to the capitalist imperatives of profit maximization and expansion under risk-averse conditions, this collection places recycled film and television texts as core to the financial model of the on-demand, post-network, and multi-platform media ecology. Many of the reboots discussed in this book were recycled through post-network and streaming platforms, such as HBO and Netflix. Writing about television revivals, Kathleen Loock suggests the "crowded contemporary media landscape" that includes a never-ending number of streaming platforms available on unlimited types of smart devices has created a third financial incentive—"the end of endings."[18] In other words, it makes economic sense and industry efficiency to extend the life of a proven cultural property rather than definitively end its narrative life altogether and invest in the more expensive creation of an entirely original media property. It is difficult to ignore the need for rebooted texts rapidly increased in 2020 with the COVID-19 pandemic and the resulting increased dependence by global audiences on streaming subscription services for entertainment. Convergence studies scholar Henry Jenkins reminds us that transmedia convergence, defined as the process of retelling a narrative across different media platforms (music, film, TV, social media, etc.), has pervaded cultural properties since before the advent of mass communication.[19] Indeed, during the medieval period, the recirculation of King Arthur tales generated endless numbers and versions of paintings, sculptures, performances, and literary texts, extending into contemporary media productions.[20] Jane Austen's many novels, including *Emma* (1815), *Pride and Prejudice* (1813), and *Sense and Sensibility* (1811), and Lewis Carrol's *Alice in Wonderland* (1915) are other early examples of transmedia cultural productions that continue to be generative across platforms and generations of audiences.[21] Today's dynamic digital media ecology and the horizontal (integration of diverse networks and media platforms) and vertical monopolies (integration of the production and distribution of content) by the top transnational media conglomerates sets up the easy convergence of rebooted content for maximum profit.[22] Jenkins's concept of transmedia convergence in conjunction with Jonathan Gray's concept of paratext provide a compelling explanation of reboots as interrelated forms of content production that recirculate narratives and maximize synergies.[23] Paratexts are references within a media text that connect the text to other related content. Paratextual references extend and redraw boundaries across original texts, either through cross-promotion and marketing, through the intentional development of narratives, and/or within fan-produced versions such as fan fiction.[24]

We return to Disney for the most explicit example of synergy, transmedia convergence, paratext, and reboots. Fans of Marvel Studios movies know to stay after the credits because there is always a preview/promotion of the next Marvel film or television program in development. Within the Disney universe, paratextual references to Marvel comics and films appear in original Marvel live-action and animated television content (e.g., the streaming production of *The Falcon and the Winter Soldier*, 2021, which referenced previous Marvel movies and comics), and Marvel films often engage in paratextual references to the comics and television content (e.g., *Captain America: Brave New World*, 2025, featuring Black actor Mackie Wilson as Captain America, which references the comics, movies, and streaming series). The paratextual references encourage fans and audiences to become versed across multiple platforms to understand the circuitous nature of the Marvel Cinematic Universe (MCU).

Streaming and digital platforms have accelerated the use of transmedia convergence and paratexts. For instance, the executive producers of Hulu's Latina-themed original production *East Los High* (2013–2017) encouraged audience engagement by developing a website for the show that converged original program content, social media content, ancillary original content, and related social and political resources relevant to the storylines. Together synergy, convergence, and paratexts provide an economic explanation for the cross-promotion and multiple platform circulation, and hint at the range of strategies used to profit from creative production and the global circulation of intellectual property. As a result of these capitalist forces, reboots, remakes, and revivals pervade our cultural universe.

Inequality in Hollywood Industries

Historically, Hollywood media productions, including reboots, have existed within a capitalist system characterized by inequalities in production, distribution, and representation. Hollywood film, television historians, and industry experts document the long-standing power and privilege of predominantly white, heteronormative men (and incrementally in the last ten years white women) in front of and behind our screens despite decades of dramatic demographic shifts in the United States.[25] The privileging of white men in decision making, creative production, and media content is not new to television and film or the formal and informal institutions of Eurocentric societies. Going to back to the early twentieth century, the radio reboot of *The Amos 'n' Andy Show* allowed white producers to cast white voice actors to perform the voices of blackface minstrel characters, a sonic form of blackface. And when executives at CBS Corporation adapted the radio show into the new television medium (1951–1953), the original white producers maintained creative control, as was the norm in this medium transition. It was not until television as a visual medium that the original producers reluctantly welcomed African American actors into the stereotypical roles.[26] Eventually protests by the NAACP over the negative representation of African American people and shifting cultural norms around stereotypic racial representations resulted in the television show ending its syndicated recirculation in 2012.

Indeed, most rebooted TV programs and films are created by US transnational media conglomerates under the ownership and executive control of white men; created, predominantly written, produced, and directed by white heterosexual men; and with content featuring white middle-class-to-wealthy men characters as the protagonists.[27] In 2023 alone the following reboots and revivals with white lead actors were rumored in production, announced, or televised: *Night Court* revival (NBC), *The Office* reboot (Peacock), *Who's the Boss* revival (Amazon Freevee), and *Frasier* revival (Paramount+). All four of those rebooted shows are anchored by the same leading male actors as their original series, and *The Office* and *Frasier* reboots are produced by the original creators.

In short, reboots are a pathway for recycling, reviving or extending the careers of mostly white actors and white men producers.[28] It is thus not surprising that several of the contemporary reboots studied in this collection are produced by the original white men creators, feature the original white lead actors, and target its original "mainstream white" yet aged audience base. To use one of the reboots in this collection as an example (see Moran and del Río, and Valdivia), *One Day at a Time*'s original producer, Norman Lear, returned as executive producer in the flipped reboot—at the age of 96. At the time of his death in 2023 at 101, he was involved in rebooting two other shows: *Who's the Boss?* and *Mary Hartman*. In another example of inequality within Hollywood productions, Colombian actress Sofía Vergara was hailed for her representational success as a Colombian Latina co-star in the hit show *Modern Family* (2009–2020, ABC). Yet her undocumented immigrant, spitfire, younger stepmother character was written by established showrunners Christopher Lloyd and Steven Levitan, both white men, who wanted to make a show about their domestic lives in Los Angeles.[29] It wasn't until later in the series that the creators diversified their initial hiring of an all-white, all-heterosexual, all-men writers' room, most of whom had previously worked with Lloyd or Levitan or were referred to them by other colleagues. *Modern Family* exemplifies the industry's established racist and sexist practices where white men in power hire other white men to write about characters and cultures different from theirs. Industry studies of film and television document that decision making and creative control throughout the past ten years have improved but remain predominantly in the hands of white men, even as US ethnic and racial minorities and non-US consumers are the fastest-growing demographic and an economically important media audience.[30]

A casting director from a racial minority background termed these informal and exclusionary hiring practices simply as "the network." The casting director argued that the social network in Los Angeles where one lives, the neighbors one has, where one's kids go to school, and who one spends one's leisure time with overdetermines who gets to work in Hollywood.[31] For ethnic and racial outsiders, especially women and LGBTQI+-of-color creators, it is difficult to break into Hollywood's hierarchical, socially segregated economic, social, and professional networks—even when, as critical race and media studies researcher Ralina Joseph documents in her book on Black women producers, those in power are themselves gender and racial minorities.[32] The perpetual heteronormative and Eurocentric whiteness in the production and content of reboots, revivals, remakes, and audience responses to these texts are symptomatic of Hollywood's informal network.

Racial Capitalism, White Nostalgia, and the Reboot

Together the concepts of racial capitalism and white nostalgia provide an explanatory framework for the analyses of inequality in this collection. Specifically, the concepts connect the previous sections on the political economy of recycled media and inequality in Hollywood industry to explain audience expectations for and resistance to nostalgic whiteness in reboots during a period of unsettling change and volatile social conflicts. By focusing on case studies produced during the emergence of Trumpism from 2015 to the present, the authors illustrate the culturally soothing function of reboots for some producers and audiences and the demand for cultural resistance to white nostalgia by others. Racial capitalism and white nostalgia are critical concepts for building an analytical framework for teaching, studying, and writing about film and television through the lens of inequality and gender, sexual, ethnic, and racial differences. By focusing on reboots from 2015 to 2024, the collection explores the tensions between the erasure and visibility of racial, gender, and sexual diversity in Hollywood productions against a troubled political moment fueled by a populist desire for the nostalgic past. Our research demonstrates the importance of popular communication and media culture as an arena for studying ethnic, racial, gender, and sexual differences and inequalities.

Racial Capitalism and Hollywood Inequality

We begin by positioning the rebooted content produced and recirculated within the inequality of transnational media corporations predominantly owned by white men from the United States and Europe. Because corporate executives rarely disrupt the informal social networks of the Hollywood industry that maximize financial profits and maintain the reproduction of ethnic, racial, and gender inequality upon which capitalism depends, we posit that Hollywood functions as a modern apparatus of racial capitalism.

Critical race theorist Cedric Robinson documented the historical relationships between society, culture, racialized inequality, and capitalism. His work also examined the work of Black artists, writers, scholars, and activists, defined as the Black Radical Tradition, to disrupt political, economic, and cultural inequality.[33] Robinson forcefully argues that the racial ideology (racialism) of European cultures produces and depends on racial hierarchies as the central mechanism for the development of capitalism and capitalist societies. Canonical American studies scholar Ruth Wilson Gilmore summarizes his thinking: "As Robinson explains in *Black Marxism*, capitalism's requirement for inequality historically coalesced through racial practices that developed between and among people, all of whose descendants may well have become white."[34] Capitalism relies on the social organization of people (not just those who identify as racially white) who are dependent on race, racial categories, and racialization to create and hierarchize social differences and the economic, political, and social value given to the lives of some and not others.[35] In the case of the United States, similar to other European societies, racialized value is embedded in social, cultural, political, and economic institutions and norms—free-market competition, individualism, liberalism, colorblindness—known colloquially as the "American Dream."

To Robinson the antidote for disrupting racial capitalism lies in studying the socially transformative potential of antiracist work. While his focus was on the Black Radical Tradition and the work of Black philosophers, sociologists, writers, and artists, among others, to undue racial inequality, we place this collection on popular forms of communication within an intersectional antiracist project that critiques the institutionalized system of inequality in Hollywood productions, distribution, and representations. Toward the end of Robinson's career, he became increasingly concerned with the conservative nature of mainstream and popular media representations, the economic structure of news, film, and television organizations shaped by the need for profit maximization, and the powerful political and social role of transnational media conglomerates and their owners. In the preface to *Cedric J. Robinson: On Racial Capitalism, Black Internationalism, and Cultures of Resistance*, Elizabeth Peters Robinson points to the influence of Ben Bagdikian's 1983 *Media Monopoly* on Cedric Robinson's growing concern with media ownership and representations: "As Cedric's project was always about casting light in hidden corners, his attention to media mismanagement and malappropriation was a natural."[36] Robinson's scholarship suggests, antiracist politics, literature, media, or in the case of this collection antiracist research, is one mechanism for undoing forms of racial inequality integral to the maintenance of racial capitalism. Cedric Robinson's racial capitalism also makes clear the importance of Black and Brown resistance and oppositional ways of reading and seeing the cultural world.

The authors in this collection share Robinson's drive to bring to light inequality within rebooted media, as well as the creative attempts by women, queer people, and ethnic and racial minorities working within US capitalist media to create cracks in an unequal system of cultural production. Obviously Hollywood-produced film and television content are not part of an antiracist tradition. However, the lack of diversity in the ownership of transnational media conglomerates and the white men who produce the majority of Hollywood film and television play a globally significant cultural and economic role that calls us on as teachers, researchers, students, and audiences to study Hollywood as a cultural force in the contemporary history of racial capitalism. To position Hollywood ownership, production, and texts as a structure of racial capitalism, we build on the work of Black and Latina/x feminists, critical communication, and critical ethnic and race scholars to characterize the television and film industry as an institution of civil society. Like other parts of Anglo-European civil society, such as schooling and education, the media is shaped by the legacies of racialism, racialization, and the racial violence of US colonization, genocide, slavery, and segregation.[37] Anjali Vats brilliantly documents the deliberate construction of intellectual property law that dispossesses peoples of color from their own cultural production. She reminds us that the accrual of intellectual ownership itself was scripted as a racialized enterprise.

Rebooting White Nostalgia

Since the 2008 election of the first mixed-race president of the United States, Barack Obama, the world has witnessed a reemergence of conservative, right-leaning, and authoritarian politics. This nationalist turn is symbolized in part by the United States' conservative election and reelection of convicted felon Donald J. Trump. Governments in Italy,

France, Spain, Germany, Denmark, Argentina, Brazil, and others are also facing a renewed emergence of nationalist political parties, whose racialized presence has not been so explicit since the 1930s with the rise of Nazism and Fascism. At the same time as this ultraconservative political turn, protests surrounding social inequalities continue to surge in the wake of the COVID-19 pandemic, creating a polarized environment for populations and media audiences.

Grassroot campaigns for gender, ethnic, and racial equality move onward even as the social and political backlash against them increases. For example, the BLM movement, which emerged in the United States as a response against racial inequalities in policing, has gone global. In 2023 protests ignited throughout France in response to the police killing in Paris of Nahel Merzouk, a young man of Moroccan and Algerian descent. Paris, like other major cities in France, has seen a sharp increase in immigrants from African countries and its former French colonies, many of them Muslim, igniting anti-Islamic and anti-immigration sentiment most recently reflected in the electoral surge by French nationalist parties.[38] Similar anti-immigrant sentiments are embedded in the anti-Latino violence sweeping across the United States during the first year of Trump's second term. Yet, in the context of this generation-defining political and social moment, the Hollywood culture industry continually reboots racial and gender nostalgia by employing the same normative white bodies in stories often created by established white film directors and television showrunners. To borrow from cultural communication theorist Stuart Hall, the world changes while nothing changes in Hollywood.[39]

We propose that economic and cultural forces drive media reboots, and that audiences' desire for nostalgic media is shaped by the contentious social dynamics that define the contemporary moment. Indeed, media industry scholar Carle Lavigne confirms that "remakes . . . have proven popular with producers and networks interested in building on the nostalgic capital of past hits."[40] Because their original popularity is already proven, the redeployment of these properties is an economically and culturally safe investment. In a media industry economic and cultural feedback loop, the corporate desire for profits motivates production executives to hearken back to the proven formulas of the nostalgic past—as in a previously successful program, movie, or genre. In turn, nostalgic film and television texts reinforce the gender, ethnic, and racial inequality within Hollywood by meeting mainstream US audiences' demand for white actors, white characters, and the safe heteronormative stories that surround them. Rebooting successful properties grounded in nostalgic whiteness and heteronormative masculinity depends on institutional inequality to limit the risk and maximize the profits of transnational media conglomerates.

While the authors in this collection engage the concept of nostalgia in a variety of ways, we define *nostalgia* as a cultural discourse that romanticizes the return to a pastoral past where US white, heteronormative power and privilege are the norm and race, ethnic, sexual, and gender differences are not significant or central to storytelling. Let us be clear: We recognize that the nostalgic past is a fantasy whose continuing narrative power illustrates the cultural stakes in this reboot project. That is, the cultural demand for nostalgic media is partially a response to the increase in post-racial media representations and production practices that emerged during the Obama era and the ensuing social conflicts surrounding the diversification of US culture, society, and politics. During the Trump era the public's precarious desire for a return to the nostalgic cultural norms of a homogeneous, idealized white middle-class class life is also echoed in nationalist political rhetoric. The nationalist rhetoric of the Trump administration has enabled an era of white hetero-centric privilege and increased public support for non-governmental and state-sanctioned violence.[41] In her introduction to a special issue on revivals, Kathleen Loock argues that "revivals rely on past TV experiences to circulate new products through the crowded contemporary media landscape, and . . . they seek to negotiate the televisual heritage of original series, feelings of generational belonging, as well as notions of the past, present, and future in meaningful ways."[42] Indeed, she argues, some rebooted texts revert to nostalgia, almost as if political and cultural events in the intervening decades did not happen, with the effect of turning back the clock to an idealized simpler time that re-centers suburban middle-class and heterosexual whiteness.

Together the collection of case studies in this book document the Trump effect through the reproduction of racial and gender nostalgia through reboots. By studying media reboots the authors illustrate how nostalgia functions and continues to reproduce inequality in productions and texts. It is a mediated form of nostalgia that consistently hearkens back to a pastoral fantasy, a historical cultural amnesia, that amplifies narratives of racial purity and white privilege associated with a romanticized pre–Civil Rights era characterized by lessened social conflict and greater happiness for white families. Additionally, the case studies in this collection illustrate the production and narrative strategies found in rebooted media content that plays on audiences' desires for nostalgia and draws in diverse audiences by superficially incorporating diverse actors and characters through post-racial colorblind casting, narratives, and humor.[43]

Some reboots drop in diverse actors, characters, and storylines free from the political and social context of their identities, as if producers just discovered ethnic, racial, and gender diversity. Diversity in these reboots take place in the myth of discovery, of a "newness" of an idealized a-political multiracial and post-racial present where racial difference does not matter at all. For example, the producers of some reboots position race, gender, and sexuality as important to the narrative and character development yet outside of racism, xenophobia, or homophobia (See Morin in this collection). Similar dynamics apply to homo-domestic fantasies present in contemporary queer narratives (see Stephanie Pérez, Rhiannon Bettivia, and Aymar Jean Christian in this collection). In relation to the whiteness of the original narratives and character, some producers of reboots incorporate racial, gender, and sexual diversity as a futuristic fantasy that only superficially moves beyond the nostalgic whiteness and representational past of the original.

Sometimes changes to the racial or gender identity of the cast and characters alienate some audiences and fail to draw in the diverse audiences sought by executives. For example, the *Charmed* reboot (2018–2022, The CW) that originally presented a trio of white sisters as powerful witches flipped the original to three mixed-race and Afro-Latina characters instead (see Báez and Alemán and Molina-Guzmán in this collection). Nevertheless, the flipped production was also met with vocal protests from both original audiences and Latina/o audiences and critics who were disappointed that only one Latina actor was cast to play a lead role (see Molina-Guzmán in this collection). At the core of these dueling protests is the tension between nostalgic audience demands and the push by audiences and activists for more complex visibility and storytelling, particularly during the Trump era of civil rights retrenchment and increased racial violence (see Hermes and Eeken, Sanders and

Harris). The burden of underrepresentation makes any diverse presence a lightning rod for pent-up desire for visibility.[44]

The economic imperatives and cultural practices of inequality that define Hollywood productions limit and make it difficult for alternative voices and visions to surface, to be seen, and to be economically sustained. Unique and significant to the reboot moment examined in this collection are the social, political, and cultural tensions and stakes around the production of representations of race, ethnicity, gender, and sexuality. Accordingly, we document the interventions of women, queer people, Latinas/os, and Black creators and audiences who engage the practice of recycling to reimagine and challenge what and whose stories are told, how those stories are told, and who gets to tell stories about their communities (See Johnson in this collection). Because the politics of race, gender, sexuality, and inequality are partially transacted through the mainstream media, we play with the concept of *(re)booting inequality* to question and critique cultural recycling in the context of racial capitalism and Hollywood's nostalgic drive and institutional legacy of ethnic, racial, and gender inequality in production and representations. Building on Antonio Gramsci's prescient analysis of popular culture as the terrain of ideological and political struggle, authors in this collection focus on recycled texts that foreground ethnic, racial, and gender difference as caught within the ideological contradictions of capitalism and the political struggles over systemic racial inequality.[45]

Nostalgia and Reboots

By studying recycled texts to understand the broader economic, cultural, and social tensions around race, ethnicity, and gender embedded in the production of and audience responses to reboots, we contribute to the burgeoning efforts of scholars/teachers, such as the ones featured in this volume, who teach and research about inequality in the media. After decades of activism by media watchdog organizations, the slow increase in more diverse reboots should be celebrated as a sign of representational progress. However, these incremental changes in diverse casting and socially updated narratives also face backlash from fans who decry the producers' move away from the whiteness of the original show—white characters, white actors, and heteronormative storylines.

Conversely, for some ethnic and racial minority and global audiences, particularly younger audiences, these rebooted productions of minoritized identities, which are often seen as lacking in representational nuance, complexity, and ethnic authenticity, do not go far enough.

Previously all-white media texts recast with or including non-white actors are sometimes met with anti-fan backlash by the original audiences of the films or television programs, audiences who are motivated in their distaste by a nostalgic desire for less politicized content and the return of favorite white actors and characters. Among the case studies in the collection, the desire for nostalgic whiteness and heteronormative masculinity is most evident in audience responses to the gender flip in the casting of *Doctor Who* and the flipped ethnic, racial, and sexual identities of the characters in *Charmed*. Focusing on anti-fan responses to the flipped reboot of *Charmed* (see Molina-Guzmán in this collection) and the thirteenth-season recast of *Doctor Who* (see Hermes and Eeken in this collection), both chapters document the perilous redeployment of Latina and white women characters and illustrate the limits of rebooted texts that challenge ethnic and racial inequality. The two case studies examine the backlash by fans when producers reboot programs by changing the gender, race, or ethnicity of the original white actors and characters. Consequently, flipped reboots, where the race, ethnicity, gender, or sexuality of the original characters re-situates the narratives within the contemporary politics of gender and racial inequality, often challenge some audiences' expectations for nostalgic texts.

Nevertheless, the contemporary reboot moment creates a space for intervention. The chapters in this collection by Meghan Sanders and Tina Harris on the BLM context of the flipped *Watchmen* reboot (2019, HBO), Báez and Alemán's reading of Latina feminism in the flipped and queered *Charmed* reboot, and Patrick Johnson's essay on Black nostalgia and young Black fandom of syndicated Black 1990s television programs point to constrained antiracist openings in Hollywood.

Book Organization

Part I: Television's Nostalgic White Revival

Working within a highly segregated industry, Hollywood decision makers rely on an informal white and masculine social network of labor that reproduces inequality in production, distribution, and representation. The informality and personal nature of Hollywood's network makes it difficult to legally challenge discrimination in Hollywood.[46] In spite of the 2015 #HollywoodSoWhite social media protests in response to the all-white winners of the Academy Awards, and numerous changes to the Academy policies with regards to its nominating and voting process, few signs of gender and racial progress are visible. The top four 2024 Oscar awards went to established racially white Hollywood figures: Cillian Murphy for Best Actor, Christopher Nolan for Best Director and Best Picture, and Emma Stone for Best Actress.

Despite great technological advances, and some representational innovations, Hollywood privileges whiteness, masculinity, and heteronormativity. Hollywood film and television executives maintain cultural and economic power by limiting access to production for marginalized storytellers. Industry reports released in 2023 document (1) the people who own the media, (2) those who greenlight new projects, (3) those who represent actors and cast the programs, (4) those who produce, write, or direct, and (5) the guilds who provide skilled technical labor are dominated by predominantly white, heterosexual, cis men.[47] Whether we study media production, archiving, texts, and/or gaming, white masculine normativity and privilege are always in the space, always a question rarely explored. The authors in this collection precisely interrogate the question of white masculine heteronormative privilege in television and film production and audience responses to reboots, remakes, and revivals, which we will refer to generally as reboots. In this section, the chapters on television revivals and remakes demonstrate how whiteness, Eurocentrism, and heteronormativity are reproduced through the practices and narrative consequences of recycling the same actors, creators, and storylines.

First, Aymar Jean Christian's (chapter 1) analysis of *Will & Grace* (2017–2020, NBC) demonstrates how the original creator's superficial engagement with queer sexuality de-politicizes the anti-queer politics of Trump and his Republican Party. Instead, Christian proposes that the supposedly updated revival reaffirms the nostalgic white, heteronormative, conservative paradigm of the original *Will & Grace*. In the essay on the short-lived *Roseanne* revival (2018, ABC), Céline Morin (chapter 2) explores the erasure of the original's working-class feminist narratives by the network and the producers' marketing of the reboot as targeting the silent Trump audiences who enabled his 2016 election. Her analysis of Roseanne Barr's racist tweets and the network's quick pivot away from the show and the actress/producer test the limits of productions grounded explicitly in white, heteronormative nostalgia and resentment.

Finally, Stephanie Pérez's (chapter 3) reading of *Sex and the City* (1998–2004, HBO) and its revival *And Just Like That . . .* (2021–, HBO Max), as well as Rhiannon Bettivia's (chapter 4) discussion of the *She-Ra* remake, *She-Ra and the Princesses of Power* (2018–2020, Netflix), focus on the troubling hypervisibility and invisibility of queer, ethnic, and racial minority voice actors and characters that are still bound within the settler colonialist Eurocentric narrative logic of the original. Both *She-Ra* and *And Just Like That . . .* (*AJLT*) attempt to remedy the original's depiction of whiteness. The *AJLT* remake diversifies the original's all-white, all-wealthy characters and New York City by including a multicultural cast of secondary characters, via girlfriends and children of the protagonists. Despite the *She-Ra* remake's diversifying the producers, voice actors, and animated characters in terms of race, sexuality, and gender identity, Bettivia locates its narrative within the same settler colonialist logics of the original. Her analysis illustrates that, even when the creator, showrunner, and executive producers are diverse, it is difficult to work against Eurocentric norms of storytelling in Hollywood.[48] Nonetheless, *She-Ra* originally and contemporarily provided a visibilization of queerness, something that was then transgressive and is now reinforcing.

All the shows in this section, except the *She-Ra* remake, brought back the original creators. The *Roseanne* revival did not but was instead executively produced by the original all-white cast. Sociologist and ethnic studies scholar George Lipsitz reminds us that the white supremacy that undergirds US society consequently informs the production of US culture as a form of the continued "possessive investment of whiteness."[49] Together the authors in this section question the recycling of inequality and institutionalized white privilege, and document the relationship between racialism, racialization, and capitalism in the cultural messages of revivals and remakes. Reboots are an important example of how gender and racial inequalities in the Hollywood industry serve the economic, cultural, and political interest of those at the top of gender and racial hierarchies, one more mechanism of white supremacy and racial capitalism. Specifically, the authors question the contemporary practices of creative producers that incorporate diversity through the development of gender, racial, ethnic, and sexual minority actors, characters, and/or narrative arcs.

In the context of contemporary US nationalist politics, the recycling of dominant culture in television revivals and remakes is grounded in a romantic privileging of conservative gender and racial norms and values. For example, Céline Morin's discussion of the revival of *Roseanne* argues that while class and gender intersected in the original series to explore its blue-collar, feminist heroine's organizational issues, the revival locates most problems outside the heteronormative family, which now acts as a sanctuary that must be preserved from socially progressive forces. The historical relationship between womanhood, family domesticity, and television in *Roseanne* is rebooted through a representation of white US American suburbs under siege from modern values like equity, historicity, subjectivities, and identity politics. Shows like the turbulent reboot of *Roseanne* perform a type of historical amnesia amplifying conservative narratives of whiteness and ethnic and racial purity while at the same time incorporating some diverse characters.

Part II: (E)-Racing Whiteness in Reboots

Focusing on reboots that reimagine the past through a more nuanced multicultural lens, the authors in the second section explore the unsettled nostalgic expectations of original audiences. Television's post-racial call for the end of ethnic and racial identity politics makes it safe and profitable to represent women, Asian Americans, Black Americans, and Latinas/os in contemporary Hollywood film and television. Shifts in audience demographics, both globally and domestically, motivate film and television producers to make reboots and revivals that target more diverse and global audiences through flipped gender, ethnic, and racial casting and socially progressive storylines. For example, in the last five years, the Walt Disney Corporation has released animated and live-action CGI remakes of its some of its most popular animated films featuring ethnic and racial minorities actors and characters such as *Mulan* (2020), *Aladdin* (2019), and *The Lion King* (2019).

In referring to a *post-racial* era in television and film, we are not suggesting that race, ethnicity, gender, and sexuality are ignored by recycled texts, because they are not. Instead, we build on the work of critical race scholar Ashley Doane, who argues "for a more nuanced view of color-blind racial ideology, one that moves beyond a simple focus on the denial of racism and instead emphasizes the ability to hold simultaneous—and contradictory—positions—for example, that racial inequality and white privilege persist, but that racism is not widespread."[50] Similarly, Brüning finds that televisual casting of a Black protagonist in a show such as *Scandal* (2012–2018, ABC) foregrounds issues of white feminism at the expense of issues of race.[51] Post-racial and postfeminist narratives depoliticize racial, ethnic, gender, and sexual difference while superficially placing them at the core of the text.

Angharad N. Valdivia (chapter 5) begins this section by revisiting three recycled programs and their deployment of whiteness and Latinidad in tension between comedic escapism and the political turmoil following the election of the forty-fifth president of the US. To do so, Valdivia provides a modified production analysis of the *Gilmore Girls* revival (2016, Netflix) and the flipped reboots *Party of Five* (2020, Freeform) and *One Day at a Time* (2017–2020, Netflix/Pop TV) featuring Latina/o casts instead of the original all-white characters. Valdivia investigates three different production and representational strategies in terms of the endurance of the show in relation to the inclusion of Latinidad and the resulting visibility in terms of the shows' engagement with ethnic specificity. She concludes that visibility of ethnic-specific Latinidad and Latina/o political and social issues is in inverse relationship to the popularity and staying power of the series. Two of the three shows contribute to the superficial celebration of representational diversity by targeting increasingly diverse audiences, but rarely decenter the economic and cultural power of Hollywood's predominantly white and cis-male-gendered media executives, producers, directors, and writers who together create and reproduce a normative white US patriarchal narrative universe for domestic and global audiences.

Animated and fantasy reboots not connected to the facsimile of the real potentially present an opportunity for innovative storylines and characters that break away from the Hollywood industry's privileging of nostalgic whiteness. However, the authors in this collection point to the difficulty of breaking away from Eurocentric narratives even in storytelling not bound by the pretense of reality. In another modified production analysis, Zhui Ning Chang and Shyamala Parthasarathy (chapter 6) explore the live-action remake of *Aladdin* (2019, Walt Disney Co.). Given Disney's long-standing tradition of recycling its texts, the authors engage the live-action remake of *Aladdin* to investigate Disney's conservative approach to representation and inclusive storytelling via a comparative case study of the 1992 animated film *Aladdin* and its recent remake. The authors compare the original animated film's exaggeration of ethnic stereotypes to the producers' live-action decision to diversify the cast and socially update the narrative. In doing so, they suggest the remake plays into equally troubling ideas about the good immigrant, racial colorism, and representations of whiteness. While Disney's remakes aim for updated historical accuracy as well as revision of some of the more controversial components of the original movies—including racist, homophobic, sexist, and Orientalist elements—Chang and Parthasarathy document the limits of Disney's approach, which must operate within the racial capitalist logics of whiteness and nostalgia.

Some media executives specifically market flipped reboots and remakes in the context of the US nationalist backlash to an increasingly diverse society. For example, Jillian M. Báez and Sonya M. Alemán (chapter 7) compare the original and reboot *Charmed* to trace the continuities and differences between the original produced by Brad Kern, who was identified as a sexual harasser during the initial Hollywood #MeToo moment, and the reboot produced by Jessica O'Toole and Amy Rardin, the creators of the *Jane the Virgin* (2014–2019, The CW), the English-language reboot of the Venezuelan telenovela *Juana la Virgen* (2002) created by Perla Farías for RCTV (Radio Caracas Televisión). Báez and Alemán outline the writers' engagement with the current politics of white masculine resentment through a narrative and character development analysis grounded in Latinx feminist and ethnic studies. Similarly, Esteban del Río and Kristin Moran's essay (chapter 8) focuses on critics' and reviewers' responses to the ethnic flipped reboot from the white family of the 1970s classic *One Day at a Time* to a single Latina-headed family. In particular, the authors document the strategies used by the reboots' Latina producer to develop Latina/o characters and tell complex and nuanced stories. Thus, the Hollywood reboots, revivals, and remakes sampled in this section present scholars, students, and audiences an opportunity to reflect on the industry's continuing racialism, production practices of inequality, and the often short-lived if not failed attempts to redress them.

Part III: Challenging White Nostalgia in Contemporary Reboots

Finally, the collection turns to the rebooting of texts that foreground racial and sexual diversity or are flipped reboots of TV and films with previously all-white or all-men casts. Both types of reboots provide cultural and financial opportunities to white women and people-of-color creators and actors. However, the development of beloved programs such as *Doctor Who*, *One Day at a Time*, *Charmed*, and *Watchmen* through racially and gender-diverse characters and storylines informed by contemporary social and cultural politics also produces moments of cultural conflict. The chapters in this section explore recycled and rebooted texts that foreground ethnic and gender difference in more complicated ways at a time when ethnic, racial, and sexual equality initiatives are under political contestations and legal attacks by the Trump administration. In particular, the authors explore how these recycled texts negotiate the tension between the expectations for gender, ethnic, and racial nostalgia by the shows' original audiences and urgent demands by ethnic, racial, and sexual minorities for respectable visibility.

Decentering whiteness is a risky proposition, but so is decentering masculinity in mainstream media productions. The gender-flipped *Ocean's 8* (2018, Warner Bros.), *Ghostbusters* (2016, Sony), and *Doctor Who* commanded lower production budgets than their previous iterations starring white men actors, presumably because the executive producers believed them to be financially riskier than featuring men in the franchise. The flipped *Ghostbusters* generated $229.1 million box office return on a $144 million budget. It was considered a "bomb" because there was only an $18.1 million profit margin after the subtraction of $70 million in theater revenue—not exactly a loss but not necessarily the numbers usually generated by franchise hits. The flipped *Ocean's 8* brought in $298 million at the box office with a $70 million budget, a very respectable more than four times return on investment—roughly the same return on investment as *Ocean's Thirteen* (2007), which featured male actors again. Sandra Bullock, one of the two principal co-stars of *Ocean's 8*, publicly defended *Ghostbusters* against the backlash, adding that women were here to stay in these major franchises.[52]

A study of audience reactions to both of these movies along the lines of the *Charmed* analysis by Molina-Guzmán and the *Doctor Who* analysis by Hermes and Eeken would likely reveal that fans reacted virulently to both the gender and racial inclusion in both of these flipped movies. Moreover, beyond the box office, and concordant with the themes of this book, both *Ocean's 8* and *Ghostbusters* flipped the gender of the protagonist but included problematic women-of-color characters. *Ghostbusters*' Patti Tolan (Leslie Jones) played out the classic sassy Black woman role. *Ocean's 8*'s ensemble cast foregrounded two of the white actors/characters—Debbie Ocean (Sandra Bullock) and Lou (Cate Blanchett) as the intellectual core boss girls. The characters of Nine Ball (Rihanna), Constance (Awkwafina), and Amita (Mindy Kaling) performed more low-level and streetwise tasks such as internet hacking, panhandling, and jewelry switching. Both flipped movies retained a racial hierarchy within the female cast. Nonetheless, studio executives re-rebooted the *Ghostbusters* franchise in 2020 with the original white men actors and a sustained marketing effort to bury the gender-flip version. The heist *Ocean's* franchise has yet to follow up *Ocean's 8*. The ratings and profitability of flipped franchise reboots do not yield consistent outcomes: Some flipped reboots are profitable and popular while others are not.

As chapters in this section demonstrate, the original audiences predictably resist the contemporary flips. The challenges and constraints Hollywood producers face in their efforts to maintain profitability while diversifying the range of narratives in the current context of white heteronormative resentment appear to make it easier to reproduce the nostalgic un-flipped versions. We are certainly within the terrain of ideology when, despite the capitalist profitability of some flipped cultural products, there remains a preference to reproduce the original nostalgic versions often featuring the original white men actors. Hermes and Eeken's (chapter 11) analysis of online responses to the gender flip of the main character Doctor Who, an alien time lord who regenerates into different human forms, examines the virulent response of mostly men. Interestingly, there has not been a similar response to the to the 2024 racial flip of the Doctor Who character to a Black man.

Anti-fandom speaks to fans' nostalgic tendencies, which are constrained by the industry's entrenched inequality and corporate demands for safe, ideologically conservative narratives. Molina-Guzmán (chapter 10) visits anti-fan responses to the flipped *Charmed* reboot that was meant to attract new audiences and culturally update storylines through diversified producers, cast, and narratives. She concludes that anti-fan Twitter responses to the ethnic and racial flip of the *Charmed* reboot spotlight audience expectations for a white, heteronormative postfeminist past, especially during a vexed social and political moment. Both case studies demonstrate the desire by original fans to relive the original shows, romanticizing an idealized past defined by heteronormative, masculine, and white nostalgia.

Reboots, such as the racial and gender flip of *Watchmen* (2019, HBO), also demonstrate the antiracist potential of television. Sanders and Harris (chapter 9) explore the decisions made by the producer of the *Watchmen* reboot to create counternarratives to contemporary notions of a post-racial ideology. To do so, the authors perform a circuit of culture analysis, exploring aspects of the series' production, narrative representations, and audience responses. Specifically, by flipping the lead character from a white man to a Black woman police officer, the writers centered the #BLM movement to de-center whiteness and the familiar white savior complex common in mainstream film and television. The narrative focus on the powerful intersectional identity of a Black woman superhero celebrates and affirms Black identity during an especially volatile sociopolitical time in the US.

Shifting to syndicated texts that center minoritized actors, characters, storylines and audiences, Patrick Johnson (chapter 12) moves past superficial diversity toward the syndication of 1990s mainstream programs produced by Black men producers, programs like *Martin* (1992–1997, Fox), *The Cosby Show* (1984–1992, NBC), and its spin-off *A Different World* (1987–1993, NBC). Johnson's study of the continuing popularity of these programs for young Black college students explores the role of these shows in producing a counter to white nostalgia. Black creative producers thus provide young audiences living in the present with an opportunity to reflect on the creation of oppositional forms of nostalgia that provide a salvo against structural racism. A representation of a Black nostalgic past like white nostalgia is idealized by young Black audiences.

Yet Black nostalgia differs from white nostalgia in that it holds hopeful possibilities for a multi-racial and multi-cultural future, a utopian hope. Johnson concludes that the continued syndication of Black-produced sitcoms privileges and celebrates Black culture and identity in equally nostalgic but culturally empowering terms.

Conclusion

The chapters in this collection present a critical reflection on the role of gender, race, and class in the remaking of television and film.[53] Contemporary producers of flipped reboots that include gender, ethnic, and racial minority characters in the name of entertainment often do so masking the ethnic and racial disparities that define Hollywood and Latina/o and African American life in the United States. Diversity in Hollywood rebooted representations ironically contributes to the popular belief that as a nation the United States is beyond caring about race, ethnicity, and gender, even as Trump policies explicitly dismantle the rights of these communities. Almost twenty years from Obama's first presidency, it is impossible to deny that the very opposite of US post-racial society is true. Instead of suggesting that diversity in reboots is evidence that audiences and producers have moved beyond whiteness as the norm, we propose that the conditions under which audiences see ethnic and racial minorities in reboots are constrained by inequality in the Hollywood industry and US society in general. Similarly, the analyses of revivals in the collection illustrate the romanticization of stories grounded in a nostalgic privileging of white, heteronormative identity, norms, and values. However, even as nostalgic reboots whitewash the past, other flipped reboots tackle contemporary racial, gender, and sexuality politics head-on. Some flipped reboot producers, by consciously including gender, sexual, and racial representations, violate the implicit colorblind production code grounded in whiteness. These socially consciously reboots engage in contemporary identity politics head-on with a range of sometimes troubling audience outcomes. The resulting ratings and profitability of diverse reboots as previously discussed speak to the difficulties in Hollywood production efforts to maintain and expand profitability while diversifying the range of narratives within the narrow confines of low-risk, acceptable innovation.

Together, the authors in this collection move beyond rehashing the homogenizing and often stereotypic gender and racial tendencies of US television and film production and texts. We begin by granting the established media studies position that mainstream media content flattens out ethnic, gender, sexual, and racial difference, and move past analysis that focuses on ethnic, gender, sexual, and racial representations as simplistic or direct negative or positive representations of reality. Instead, the authors tease out the cultural tensions between the production of media texts that look backward to privilege a racialized and gendered nostalgic past and productions that romanticize the present through a post-racial and postfeminist future that depend on superficial diversifications of casts, characters, and storylines. Collectively we critique the inequality embedded in rebooted texts while questioning the incremental diversity found in contemporary reboots in the context of a nostalgic backlash grounded in white resentment.

NOTES

1 Travis L. Dixon and Charlotte L. Williams, "The Changing Misrepresentation of Race and Crime on Network and Cable News," *Journal of Communication* 65, no. 1 (2015): 24–39, https://doi.org/10.1111/jcom.12133.

2 Lisa Marie Cacho, *Social Death: Racialized Rightlessness and the Criminalization of the Unprotected* (New York University Press, 2012).

3 For discussions of racial capitalism and culture, see Jodi Melamed, *Represent and Destroy: Rationalizing Violence in the New Racial Capitalism* (University of Minnesota Press, 2011). For a discussion of the economic structures of production and race, see Anamik Saha, *Race, Culture and Media* (Sage, 2021). For a discussion of gender and sexuality and the political economy of media production, see Eileen R. Meehan and Ellen Riordan, *Sex and Money: Feminism and Political Economy in the Media* (University of Minnesota Press, 2002).

4 Anjali Vats, *The Color of Creatorship: Intellectual Property, Race, and the Making of Americans* (Stanford University Press, 2020).

5 Mohamad Moslimani et al., "Key Facts About the U.S. Black Population" (Pew Research Center, January 18, 2024), https://pewrsr.ch/48ZiMyw.

6 Luis Noe-Bustamante, Lauren Mora, and Mark Hugo Lopez, "About One-in-Four U.S. Hispanics Have Heard of Latinx, but Just 3% Use It" (Pew Research Center, August 11, 2020), https://pewrsr.ch/2XNrKfR.

7 Mark Hugo Lopez, Jens Manuel Krogstad, and Jeffrey S. Passel, "Who is Hispanic?" (Pew Research Center, September 5, 2023), www.pewresearch.org.

8 Elana Levine and Lisa Parks, "Introduction," in *Undead TV: Essays on Buffy the Vampire Slayer*, ed. Elana Levine and Lisa Parks (Duke University Press, 2007), 1–16.

9 Comcast, National Amusements, Paramount Global, ViacomCBS, Sony, Walt Disney, Warner Brothers, and NBCUniversal are all examples.
10 See Jonathan Gray, *Show Sold Separately: Promos, Spoilers, and Other Media Paratexts* (New York University Press, 2010); Timothy Havens and Amanda D. Lotz, *Understanding Media Industries* (Oxford University Press, 2012); Amanda D. Lotz, ed., *Beyond Prime Time: Television Programming in the Post-Network Era* (Routledge, 2009); Amanda D. Lotz, *Netflix and Streaming Video: The Business of Subscriber-Funded Video on Demand* (Polity, 2022).
11 Eileen R. Meehan, "Transindustrialism and Synergy: Structural Supports for Decreasing Diversity in Commercial Culture," *International Journal of Media and Cultural Politics* 1, no. 1 (2005): 123–26, https://doi.org/10.1386/macp.1.1.123/3.
12 Marisa Dellato, "The World's Largest Media Companies in 2023: Comcast and Disney Stay on Top," *Forbes*, June 8, 2023, www.forbes.com.
13 Meehan, "Transindustrialism and Synergy."
14 Diana Leon-Boys, *Princess of the Periphery: Disney's Flexible Latina Girl* (Rutgers University Press, 2023).
15 Michelle Hilmes, "The Whole World's Unlikely Heroine: Ugly Betty as Transnational Phenomenon," in *TV's Betty Goes Global: From Telenovela to International Brand*, ed. Janet McCabe and Kim Akass (I.B. Tauris, 2013), 26–44.
16 Jeremy Tunstall, *The Media Were American: U.S. Mass Media in Decline* (Oxford University Press, 2007).
17 Tunstall, *The Media Were American.*
18 Kathleen Loock, "American TV Series Revivals: Introduction," *Television & New Media* 19, no. 4 (2018): 300, https://doi.org/10.1177/1527476417742971.
19 Henry Jenkins, "To Understand the Futures of Film-Going, We Must Know Its Histories," in *Entertainment Values: How Do We Assess Entertainment and Why Does It Matter?*, ed. Stephen Harrington (Palgrave, 2019): 269–77.
20 Amanda A. Klein and R. Barton Palmer, *Cycles, Sequels, Spin-offs, Remakes, and Reboots: Multiplicities in Film and Television* (University of Texas Press, 2016).
21 Sparrman (2020) identifies Lewis Carroll's *Alice in Wonderland* (1915) as an early example of transmedia cultural production that continues to be generative. For more on transmedia, see Jenkins, "To Understand the Futures of Film-Going"; for more on paratexts, see Gray, *Show Sold Separately*, and Jonathan Gray, "Text," in *Keywords for Media Studies*, ed. Laurie Ouellette and Jonathan Gray (New York University Press, 2017).
22 For an overview of the monopolistic organization of media industries, see Ben H. Bagdikian, *The Media Monopoly* (Beacon Press, 2000); Randy Nichols and Gabriela Martinez, eds., *Political Economy of Media Industries: Global Transformations and Challenges* (Routledge, 2020).
23 Jenkins, "To Understand the Futures of Film-Going"; Gray, *Show Sold Separately.*
24 Gray, "Text."
25 For a historical analysis on the role of white identity in Hollywood, see Daniel Bernardi, ed., *The Birth of Whiteness: Race and the Emergence of U.S. Cinema*

(Rutgers University Press, 1996); Daniel Bernardi, ed., *Classic Hollywood, Classic Whiteness* (University of Minnesota Press, 2001); Daniel Bernardi, ed., *The Persistence of Whiteness: Race and Contemporary Hollywood Cinema* (Routledge, 2008).

26 Bernardi, *The Birth of Whiteness*; Bernardi, *Classic Hollywood*; Bernardi, *The Persistence of Whiteness.*

27 Although they're not broken down by reboots, we can infer from the following reports that similar trends would apply: Stacy L. Smith, Katherine Pieper, and Sam Wheeler, *Inequality in 1,600 Popular Films: Examining Portrayals of Gender, Race/Ethnicity, LGBTQ+ & Disability from 2007 to 2022* (USC Annenberg Inclusion Initiative Report, August 2023); Ana-Christina Ramón, Michael Tran, and Darnell Hunt, *Hollywood Diversity Report 2023* (UCLA Division of Sciences Report, 2023).

28 For discussion of the term *culture industry*, see Theodor W. Adorno, *The Culture Industry: Selected Essays on Mass Culture*, ed. Jay Bernstein (Routledge, 1991); Anamik Saha, *Race and the Cultural Industries* (Polity, 2017).

29 Isabel Molina-Guzmán, *Latinas and Latinos on TV: Colorblind Comedy in the Post-Racial Network Era* (University of Arizona Press, 2018).

30 Ramón, Tran, and Hunt, *Hollywood Diversity Report 2023.*

31 The comment was made by a casting director at a private University of Southern California symposium in 2010.

32 Ralina L. Joseph, *Postracial Resistance: Black Women, Media, and the Uses of Strategic Ambiguity* (New York University Press, 2019).

33 The Black Radical Tradition refers to the diasporic and pan-African work of artists, scholars, and activists contesting Western colonization, slavery, and the contemporary legacy of Black disenfranchisement. See Cedric J. Robinson, *Black Marxism: The Making of the Black Radical Tradition* (University of North Carolina Press, 2000).

34 Ruth W. Gilmore, "Foreword," in *On Racial Capitalism, Black Internationalism, and Cultures of Resistance*, by Cedric J. Robinson, ed. H. L. T. Quan (Pluto Press, 2019), xii.

35 Cacho, *Social Death.*

36 See Ben H. Bagdikian, *The Media Monopoly*, 4th ed. (Beacon Press, 1992); Robinson, *On Racial Capitalism*, xxi

37 Stuart Hall, "Gramsci's Relevance for the Study of Race and Ethnicity," *Journal of Communication Inquiry* 10, no. 2 (1986): 5–27, https://doi.org/10.1177/019685998601000202.

38 Roger Cohen, "In Calling Elections in France, Macron Makes a Huge Gamble," *New York Times*, June 10, 2024.

39 Stuart Hall, "Race, Culture, and Communications: Looking Backward and Forward at Cultural Studies," *Rethinking Marxism* 5, no. 1 (1992): 10–18, https://doi.org/10.1080/08935699208657998.

40 Carle Lavigne, ed., *Remake Television: Reboot, Remake, Recycle* (Lexington Press, 2014), 1.

41 Griffin Sims Edwards and Stephen Rushin, "The Effect of President Trump's Election on Hate Crimes," SSRN (2018), http://dx.doi.org/10.2139/ssrn.3102652.

42 Loock, "American TV Series Revivals," 299.

43 See Amy Holdsworth, *Television, Memory and Nostalgia* (Palgrave Macmillan, 2011); Kristen J. Warner, "The Racial Logic of *Grey's Anatomy*: Shonda Rhimes and Her 'Post-Civil Rights, Post-Feminist' Series," *Television and New Media* 16, no. 7 (2015): 631–47, https://doi.org/10.1177/1527476414550529; Molina-Guzmán, *Latinas and Latinos on TV*.

44 For a discussion of the burden of representation, see Isaac Julien and Kobina Mercer, "Introduction: De Margin and De Centre," *Screen* 29, no. 4 (1988): 2–11.

45 Stuart Hall speaks on Antonio Gramsci in *The Hard Road to Renewal* (Verso Books, 1988).

46 In 2003, the Equal Employment Opportunity Commission filed a lawsuit against Universal Studios because of racial discrimination in hiring. Universal won the case in 2007. See US Equal Employment Opportunity Commission, "EEOC sues universal studios for race discrimination," news release, September 30, 2003, https://eeoc.gov.

47 Smith, Pieper, and Wheeler, *Inequality in 1,600 Popular Films*; Ramón, Tran, and Hunt, *Hollywood Diversity Report 2023*.

48 N.D. Stevensen, who created, wrote, and produced the remake of *She-Ra*, identifies as non-binary and transmasculine.

49 Stuart Hall, Jessica Evans, and Sean Nixon, eds., *Representation: Cultural Representations and Signifying Practices*, 2nd ed. (Sage, 2013); George Lipsitz, *The Possessive Investment in Whiteness: How White People Profit from Identity Politics* (Temple University Press, 1998).

50 Ashley Doane, "Beyond Color-Blindness: (Re) Theorizing Racial Ideology," *Sociological Perspectives* 60, no. 5 (2014): 17, https://doi.org/10.1177/0731121417719697.

51 Kristina Brüning, "Olivia Pope: A Black Post-Feminist Subject? Analyzing *Scandal*'s Intersecting Post-Feminist and Colorblind Discourses," *Feminist Media Studies* 19, no. 4 (2019): 463–78, https://doi.org/10.1080/14680777.2018.1508049.

52 Jessica Rawden, "Sandra Bullock Says the Reaction to Female Ghostbusters Movie was Unfair," *CinemaBlend*, June 7, 2018, www.cinemablend.com.

53 Molina-Guzmán, *Latinas and Latinos on TV*.

PART I

Television's Nostalgic White Revival

1

Will & Grace

Branding Whiteness from Broadcast to Streaming

AYMAR JEAN CHRISTIAN

READING NOTE: *Will & Grace* was hailed as groundbreaking in 1998 for its representation of gay men. This chapter revisits the original in relation to its 2017 revival. The essay documents how the producers of *Will & Grace*'s revival continued privileging white middle-class identity and the normative value of heterosexuality through the "horrible white people" genre. In the context of the 2016 Trump presidency, *Will & Grace*'s 2017 revival reinforces network executives' need to attract SLUMPY (socially liberal urban-minded professionals) audiences through reviving the careers the established white actors and producers of their youth and thus reinforcing the racial inequality of television production.

Introduction

Will & Grace was a revolutionary series when it premiered on NBC in 1998: the first sitcom led by an openly gay character (though it would take two seasons to show two men kiss on broadcast prime time). When I was coming out of the closet at the exact same time the original aired, the hit show filled many needs and desires for me: mainly, to grow into a handsome, successful, culturally sophisticated out gay man with a fabulous apartment in New York's Upper West Side. At the time I was not aware I was being conditioned to desire whiteness and its bourgeois entrapments, nor was I aware of how this aspiration marginalizes people who look like me.

Through the lens of the Millennial "horrible white people" genre, this chapter deconstructs *Will & Grace* through its two pilots—the original from 1998 and the reboot-revival from 2017. I focus on the pilots as the episode network executives care most about; most shows, especially in the 1990s, would not get a green light for a series without a pilot on which executives offered extensive notes (here, NBC). Pilots most heavily reveal the network's hand through the notes executives give. Thus, pilots are also most representative of the brand image networks want to project. Through an analysis comparing the two *Will & Grace* pilots, I show that even in the wake of a country changed by the election of an explicit white supremacist, *Will & Grace* and NBC cannot make explicit their own complicitly with white supremacy, even after depicting a pillow fight in Trump's Oval Office. In the conclusion I connect Trump to NBC and make a case for reparations from the network for the horrible white people it has platformed. In all, the *Will & Grace* reboot represents the kind of "cultural recycling" that perpetuates Hollywood's inequalities of racial capitalism while also representing liberal white complicity in a broader backlash against people of color advocating for change in the post-Trump era, as Isabel Molina-Guzmán and Angharad Valdivia write in the introduction.

Created by David Kohan and Max Mutchnick, *Will & Grace* is often seen as one of the most popular sitcoms for television's SLUMPY demographic—Ron Becker's term for socially liberal, urban-minded professionals.[1] Part of broadcast TV's strategy to brand itself as cool and gentrify its audiences, the SLUMPY demographic represented the gentrification of cities, as a generation of white people whose parents moved to the suburbs longed for urban living. From *Seinfeld* to *Frasier* and *Friends*, NBC profited from a genre that misrepresented the reality of urban diversity and undervalued the importance of Black audiences through its programming lack of racially diverse representations.[2] During its heyday *Will & Grace* stood alone as a broadcast TV series led by a gay character. Cable and, later, streaming would change that. By the early 2020s, GLAAD found that 12 percent of all TV characters were LGBTQ, many of them people of color. *Will & Grace*, then, symbolized television's transition from seeking mass audiences to more culturally specific ones as a result of the increase in the number of niche TV channels. The growth of TV in the 2010s not only led to more queer characters but also coincided with more diverse representations of white people. With more shows about white people, a subgenre of series emerged to expand televisual whiteness: the "horrible white people" comedy.[3] Within this context NBC decided to revive *Will & Grace*.

The NBC/Hulu reboot reveals that *Will & Grace* has always been a sitcom explicitly about the class privilege afforded by white able-bodied cis heteronormativity. The show focused on poking fun at heteronormativity, using the relationship between a gay man and straight woman to mock the worst of straight relationships and suggesting how perfect opposite-gender relationships can be when sex is taken out of equation. Yet *Will & Grace* has not been as adept at making explicit its critique of whiteness, as it enables various forms of privilege, with marriage chief among them. In its first run, from 1998 to 2006, *Will & Grace* routinely "punched down" toward people of color, trans people, fat people, disabled people, and even lesbians as the butts of jokes—often with an ironic wink suggestive of satire.

In the original *Will & Grace* series, the writers find humor in Will, Grace, Grace's employee Karen, and Will's friend Jack all acting horribly to strangers, lovers, and each other. Will is often horrible to Jack, policing his friend as too gay or effeminate; and Karen to Grace, ridiculing her for her lack of wealth or feminine grace. Thus, the comedic engine of the show revolves around white people being horrible to each other because of gender, sexuality, and class, obscuring how their whiteness nevertheless mitigates or allows them to survive these diversions from normativity. Beyond the four lead characters, the original series featured regular cameos of butches and studs walking into their fabulous Manhattan apartment only for the leads to make stereotypical jokes about loving Home Depot or lacking fashion sense, a form of gender and class policing. Of course, the creators might say these jokes wring comedy from the stupidity of stereotyping, but without a non-horrible "straight" character to represent an equitable perspective, it is hard to see where viewers might find the lesson.[4]

The show avoids shaming too many walk-on characters for their race or ethnicity, except Karen's maid Rosario, admittedly a complex figure. Played by white Jewish actress Shelley Morrison, Rosario, a Latina maid, was not servile and "spoke back" to her boss in ways that suggested equanimity but really positioned the show as "progressive" to mask its dog-whistles to Log Cabin Republicans and mainstream viewers. At once an overworked, consistently disrespected servant to Karen, a rich

Republican socialite, Rosario still lacked agency over her life and functioned largely as a foil to advance Karen's storylines, naturalizing how the Latinx immigrant workers whom rich white people hire are rightfully theirs to exploit. In the eighth and final season, production added more diversity by giving Will a boyfriend, played by Taye Diggs, who did not last long and, frankly, lacked interiority or character motivation, offering little change to the persistent erasure of Black gay men and women on television as documented by television scholar Alfred Martin.[5]

In the 2017 reboot, announced in the wake of the election of President Donald J. Trump, the topic of whiteness is difficult to avoid, yet somehow the show manages to do it. Instead, the show leans more heavily in poking fun at the emptiness of liberal politics by showing how class aspiration mitigates any real resistance to fascism or nationalism, exemplified by the president, who, conversely, won by blowing the racist dog-whistle louder than any presidential candidate since George Wallace. This focus on class is intended to be reflexive, a way for the show to name that it is out of touch with the average US American, whom broadcast networks felt they lost after Trump's election.[6] While laudable, this focus on class obscures a critique of whiteness, which is intimately related to class.[7]

Proto-Horrible White People

The genre of "horrible white people" emerged in full force in the streaming era with series like *Louie* (2010–2015, FX), *Girls* (2012–2017, HBO), *Difficult People* (2015–2017, Hulu), and *Search Party* (2016–2017, 2020–2022, TBS/HBO Max).[8] It has roots in *All in the Family* (1971–1979, CBS), whose lead character, Archie Bunker, represented the conservative foil to the liberal values of his family, and then *Seinfeld* (1989–1998, NBC), whose "antisocial" leads had no consistent foil but largely "foregrounded race relations rather than gender," as Angharad Valdivia writes in this volume.[9] Interestingly, both *All in the Family* and *Seinfeld* emerged at critical moments of broadcast television's reckoning with its own whiteness, revealing the medium's complicity in racial capitalism. At the height of broadcast TV's popularity, the 1970s brought some of the first culturally Black TV shows as broadcast TV tried to catch up with the aftermath of the 1960s, the death of Dr. King, the rising Black power movement and blaxploitation film, and government pressure following Federal Communications Commission Chairman Newton Minow's castigation of the medium's commerciality in the decade prior. The 1990s intensified TV's interest in horrible white people, as broadcast TV networks greenlighted even more Black TV shows in response to cable's siphoning of white viewers from the legacy networks ABC, CBS, and NBC.[10]

The original *Will & Grace* is an early instance of a broadcast network trying to find new ways of representing whiteness amid concerns over the US's increasing diversity and network TV's declining ratings. The streaming-era reboot emerges in an advanced stage of representing horrible white people and the TV market's diversification, so the show goes farther into this anxiety. Both periods reveal white anxiety over their own cultural irrelevance. In the streaming era, with the increase in global distribution and independent production from more diverse creators on social media, Hollywood needs a new way to represent whiteness that still centers white people but with awareness of growing race, class, and gender diversity: "Contemporary Hollywood is caught between the force of historically established white patriarchal structures of cultural production, and the rising currents of changing demographics, economics, and technology."[11]

TV's desire for—and anxiety over—cultural relevance drives series development in both periods. Shows try to make you laugh at how horrible white people can be, walking the thin line between tragedy and comedy amid increasing inequalities of power, while still centering whiteness. Taylor Nygaard and Jorie Lagerway write that these shows "privilege Whiteness in their aesthetics, in the uneasy tension of mixing comedy and drama,"[12] but stick to the comedy format to avoid the difficult conversations around race, power, and inequality. Molina-Guzmán calls this "hipster racism" and connects it to producers wanting to balance acknowledging inequality without losing a profitable white audience:

> because the economic imperatives of commercially supported network television are heavily connected to advertisers' continuing demands for young, wealthy, white audiences/consumers, hipster racism in post-racial era network TV is an effective comedic tool for allowing producers to

> walk the fine line between maintaining majority-white audiences and attracting ethnic and racial minority viewers.[13]

We see this "fine line" between keeping the white audience while courting other viewers in the broad changes in the United States during TV's great expansion. From the 1970s to the 2010s, the number of white viewers started declining while class inequality in the US was increasing. The number of people with incomes over $100,000 was not growing as fast as those with less. NBC benefited the most during this transition by frequently touting to advertisers that its viewers were the wealthiest.[14] It didn't matter that ratings for shows like *Will & Grace* were declining, because NBC could charge a premium to sell those viewers luxury goods (the rhetoric of gay men having more disposable income didn't hurt). The result is what Hunter Hargraves calls "uncomfortable television," shows that gave white viewers, in part, the license to laugh at or deconstruct their own increasing privilege in a diversifying America.[15]

Why then was *Will & Grace* rebooted through a revival despite the original's declining ratings and cultural relevance? As with reboots in general, it was a brand, a piece of intellectual property that could confer to NBC the "buzz" necessary to tickle America's funny bone or scratch the itch to laugh at whiteness and privilege in the Trump era, while "feeding a troubling nostalgia addiction," as Molina-Guzmán and Valdivia write in the introduction to this volume. The reboot ended up being one of the more successful of the time, lasting three seasons, whereas others like *Party of Five*, *Saved by the Bell*, *Mad About You*, *Murphy Brown*, *The X-Files*, *Roseanne*, *Sabrina the Teenage Witch*, and *Gossip Girl* lasted less. Perhaps it worked because it became a safe vessel for whiteness in a time of heightened white supremacy, tapping into the multiple ways whiteness functions in society. According to Cheryl Harris in her famous essay "Whiteness as Property," "Whiteness has functioned as *self-identity* in the domain of the intrinsic, personal, and psychological; as *reputation* in the interstices between internal and external identity; and, as *property* in the extrinsic, public and legal realms" (italics added).[16] By operating on the level of self-identity (how viewers connect to characters) and reputation (how the love of characters expands the show's popularity), whiteness becomes the most valuable piece of intellectual property in media: a brand, an authentic story that soothes the rough edges of complex cultural inequalities.[17]

The *Will & Grace* reboot's liberal "soft" whiteness differentiates it from Trump's aggressive representation of whiteness at the same time, comforting white viewers' self-identity and reputation: a valuable commodity at a time when the very unfunny violence of whiteness was inescapable. This replicates what many other scripted and even unscripted (news and reality) TV series did in the Trump era: "Media portrayed race and racism as qualities of personal meaning and divergent significance, as a mode of consumption and appropriation, rather than a means by which issues of inequality and disadvantage could be addressed," as Khadijah White argues.[18] Race has always shaped how post-cable TV networks have branded themselves, as Jennifer Fuller finds of cable TV's early fascination with Black and Latino stories to differentiate themselves from whitewashed broadcast TV in the early 2000s, and as Patrick Johnson finds of reruns in this volume.[19] In the streaming era, with more diverse audiences and more media for them to consume, representing all forms of identity becomes important to brand management.

But what does a studio do when its oldest and most valuable intellectual properties are racist? NBC sought buzz from the innovative realization that gay people can be horrible white people too: "the normalcy of gayness was stressed at the expense of queer identities and practices that would seriously challenge existing social and economic structures," as Eve Ng writes.[20] The difference of gayness becomes normal (and individualized) through white class privilege, while the white class privilege becomes less recognizable when refracted through gayness. As with hipster racism, *Will & Grace* "walks a fine line" that ultimately allows viewers to avoid difficult conversations about the real consequences of how horrible white people can be. Instead, horrible white people become special, quirky individuals we can laugh and connect with as representations of deeper cultural concerns.

Will & Grace (1998): Heteronormativity Is a Sham, or Is It?

Will & Grace starts with the titular characters in bed, speaking flirtatiously, and flirting with the audience's expectations of heteronormativity. "Come over, Grace, you know you want to," Will says as he watches *ER* (even if the show flops, NBC execs have at least used cross-promotion to remind the audience their hit show *ER* is next at 10 p.m.). Grace tells Will she can't, because she went shopping for a camisole that day and it was effective, evidenced by the man revealed to be in her bed, her boyfriend Danny. A cishetero audience member stumbling on this series by accident (the show premiered at 9:30 p.m.) might be confused as to why this man is flirting with this woman who already has a man in her bed. But Will outs himself immediately after stating he doesn't need her man: He has George Clooney (*ER*'s breakout hunk).

The pilot further marginalizes heteros by starting the first act with a bro-y activity—the card game—but it doesn't stop there, and quickly we learn that gay, disabled, and fat people will also be punchlines just as often as heteros. The second scene introduces Will's friend Jack (a masterclass in camp performance by Sean Hayes) singing show tunes instead of playing the game. In this sitcom, straight activities will always be disrupted by gay antics! The scene is scaffolded by jokes about how gay Jack is. So gay, everybody knows, from dead people to Grace's dog, and yes even "blind and deaf" people. Anyone whose body deviates from normative beauty is up for ridicule. Jack later mocks Will for gaining weight and going bald, setting up a punchline that would last the entire series, despite the fact that Eric McCormick is very visibly neither fat nor bald; this is supposed to be a joke, but becomes less funny when you know that LGBTQ people are more likely to experience eating disorders than cis/hetero people.[21]

The writers quickly establish class as the primary means through which audiences can relate to the leads. What makes *Will & Grace* relatable to the presumably not all gay SLUMPY demographic is their pursuit of upward mobility. In the next scenes we learn that Will is a lawyer whose main client is a conservative Texan executive gobbling up companies, and that Grace is an interior designer who will tolerate her rich, perpetually late, callous, and proudly conservative assistant Karen, who mocks her constantly, solely because Karen's rich friends are the base of her clientele. Karen, who never regrets marrying for money, is here to be the voice of the patriarchy. Assuming the thirty-year-old Grace is ten years older, Karen implores Grace to "close the deal" with her boyfriend Danny, despite doubts of his worth. (It should be noted here that the pilot features several references to bad mother–child relationships that also position it as a satire of the traditional family, with Karen acting as just one of these bad mothers to Grace). There is comedy in this tragedy and a touch of critique, showing how liberal characters like Will and Grace, in their pursuit of the good life, must compromise their politics for capital gain. We know now that the show will wring humor from the indignities the bourgeois must endure in late capitalism. But given US television's tendency to raise characters' economic status over multiple seasons to drive the plot and satisfy the myth of the American dream,[22] Will and Grace's economic precarity will be short-lived. (By the end of the series, Will is a partner in a big corporate law firm; Grace's firm is a success; and they both own property in pricey Manhattan.)

Before they *tell* us in the end, in the next scene the writers *show* that Grace's real soul mate is a man who loves her for everything but her sex, undercutting Karen's case for marriage. To do this the show creates a party game called "the $25,000 Pyramid." Unlike with the guys' card game, we get to witness this game—and we will again in the opening scene of the 2017 reboot. The Pyramid underscores how much more in sync than straight people a gay man and his best friend can be—"you give, I receive" Grace says, to which Will quips, "just like God intended." The writers use the Pyramid to perform some lightning-fast pop-culture quizzes and ideological exposition. First, a jab to heteronormativity. Will's clue: "Your parents' marriage." Grace gets it immediately: "Things that are dead!" But next, a nod to white gay relations outside the institution of marriage. Will's clue: "My one-night stand on Fire Island." Grace: "Latin things!" It's a gesture to ethno-sexual conquest reminiscent of colonial relations on the bougie vacation island that favors New York's gay male elite. But we aren't given much time to process it. There are three more clues after that one before the end of their turn, which finishes with Will saying "each other" and Grace answering "Things that you lean on!"[23] Audiences learn again of heterosexuality's failings from their two boring straight friends: "Grace and Danny never play this well." Here we see how the show both critiques heteronormativity and yet subtly reconstructs it.[24]

Sprinkled in the unfolding of the A-plot—chiefly, Grace's engagement to Danny and subsequent failed wedding—we get some cute moments of casual ignorance, including Will using the transphobic trope that transwomen are just gay men to insult Jack, and Karen mangling

Spanish to insult her housekeeper, Rosario (not cast in the pilot), even after Will gives Karen the correct pronunciation of the words she's trying to say. Here, by marginalizing trans people and people of color, the show centers cis-ness and whiteness as neutral, comforting cisheterosexual SLUMPY viewers who may not relate to its gayness or distancing of sexual relations between men and women.

The pilot drags heteronormativity as a sham, uplifting white gay–female relations as the only relation of value, at the expense of people of color and othered bodies. Hetero marriage just *is*, which is all Karen can muster to say about it after Grace's falls apart so spectacularly. The pilot ends with Will and Grace in a bar, Grace in a wedding dress, and the whole bar celebrating their union. Grace says Will is her soulmate, but lest we fear the showrunners have gone too far in pushing the two as a real partnership—which would smell too much of corporate brand-safe co-optation—after the bar pressures them to kiss we are assured: Will feels nothing. His desire is not centered and won't be for the first season. The pilot confirms the engine of the show will be his non-sexual relationship with a woman and their pursuit of the American Dream. In this way, *Will & Grace* pokes fun at traditional marriage between a man and a woman, historically an institution for racial and class uplift,[25] only to reconstitute it—just without sex. Throughout the series, the joke persists that, given that so many marriages are sexless, Will and Grace are actually the perfect couple.

Will & Grace Pilot (2017): Whiteness as (In)visible

The writers maintain the show's thin critique of heteronormativity in the reboot, but by 2017 the show gets overtaken by "the culture wars." The pilot (S1, E1) opens with the Pyramid game, and Will and Grace are still the perfect match. Gone is any apparent doubt about the inevitability of their partnership. They're still single, but they will always have each other. Meanwhile Karen will always have a martini, pills, and the ability to black out with her eyes open. Jack wakes the sleeping Karen by shaking her pills. She jumps up asking who won the election. Will and Grace say, despondently: Her guy. It's a wink to fans: We know that means Trump, both because Will and Grace are furrowing their lips and because fans know by now Karen has not only voted for but also befriended every Republican president since and including Richard Nixon. We are supposed to love Karen anyway because she's the ultimate diva, as cruel as Cruella but as cute as a Disney princess. This pilot shows whiteness's weak resistance amid political fascism and its strong commitment to white interpersonal relationships and partnerships.

The writers wring comedy from the weak political engagement of the white liberal bourgeoisie in their class aspirations and pursuit of sexual relations and contrast it with conservatives' uncompromising commitment to power. The rest of the episode exorcises our anxieties about Trump and avoids viewers falling out of love with the Trump-loving Karen by presenting the politically lazy Will and Grace each engaged in Faustian bargains. Will has his performative wokeness exposed after we learn of his "heroic" angry emails to his attractive anti-environment congressman Steve Sandoval, who wants to gut the EPA. The emails are not activism but merely a way for him to flirt his way to an "Anderson Cooper" or to marrying a rich and famous gay guy. Partnership is a path to power, politics be damned. Grace makes no pretense to wokeness, at least not anymore. She uses her "pussy hat" to sneak candy into the movies. Still, her loose ethics are challenged by Karen, who has convinced Melania Trump to hire Grace to redecorate the Oval Office. She resists, but she wants the job.

The reboot poses a politically charged question that suggests an understanding of the stakes of the cultural moment: What will it take to get white liberals to commit to their values over their racialized class and sexual interests? Will and Grace both know their actions are hypocritical, but the pursuit of dream partnerships and career coups wins out, and they are both at the White House by act 2 (though not before we get a quick scene with Anthony Ramos as Grace's new employee, who is reluctant and perhaps disempowered to disclose that Karen has been spewing offensive anti-Latino rhetoric in the office). Most of act 2 is a pastiche of cheap Trump jokes that don't rank in a crowded field that includes every comedian on the internet. Karen continues to think rich people are above it all, and Jack is still coming up with silly business ideas with his name anchoring the corny brand. We've heard these jokes before, either in *Will & Grace* ten years ago or on Twitter six months ago.

The episode climaxes with Will and Grace confronting each other in the Oval Office, resulting in a pillow fight after the president's assistant leaves stating she "can't watch another husband-and-wife fight in this office." It is a hint of the pitfalls of heterosexual marriage, with dark undertones given Trump's history of sexual violence and Melania Trump's public displays of displeasure with him. That the fight is turned into a joke comforts the SLUMPY audience's feelings of superiority, especially when compared to the emergent fascist public's continuing attack on the rights of women. But the scene is only funny because it reduces these dynamics to an interpersonal relationship of a man, who is decidedly the worst, while avoiding how race, class, nationalism, homophobia, and transphobia were critical to this toxic marriage getting to the White House in the first place.

In New York, Will and Grace make up, with Will saying that chastising Grace makes him want to be a better person, and Grace saying it makes her try to be a better person, implying that they're both horrible people, but they know it and regret it, and that makes them perfect for each other. Grace's threat to move out was for show anyway: Her suitcase is empty. She's never going to leave Will. They're the perfect couple—rich, white, and eligible but refusing to marry or have sex or kids.

We're back to the original narrative of the show. In over a decade not much has changed. The writers assure us, though, that this time is different. Why? Because this time, "we *know* it's going to be exactly the same," which is what Will tells Grace of their relationship and, implicitly, the show itself. The reboot assures its audience that even as it flirts more directly with politics than it has in the past, it will not disrupt the show's silence on whiteness as the hidden culprit for Will and Grace's ignorance and lack of political fortitude. An astute viewer can see this, but if you don't want to think too hard, Will and Grace are still our favorite, clueless, harmless liberal couple.

Conclusion

The *Will & Grace* revival lasted three seasons and relied on network TV's nostalgia for the brand of cultural relevance they created with the SLUMPY demographic, a demographic that by 2017 had drastically changed. By 2017 the SLUMPY demographic have more options than broadcast TV, increasing legacy networks' anxiety over the value of their old-fashioned intellectual property. Social media platforms and big-data-driven streaming services have raised the bar for political satire and comedy through their circulation of content foregrounding the many ways people can be queer, including how white professional queers can marginalize the interests of their Black, Brown, poor, trans, disabled kin. We see this anxiety about the cultural shifts of the SLUMPY audience in other reboots that continue to center white cishetero leads such as *And Just Like That . . .* and *The Matrix*, which surround their normative leads with trans and nonbinary people of color, keeping them on the margins of the narrative and thinly written but a little more visible—what Kristen Warner calls "plastic representation." Plastic representation allows TV to stay culturally relevant without having to empower people of color in the writers' room.[26] We also see plastic representation in the many reboots that replace white leads with characters of color, including others in this volume like *Charmed*, *One Day at a Time*, and *Party of Five* in addition to more politically focused reboots like *Queer as Folk*.

NBC's brand greatly benefited from *Will & Grace*'s legacy for opening space for gay representation. Everyone loves to give NBC and *Will & Grace* credit for changing the cultural terrain that eventually shifted public opinion on gay marriage while opening the doors for other forms of intersectional representation. By the time of the reboot, GLAAD reported increasing number of LGBTQ series regulars (by 2022 half would be people of color), and gay marriage had been won nationally (after a decades-long well-funded campaign to give gay people the right to the normative institution and its benefits at the expense of funding activism for issues like LGBTQ homelessness or queer-affirming care for senior citizens)—though by the time the reboot ended in 2020, fears were already brewing that gay marriage would be lost and gains in rights for people of color would be threatened, driven by Supreme Court justices handpicked by the president *Will & Grace* (2017) makes into a joke.

Few people give NBC credit for Trump, but his NBC series *The Apprentice* picked up where *Will & Grace* left off in the mid-2000s. The spin-off series *Celebrity Apprentice*, which premiered after the 2007–2008 writers' strike, encouraged corporations to order reality TV to circumvent the rising cost of union labor. Both *Apprentice* series ran up to and through Trump's bid for and ascendancy to the presidency, ending in 2015 and 2017. NBC's *Apprentice* was critical in promoting the fiction of Trump as a successful businessman, which was fundamental to his qualifications for presidency, despite the fact that his businesses have lost hundreds of millions of dollars and faced thousands of lawsuits for how they have treated workers and customers. In an episode of the Netflix documentary series *Dirty Money* called "The Confidence Man," which explores Trump's many business failings, the producers of *The Apprentice* describe how they renovated the Trump Organization's dilapidated midtown office to look almost presidential, inspired by the climactic scene in the film *Network*.[27] To the producers, it was camp, a joke. But not to all viewers. The documentary shows how *Apprentice* fans became Trump voters, who, reveling in the splendor of his (fake) palatial office, couldn't possibly believe he lacked business acumen or ethics because of NBC's gloss.

Will & Grace follows a lineage of television programs where irony engages audiences in double entendre. Jokes and references represent a progressive stance or satirize a conservative one, in this case regarding issues of sexuality and class. But jokes that are made at the expense of other marginalized communities center normative whiteness, with its associated components of gender, class, education, location, et cetera. Even more so, television and media studies research questions whether the double or multiple entendre is processed as such by audiences, as Sut Jhally famously showed decades ago with *The Cosby Show*, which, contrary to the aims of its creator, actually increased anti-Black sentiments by framing the Cosby family as the exception to the stereotype.[28] *Will & Grace* positions its leads as exceptions to capitalist heteronormativity and its associations with white supremacy but ends up reifying it. The creators of *The Apprentice* thought they were satirizing corporate New York: How could anyone believe an effective capitalist would treat even high-value workers so capriciously? The reality is that white supremacy and capitalism are remarkably adept at disposing of those who do not fit its ideal as a strategy to hold on to power: Both Trump and Will and Grace, despite their obvious incompetency, have whiteness to support their claims to capital. That is all they need, and, despite producers' efforts, it's not funny. Both *Will & Grace* and *The Apprentice* show the limits of satirizing the hollowness of whiteness's power without naming it explicitly: Not everyone's in on the joke! Many take the satire at face value—once more over-valorizing bourgeois whiteness without acknowledging its privilege over otherly racialized and less economically wealthy segments of the population.

Discussion Questions

1. Discuss the role of whiteness, white identity, and heteronormativity in the original and the revival.
2. What role does capitalism play in the production of the original and the revival?
3. Identify one example of how the revival continues the originals production and representation of inequality.

NOTES

1 Ron Becker, "Gay-Themed Television and the Slumpy Class: The Affordable, Multicultural Politics of the Gay Nineties," *Television & New Media* 7, no. 2 (2006): 184–215, https://doi.org/10.1177/1527476403255830.

2 Herman Gray, *Watching Race: Television and the Struggle for Blackness* (University of Minnesota Press, 1995); Alfred L. Martin, Jr., *The Generic Closet: Black Gayness and the Black-Cast Sitcom* (Indiana University Press, 2021); Kristal Brent Zook, *Color by Fox: The Fox Network and the Revolution in Black Television* (Oxford University Press, 1999).

3 Taylor Nygaard and Jorie Lagerwey, *Horrible White People: Gender, Genre, and Television's Precarious Whiteness* (New York University Press, 2020).

4 Audience theory suggests that viewers might interpret these interventions in a range of possible ways. The dominant reading might very well be the derisive one, though there are likely to be members of the audience reading against the grain.

5 Martin, *The Generic Closet.*

6 Lacy Rose, "TV Networks, Studios Shifting Program Strategies in the Trump Age: Are We Telling the Right Stories?," *Hollywood Reporter*, December 16, 2016, www.hollywoodreporter.com.

7 Cathy J. Cohen, "Punks, Bulldaggers, and Welfare Queens: The Radical Potential of Queer Politics?," in *Black Queer Studies*, ed. E. Patrick Johnson and Mae G. Henderson (Duke University Press, 2005), 21–51; Audre Lorde, "Age, Race, Class, and Sex: Women Redefining Difference," in *Sister Outsider: Essays and Speeches* (The Crossing Press, 1984), 114–23.

8 Nygaard and Lagerway, *Horrible White People.*

9 Drawing on Kirsten Marthe Lentz, "Quality Versus Relevance: Feminism, Race, and the Politics of the Sign in 1970s Television," *Camera Obscura* 15, no. 1 (2000): 44–93, https://muse.jhu.edu/article/7943/pdf.

10 Jennifer Fuller, "Branding Blackness on US Cable Television," *Media, Culture & Society* 32, no. 2 (2010): 285–305, https://doi.org/10.1177/0163443709355611; Gray, *Watching Race.*

11 Isabel Molina-Guzmán, "#OscarsSoWhite: How Stuart Hall Explains Why Nothing Changes in Hollywood and Everything Is Changing," *Critical Studies in*

Media Communication 33, no. 5 (2016): 443, https://doi.org/10.1080/15295036.2016.1227864.

12 Nygaard and Lagerway, *Horrible White People*, 7.

13 Isabel Molina-Guzmán, *Latinas and Latinos on TV: Colorblind Comedy in the Post-Racial Network Era* (University of Arizona Press, 2018), 48.

14 Rick Kissell, "Upscale Viewers Enrich CBS, ABC," *Variety*, November 4, 2004, https://variety.com.

15 Hunter Hargraves, *Uncomfortable Television* (Duke University Press, 2022).

16 Cheryl I. Harris, "Whiteness as Property," *Harvard Law Review* 106, no. 8 (1993): 1725.

17 Sarah Banet-Weiser, *Authentic™: The Politics of Ambivalence in a Brand Culture* (New York University Press, 2012).

18 Khadijah Costley White, *The Branding of Right-Wing Activism: The News Media and the Tea Party* (Oxford University Press, 2018), 122.

19 Fuller, "Branding Blackness and U.S. Cable Television."

20 Eve Ng, "A 'Post-Gay' Era? Media Gaystreaming, Homonormativity, and the Politics of LGBT Integration," *Communication, Culture & Critique* 6, no. 2 (2013): 261, https://doi.org/10.1111/cccr.12013.

21 Lacie L. Parker and Jennifer A. Harriger, "Eating Disorders and Disordered Eating Behaviors in the LGBT Population: A Review of the Literature," *Journal of Eating Disorders* 8, no. 1 (2020): 1–20, https://doi.org/10.1186/s40337-020-00327-y.

22 Herman Gray, "Television, Black Americans, and the American Dream," *Critical Studies in Mass Communication*, 6, no. 4 (1989): 376–86, https://doi.org/10.1080/15295038909366763; Sut Jhally and Justin Lewis, *Enlightened Racism: "The Cosby Show," Audiences, and the Myth of the American Dream* (Routledge, 1992).

23 See "Will & Grace Play a Crazy Game of Pyramid | Will & Grace," *Will & Grace*, September 8, 2022, video, 3:00, https://youtu.be/ZXWoYxtgYAE.

24 Mary Beltrán, "The Hollywood Latina Body as Site of Social Struggle: Media Constructions of Stardom and Jennifer Lopez's 'Cross-Over Butt,'" *Quarterly Review of Film and Video* 19, no. 1 (2002): 71–86, https://doi.org/10.1080/10509200214823; Bernadette Marie Calafell, "Ricky Martin's Body as a Text," in *Latina/o Communication Studies: Theorizing Performance* (Peter Lang, 2003), 88–199.

25 Natalia Sarkisian and Naomi Gerste, *Nuclear Family Values, Extended Family Lives: The Power of Race, Class, and Gender* (Routledge, 2012).

26 Kristen J. Warner, "In the Time of Plastic Representation," *Film Quarterly* 71, no. 2 (2017): 32–37, https://filmquarterly.org.

27 *Dirty Money*, season 1, episode 6, "The Confidence Man," directed by Fisher Stevens, aired January 26, 2018, on Netflix.

28 Jhally, *Enlightened Racism*.

2

From "Domestic Goddess" to "Angry White Woman"

Reaching for Trumpist Audiences in the Roseanne *Revival*

CÉLINE MORIN

Reading Note: As an exemplar of rebooted texts produced in the context of Donald Trump's presidential election, this chapter contrasts the socialist feminist critique of the original with the themes of white aggrievement in the reboot. Both the reboot producers and network executives situate the program as an attempt to encourage political dialogue and reach marginalized audiences—white, disaffected Trump voters. Yet, as the author documents, the show's transition from the original's storylines grounded in gender and economic inequality to the reboot's storylines shaped by perceptions of racial and cultural displacement contribute to the political polarization around immigration, sexual reproduction, gender fluidity, and the environment, among other issues.

Introduction

The reboots highlighted in this collection show just how atypical the *Roseanne* reboot[1] launched by ABC in 2018 really was: It was a significant attempt from a major US network to reach a new "pro-Trump audience." Turning its back on the feminist and working-class perspective of the original show (1988–1997), ABC greenlighted a rebooted *Roseanne*, defending it as a "cultural forum" at a time of national division, when political polarization led people to consider others, Democrats or Republicans, not as adversaries to debate with but as "enemies to be destroyed,"[2] therefore damaging the very foundations of democracy. Thus, there are two diametrically opposed reboot strategies. The first consists of adopting new representations of subaltern populations, which implicitly or explicitly critique the lack of diversity in the original productions. (The rebooted *Charmed* in fact attracted complaints from the original actresses, particularly Holly Marie Combs and Rose McGowan, as discussed by Molina-Guzmán in this volume.) The target audiences for that first strategy are clearly younger audiences, who are presumably more open-minded about issues of equality, in addition to fans of the original shows. The other strategy, similar to the *Will & Grace* reboot, and better embodied by the *Roseanne* reboot, is to cloak its more conservative representational politics in honorable intentions: reconciling politically polarized audiences to attract a conservative or reactionary audience that the 2016 and 2024 US presidential elections helped crystallize, but that the television industry had yet to identify clearly.

Originally aired in March 2018, the new *Roseanne* drew a lot of media attention in the United States and abroad. Some media reports praised the show's stated ambition of establishing dialogue between families perceived to be divided by the 2016 presidential election.[3] Others questioned its creator's political about-face. Roseanne Barr identified as a radical feminist and a socialist in the 1980s, only to become a fervent supporter of Donald Trump in 2016.[4] Using the nuclear-family household—television's best-charted territory since its beginnings—the reboot storylines revolved around the Conner family's economic difficulties. As this essay shows, however, they soon turned to championing the "family crisis," a discourse popular among social conservatives.[5] Discourses of the family in crisis focus on dismantling economic redistribution and welfare programs or emphasize countercultural resources that staunchly defend heteronormative familialist solidarity. This article explores the new *Roseanne* storylines about the definition of "Trumpism" in which the family must be preserved in the face of financial difficulties and modern values such as surrogate motherhood, youth emancipation, or immigration. While class and gender intersected in the original series to explore its blue-collar, feminist heroine's organizational issues, the reboot locates most problems outside the heteronormative family, a family that now acts as a sanctuary that must be preserved.

While nuclear-family homes have historically "made room for TV," as Lynn Spigel illustrated,[6] studying the *Roseanne* revival provides an opportunity to see how television makes room for a neoliberal, somewhat Trumpist reading of family structures and values. As a medium that has historically played an important role in representing normative notions of the family, what room has network television (and particularly a family network like ABC, owned by Disney) made for the idea of families in crisis?

ABC chose a very specific television series to appeal to Trump voters. *Roseanne* represented a crucial turning point in the history of television, particularly in terms of its crystallization of feminism on US American TV.[7] Yet the reboot storylines and characters work together to represent a feminist backlash. This representational move is all the more surprising when one considers the work Roseanne Barr did in the 1980s: poking fun at television's historical tropism toward perfect housewives, sharing her difficulties as a female showrunner, shedding light on radical feminist issues, and insisting on the need for politicizing family relations rather than simply encouraging women to find emancipation through work. As Janet Lee pointed out,[8] a "distinguishing feature of this series which sets it apart as a vehicle of resistance, is that it is woman-centered entertainment. . . . Roseanne, her will, feelings and perspective come through as central narrator and protagonist. Importantly she is situated, and thus gender is located, within a social totality." Roseanne's main issues were located both within the public sphere—where her working-class status gave her little agency over her material conditions—and within the private sphere, where she both asserted herself as a long-oppressed subject and fought for maintaining the stability of her family. In a nutshell, "Roseanne continually underscore[d] the thin line between blue-collar respectability and white-trash degradation," leading to explicit critiques of Reaganian policies.[9]

The production politics of the reboot, however, depend on writing fictional stories based on a certain vision of Trumpism, combining "nationalism and popular sovereignty"[10] with "the family" standing in for "the people." Indeed, familialist protectionism is omnipresent: The characters' material conditions are constantly being undermined by threats to the family's stability, prosperity, and tranquility, making parochialism one of the cornerstones of rebooted texts.[11] In so doing, the series reconnects class predominantly with whiteness rather than gender. Interestingly, in another chapter, Stephanie Pérez shows how the reboot of *Sex and the City*, titled *And Just Like That . . .* , subtly incorporates whiteness as an unspoken yet operative factor in its portrayal of supposed inclusivity. In *Roseanne*, this protectionist stance is fueled by a dichotomy between economics and culture. "Serious" and "dangerous" issues, such as unfair competition from undocumented workers, gestational surrogacy, and more, threaten the well-being of the family, whereas practices and values presented as less "tangible," including intergenerational communication and environmental responsibility, are characterized as non-issues. Some historical perspective is required here. On the one hand, the intertwined history of family values and the alliances between neoliberalism and social conservatism[12] allows for a better understanding of why the series was so eager to criticize the nuclear family in the 1980s and 1990s, and so determined to defend it nowadays. On the other, the intertwined history of the nuclear family, postwar suburbs, and television are crucial to understanding the role of the "family in crisis" in recent political conflict.

This study is based on a systematic analysis of *Roseanne* reboot episodes, enhanced by an analysis of discourses from creative and production teams, and promotional appearances by the actors on television and in the press. I begin by analyzing ABC's promise that Roseanne would provide a "cultural forum" as well as network executives' strategies to reach a "pro-Trump audience." I then draw a comparison between 1998's *Roseanne* and the 2018 reboot showing how the original feminist critique of the nuclear family evolved into familialist protectionism that addresses a renewed neoliberal defense of "family responsibility" discourses embedded in Trumpism.

A "Cultural Forum" for Trumpism

The factors that enabled a show as atypical as the original *Roseanne* to reach the airwaves, as well as the difficulties Roseanne Barr encountered in keeping the upper hand during production, have been extensively documented by academics.[13] Repeated attempts to dispossess Barr of her show (plans to insert two other major female characters, script changes, infantilization, and more) both undermined and fueled the original production. Yet ABC's efforts to improve American sitcoms—and the 1988 Writers Guild of America strike—allowed Barr to benefit from a slack in editorial oversight. While production of the original *Roseanne* responded nimbly to those various tensions in a context of reduced content, production of the reboot is due far more to ABC's determination to tap into Trumpism to expand its audience reach, and in so doing, to offer their own definition of it.

ABC executives and *Roseanne*'s creative team explicitly stated their hope the reboot would turn Trump voters into a renewed network television audience.[14] Since political polls had overlooked Trump voters in the 2016 election, executives feared that television market research might have also neglected potential viewers. Implicitly the executives and producers endorse the idea that Donald Trump was elected by working-class voters (which is in itself a controversial assumption[15]). Thus, ABC proposed a show grounded in Trumpist arguments about the "family in crisis."[16] In other words, the reboot storylines focused on working class's prejudices due to the nuclear families' lost ability to protect their members from the economic and cultural dangers of modernity. From promotion to representation, the new *Roseanne* promised to be an accurate depiction of working-class Americans. Underlying the reboot was the idea of a representation for "economic minorities." Sara Gilbert, who plays Roseanne's daughter Darlene, and who co-produced the reboot, explains: "We did have a wonderful opportunity to talk about this [tension] in the context of a family, and I think part of what's going on is that people feel like they can't disagree and still love each other or still talk to each other."[17] Short of finding compromises, pro-Trump and anti-Trump, pro-Trumpism and anti-Trumpism advocates could at least finally engage in entertaining discussion once again.

The democratic ideal of public dialogue and debate informed production behind the scenes and representation on screen. A diverse writing room would work at representing ideological and intergenerational conflicts within the rebooted Conner family. In this sense, changes such as the new, more central role given to Roseanne's daughter, Darlene, and the addition of grandchildren, particularly a Black granddaughter, were seen as the guarantors of renewed ideological syncretism. Off screen, the hiring of feminist comedian Whitney Cummings as showrunner and the liberal comedian and openly lesbian Wanda Sykes as writer and consulting producer was supposed to offer progressive insights into Trumpian times. However, creative dissensions soon emerged: Cummings, who described how she was treated like "the progressive 'lib-tard' in the room," talked about how difficult it was to incorporate liberal ideas into the show,[18] while Sykes resigned immediately after Barr's racist tweets. This implosion attests to the creative constraints that weighed on the "liberal side" of the writing room.

The reboot's goal of creating a "cultural forum" in Trumpian times was made more appealing by the fact that the first series had produced an exploration of the household as a public sphere for family issues: From 1988 to 1997 on ABC, the show addressed the everyday life of a working-class family, composed of Dan (John Goodman) and Roseanne (Roseanne Barr) and their three children, D.J. (Michael Fishman), Darlene (Sara Gilbert), and Becky (Alicia Goranson, then Sarah Chalke). The original show grew out of Roseanne Barr's stand-up comedy, in which she referred to herself as a "domestic goddess," poking fun at home life and deconstructing motherhood and femininity. This made Barr an icon for feminist rebellion, while also saddling her with extensive negative publicity.[19] The first show focused on progressive policies that had been hitherto unseen on national networks: gay marriage, abortion, divorce, sexually active teens, and more.[20]

The reboot's ideological shift is all the more glaring in that other contemporary series focusing on working-class characters managed to approach multiculturalism as an individual or relational resource rather than a threat. Series like *Jane the Virgin*, *Superstore*, *Black-ish*, *Fresh off the Boat*, and *One Day at a Time* address economic justice and social justice as being complementary rather than in competition with each other. These series emphasize intergenerational female solidarity.[21] In *Jane the Virgin*, which is about a family with Venezuelan roots, and *One Day at a Time*, in which the family's background is Cuban, three generations of women living under the same roof act as incarnations of evolving femininity and feminism. Thus, there was nothing random about *Roseanne*'s derisive nod to those other series when, in the reboot, Dan wakes up from a late nap and asks what they've missed: "All the shows about Black and Asian families," to which Roseanne sarcastically replies, "They're just like us . . . There, now you're all caught up."[22] That brief exchange references the sense of threat opening representational spaces to minorities engenders.

"Us" Versus "Them": The White Family as Economic Minority

The key populist factor in promotional appearances for the show was an insistence on a divide between "us" (the creators, attentive to working-class issues) and "them" (Hollywood elites). Roseanne Barr explained that she had "always tried to portray a realistic picture of American working-class people," adding that "it was working-class people who elected Trump, so I felt that was very real."[23] Endorsing the notion of a divide between the "people" and the "elite," Sara Gilbert defended the reboot: "This is a working-class family. I think sometimes people in Hollywood do working class through the lens of people who are privileged."[24] On the set of *The View*, Sara Gilbert emphasized that "people in the Conners' situation would be making less money now than they were then, and that's without even factoring inflation in, and that's twenty years ago. So we wanted to make sure going in that we're accurately representing the struggle of the middle class." On the same episode of *The View*, Roseanne Barr explained that "'Hispanic and Thai populations' were now 'dominant' in the city that inspired Landford, so that 'we're the minority now.'" Within the reboot "economic minorities" stand for the relegated white, working-class American family.

ABC's executives adopted a similar stance. Ben Sherwood, the president of Disney and ABC's television group, acknowledged that after Donald Trump was elected, "We looked at each other and said, 'There's a lot about this country we need to learn a lot more about, here on the coasts.'" Channing Dungey, president of ABC Entertainment, added, We had spent a lot of time looking for diverse voices in terms of people of color and people from different religions, and even people with a different perspective on gender, but we had not been thinking nearly enough about economic diversity and some of the other cultural divisions within our own country. That's been something we've been really looking at with eyes open since that time."[25]

The *Roseanne* reboot proved to be a complex alliance between various players trying to produce a story about the definition of "Trumpism" rather than, as Barr and Gilbert often stated, a simple discussion over "the" working-class situation in a Trumpian context that would be predefined and stable. The first episode's 18 million viewers—and their correlation with "red" states, where a majority voted for Donald Trump—would tend to show that the network's aim was true. While the coveted correlation between its audience, the working class, and Donald Trump voters was not obvious, there was a clear association with the traditional Republican vote. As *The New York Times* pointed out, "The top markets for the debut read like a political pollster's red-state checklist: Cincinnati; Kansas City, Missouri; Tulsa, Oklahoma. Liberal enclaves like New York and Los Angeles did not crack the top 20."[26] The voice Roseanne Barr had historically given to radical feminism had turned into a television referendum on Trump and the white working class that was now represented as a minority, or at least as one having been reduced to the status of a "silent majority."

On May 29, 2018, Barr tweeted "Muslim brotherhood & planet of the apes had a baby." The tweet was a reference to Valerie Jarrett, an African American lawyer and top adviser to Barack Obama. Despite Barr's apology on Twitter, Channing Dungey, president of ABC Entertainment, announced, "Roseanne's Twitter statement is abhorrent, repugnant, and inconsistent with our values, and we have decided to cancel her show." Bob Iger, CEO of Disney, ABC's parent company, tweeted, "There was only one thing to do here, and that was the right thing." Donald Trump defended Roseanne Barr, outraged that he himself had often been insulted on ABC without ever receiving an apology from Bob Iger. A spin-off entitled *The Conners*, about the rest of the family, but without Roseanne, began to air in 2019.

1988–2018: The Ideology of the "Family Crisis"—From Feminist Critiques to Family Protectionism, Trumpism in a Classic Sitcom

Representing "Economic Minorities"

Considering both the links between neoliberalism and the family[27] and those between the nuclear family and the American sitcom,[28] the new importance given to Trumpism in a sitcom like *Roseanne* starts to make sense. We are left, however, with trying to understand how the "family crisis" is represented in the new *Roseanne*.

Characters, relationships, story arcs, and situations are distributed across two landscapes pitched as opposites: a certain representation of the "economy" competes with a certain representation of "culture." The economic stakes, which are indeed "reduced largely to the lived immediacy of jobs and taxes,"[29] impact on the relational balance of the family and thus on the characters. An entire story arc about surrogate motherhood revolves around the economic confiscation of offspring and the exploitation of working-class bodies by higher classes. It pits Roseanne's daughter, Becky, against a rich white woman named Andrea, who offers Becky $50,000 to carry her child. The imbalances in the two characters' motivations glazes over her reasons for resorting to surrogacy. While the series does delve into what led Becky to consider becoming a surrogate mother ("If I do this, I can pay off my credit cards, I could buy a new car, maybe put something down on a house. I can't do that working at the restaurant"), many scenes are devoted to Roseanne and Dan's refusal to support her project ("That's like selling off one of our grandkids!" for Roseanne). The motivations driving Andrea to seek a surrogate are totally overlooked. Instead, the scenes and dialogue focus overwhelmingly on the economic and cultural gap between Becky and Andrea.

The latter woman is a pleasant but somewhat unfathomable character, unaffected by material or emotional concerns, unfamiliar with "real" problems. Becky's body is torn in several directions—between her own financial difficulties; Andrea, who wants to use it; and Roseanne and Dan, who want to control it. While the first *Roseanne* pitched the heroine's *physicality* as both a difference she owned and a resource for resistance, the second *Roseanne*'s approach to the *body* is disarticulated from female bodily integrity, focusing purely on a class relationship where the working classes are even dispossessed of their offspring.

Other narrative elements stress the culturist excesses of modernity, including self-expression, personal development, intergenerational dialogue, children's accountability, and even gender fluidity. For example, the character of Jackie has become an insecure, divorced life-coach. Bordering on hysteria, she lectures everyone, peppering them with out-of-touch advice and comments. Alongside the threats that are constructed as "material," three main stances are relentlessly derided for their supposed superficiality: the culturalism of a "disconnected" left; personal expression, which is criticized for its disengagement from material problems; and collective struggles, focused on environmental responsibility, which are portrayed as superficial because they are reduced to individual actions.

Jackie is an explicit counterweight to her sister's Trumpism. Throughout the season, Jackie shows up to give grandiloquent speeches or to uphold principles, seeking solutions only through discourse. Jackie embodies a wobbly articulation between reflexive individualism (fueled by personal insecurity—"You think I'm smart, don't you?" she anxiously asks at one point) and feminist ideology, but without her character's having a significant effect on the narrative processes. She interacts, deconstructs, reconsiders, supports without judgment . . . but accomplishes nothing.

Even Roseanne's grandson Mark's gender performance is subjected to a dichotomy between materiality and culture. When Mark's attraction to "feminine" clothes and activities begins to draw attention, he immediately reassures his grandmother that he does feel "like a boy." Furthermore, his possible attraction to boys is alluded to only theoretically. The material repercussions of Mark's gender expression are expressed through concern that he will be teased and bullied at school. Bullying is depicted through derogatory speech and physical threats, and it is eventually resolved though the support and protection provided by his family. Interestingly, gender is therefore one of the only areas where progressive culture is socially accepted.

Prioritizing Economic Issues over Cultural Ones

Culturist excesses are also ridiculed when young people try to assert themselves. The dichotomy between important "materiality" and superficial "culture" is depicted through a generational divide. Often Roseanne and Dan are portrayed as the only ones who realize that progressive values, desires, symbols, and individualism are obstacles to the Fordian family's survival. Whether it is in response to their grandson Mark's gender expression, their granddaughter Harris's teenage self-assertiveness, or their daughter Darlene's desire for creative work, Dan and Roseanne reassert their authority grounded in their experience of material hardship. Dan, for example, is outraged to see Darlene consider refusing a sexist job—but one that offers comprehensive health insurance—and attempts to explain to her "how the world works," and how her earlier problem-solving had been nothing but luck.

Environment, health, humanitarian work, and spirituality are also extensively derided. Through the characters of Andrea and David, those collective struggles are embodied as nothing more than pretexts for bourgeois women's or deadbeat men's selfish, individualistic quests. The desire for distinction is embodied by Andrea and her constant gifts: monthly deliveries of organic pears, ionized water in glass bottles, and potpourri. Her gifts come across less as reflections of her concern for Becky's health or the planet than as symbols of her upper-class values, which are saturated with distinctive markers.

Humanitarian work and spirituality are represented through David, Darlene's former companion, who abandoned their household. David returns from a humanitarian journey during which he meets Blue, whose first name and the fact that she does not want to "merge their spiritual paths until [Darlene and David] sign [their] divorce papers" represents modernity individualism through the privileging of New Age ideologies. Darlene is outraged by this new romance, stressing the "material/post-material" imbalance of the situation: "While I have been picking up kids' clothes, dealing with meltdowns, cleaning up vomit, you're dating a crayon?!"

David's appearance, with his crumpled and dirty clothes, messy beard, greasy hair, and the awkward look on his face, brings into relief the ambivalence of the transformation, signs of both his humanitarian commitment and his failings as a man and a father. Just as Andrea's motivations for turning to gestational surrogacy are glazed over, David reveals that his humanitarian commitment was a charade, a smokescreen hiding his lack of courage. "When I left you and the kids, I rationalized that it was okay because I was helping people. The truth is, I left because my brother died and I was overwhelmed with all the responsibility and I . . . I just ran. And once I was out there, I was ashamed." In the end, the broad spectrum of cosmopolitics encompasses practices so diverse that agro-ecological engagement, humanitarian work, and the quest for inner balance are all addressed, yet they are deprived of any political, collective, or economic value. Instead, they are reduced to nothing more than individual interests: the search for social distinction and the flight from family responsibility.

Defining Trumpism in Television

When the reboot's themes are grounded in the "cultural" (spirituality, personal development, organic food, etc.), the characters wield

Hogarthian resources to keep this strangeness at bay. Bolstered by the sitcom's distinctive canned laughter, sarcasm, jokes, and other ironic markers help the family face the difficult or incongruous situations they encounter. When the theme is presented as "economic" (surrogacy, the father's absence, immigration, unemployment), Roseanne's iconic sardonic laughter, which has always concluded the credits, is no longer enough: The family members all pitch in to try to counteract those redefinitions, although usually in vain. When Becky is unable to see her surrogacy through, for example, it is not because Roseanne and Dan convinced her to stop, but because her body is no longer fertile enough.[30] Worse, the family is sometimes forced to participate in its own dispossession, as when Dan, who loses a construction contract to immigrants, finds himself obliged to hire workers off the books in order to avoid bankruptcy.[31] Ultimately, the Conners' agency is focused on problems coded as "cultural" rather than "economic."

The irony is that this dichotomy, which prioritizes economic problems over cultural expressions, is itself cultural. As Lawrence Grossberg points out, we see to what extent "Trump's politics are cultural": "the problem space is reconstructed so that matters of both economics (reduced largely to the lived immediacy of jobs and taxes) and democracy (the relations between majorities and minorities) are displaced into the relations of nationality and difference," in such a way that "political polarization is translated into cultural polarization."[32] The reboot articulates economic threats to the working class with racial affects expressed as subaltern. In this sense, the new Roseanne amalgamates and homogenizes complex elements by depicting racial issues through the prism of white, working-class hardship and deprivation. The show not only engages in "inferential racism"[33] by never really questioning its whiteness, as has been extensively studied;[34] it actually conceals it behind a populist definition that merges "the" nuclear family and "the" working class, both portrayed as being endangered.

Conclusion

From "Domestic Goddess" to "Angry White Woman," what happened to *Roseanne*? From 1988 to 1997, Roseanne struggled against the inequitable structuration of the nuclear family and screamed its injustice at her family. But the reboot disarticulated the working-class perspectives from radical feminism in order to re-articulate them within whiteness, promoting a protectionist stance on the nuclear family that had been so heavily criticized in the first series.

As the promise of "disagreements between people that still love each other or still talk to each other" unfolds within family discussions, the progressive characters struggle to be credible in their arguments because the starting point is infused with anti-modern ideology. To figure out how to deal with such turbulence, intense clashes take place within the family where these practices are described as "*very* modern!" or "so politically correct." The series relentlessly rejects or makes fun of modern constructs like egalitarianism, historicity, identity politics, and subjectivities. The new *Roseanne* opposes "economics" and "culture," and it disqualifies "culture" as no longer offering a resource for characters by making the uniformly contradictory interests of homogenized social groups more glaring than ever: parents versus children, white people versus ethnic immigrants, the working class versus the upper class.

The values of advanced modernity are generally fought when they are associated with economic threats, or ridiculed when they are confined to culturalism, intellectualism, and expressivism. The definition of modernity given in *Roseanne* invariably brings its back to a danger, insofar as its egalitarianism turns into relativism. That is precisely where the fictional Trumpism of the new *Roseanne* lies: in its ironically cultural definition of an organic crisis based on a hierarchy of "economics" over "culture" and in its methodical delegitimization of identity politics, constructed as competing with working-class economic interests. The crux of this reboot's Trumpism lies less in combining certain degrees of "economics" and "affects" than in doing so by simultaneously propelling "culture" to the most postmodern recesses of modernity.

Discussion Questions

1. Why was the *Roseanne* revival cancelled and what does the cancellation tell us about the limits of nostalgia in reboots?
2. Identify three examples of Trumpism and nationalism in the *Roseanne* revival. Do you think the inclusion of nationalistic storylines contributed to the cancellation? Why or why not?

NOTES

1 The 2018 Roseanne could be defined as both a reboot and a revival, considering how it incorporates old and new characters around updated themes and storylines.

2 Chantal Mouffe, *The Return of the Political* (Verso Books, 2006).

3 Andrea Park, "5 Ways the 'Roseanne' Reboot Embraces Modern America," *CBS News*, March 29, 2018, www.cbsnews.com; Lynn Elber, "ABC's 'Roseanne' Revival Aims to Keep It Real," *Detroit News*, March 26, 2018; Emily St. James, "The *Roseanne* Revival Is Incredibly Honest About Life in Trump's America," *Vox*, March 28, 2018, www.vox.com; Lisa Fogarty, "The 'Roseanne' Reboot Is Exactly What We Need Right Now," *Good Housekeeping*, April 10, 2018, www.goodhousekeeping .com.

4 Eugene Scott, "How 'Roseanne' Reinforces a Myth About Trump Supporters," *Washington Post*, March 30, 2018; Rob Sheffield, "Why the New 'Roseanne' Reboot Just Plain Sucks," *Rolling Stone*, March 30, 2018, www.rollingstone.com; C. Nicole Mason, "'Roseanne' was About a White Family, but Was for All Working People. Not Anymore," *Washington Post*, April 3, 2018; Jared Yates Sexton, "The New *Roseanne* Ignores the Very Real Racism of Many White Working-Class Families," *Elle*, March 30, 2018, www.elle.com.

5 Melinda Cooper, *Family Values: Between Neoliberalism and the New Social Conservatism* (Zone Books, 2017).

6 Lynn Spigel, *Make Room for TV: Television and the Family Ideal in Postwar America* (University of Chicago Press, 1992).

7 Susan J. Douglas, *Where the Girls Are: Growing Up Female with the Mass Media* (Three Rivers Press, 1995); Kathleen Rowe, "Roseanne: Unruly Woman as Domestic Goddess," *Screen* 31, no. 4 (1990): 408–19, https://doi.org/10.1093/screen/31.4.408; Kathleen Rowe, *The Unruly Woman: Gender and the Genres of Laughter in Understanding Inequality* (University of Texas Press, 1995).

8 Janet Lee, "Subversive Sitcoms: *Roseanne* as Inspiration for Feminist Resistance," *Women's Studies* 21, no. 1 (1992): 87–101, https://doi.org/10.1080/00497878.1992.9978928.

9 Tison Pugh, "Feminism, Homosexuality, and Blue-Collar Perversity in *Roseanne*," in *The Queer Fantasies of the American Family Sitcom*, ed. Tison Pugh (Rutgers University Press, 2018); Judine Mayerle, "*Roseanne*—How Did You Get Inside My House? A Case Study of a Hit Blue-Collar Situation Comedy," *Journal of Popular Culture* 24, no. 4 (1991): 71–88, https://doi.org/10.1111/j.0022-3840.1991.2404_71.x.

10 Lawrence Grossberg, *Under the Cover of Chaos: Trump and the Battle for the American Right* (Pluto Press, 2018).

11 Meaghan Morris, "On the Future of Parochialism: Globalization, Young and Dangerous IV and Cinema Studies in Tuen Mun," in *Film History and National Cinema: Studies in Irish Film 2*, ed. John Hill and Kevin Rockett (Four Courts Press, 2005).

12 Cooper, *Family Values.*

13 Mayerle, "*Roseanne*—How Did You Get Inside My House?"; John Lahr, *Show and Tell: New Yorker Profiles* (The Overlook Press, 2000); Lawrence J. Epstein, *The Haunted Smile: The Story of Jewish Comedians in America* (Public Affairs, 2001); Lynn C. Spangler, *Television Women from "Lucy" to "Friends": Fifty Years of Sitcom and Feminism* (Praeger, 2003); Alessandra Senzani, "Class and Gender as a Laughing Matter? The Case of *Roseanne*," *Humor* 23, no. 2 (2010): 229–53, https://doi.org/10.1515/HUMR.2010.011.

14 John Koblin and Michael M. Grynbaum, "'Roseanne' Reboot Sprang from ABC's Heartland Strategy After Trump's Victory," *New York Times*, March 28, 2018.

15 Grossberg, *Under the Cover of Chaos.*

16 Cooper, *Family Values.*

17 Megan Vick, "The *Roseanne* Cast Defends the Decision to Make Roseanne a Trump Voter," *TV Guide*, October 1, 2018, www.tvguide.com.

18 "Whitney Cummings on 'Roseanne': 'I Was the Progressive Lib-Tard in the Room' | Comedy Showrunner Roundtable," *Hollywood Reporter*, June 11, 2018, video, 4:53, www.hollywoodreporter.com.

19 Barbara Ehrenreich, "The Wretched of the Hearth: The Undainty Feminism of Roseanne Barr," *New Republic*, April 2, 1990, 28–31; Allison Fraiberg, "Between the Laughter: Bridging Feminist Studies through Women's Stand-Up Comedy," in *Look Who's Laughing: Gender and Comedy*, ed. Gail Finney (Routledge, 1994); Philip Auslander, "'Brought to You by Fem-Rage': Stand-Up Comedy and the Politics of Gender," in *Acting Out: Feminist Performances*, ed. Peggy Phelan and Lynda Hart (University of Michigan Press, 1993), 315–36.

20 Pugh, "Feminism, Homosexuality, and Blue-Collar Perversity in *Roseanne*."

21 Zazil Reyes García and Claudia A. Evans-Zepeda, "Intergenerational Mujerista Latinidad: A Comparative Media Analysis of *One Day at a Time* and *Jane the Virgin*," *Critical Studies in Media Communication* 40, no. 5 (2023): 277–90, https://doi.org/10.1080/15295036.2023.2264936.

22 *Roseanne*, season 10, episode 3, "Roseanne Gets the Chair," written by Sid Youngers, directed by John Pasquin, aired April, 3 2018, on ABC.

23 Emma Dibdin, "The Conners Will Be 'Politically Divided' in 'Roseanne' Reboot," *Good Housekeeping*, January 8, 2018, www.goodhousekeeping.com.

24 Debra Birnbaum, "Sara Gilbert on Life After 'Roseanne,' Guiding the Reboot and the Upcoming 'Living Biblically,' *Variety*, February 14, 2018, https://variety.com.

25 Koblin and Grynbaum, "'Roseanne' Reboot Sprang from ABC's Heartland Strategy."

26 Koblin and Grynbaum, "'Roseanne' Reboot Sprang from ABC's Heartland Strategy."

27 Cooper, *Family Values.*

28 Spigel, *Make Room for TV.*

29 Grossberg, *Under the Cover of Chaos.*

30 *Roseanne*, season 10, episode 4, "Eggs Over, Not Easy," written by Morgan Murphy, directed by John Pasquin, aired April 10, 2018, on ABC.

31 *Roseanne*, season 10, episode 9, "Knee Deep," written by Bruce Rasmussen, directed by Gail Mancuso, aired May 22, 2018, on ABC.
32 Grossberg, *Under the Cover of Chaos*.
33 Stuart Hall, "The Whites of Their Eyes: Racist Ideologies and the Media," in *The Race and Media Reader*, ed. Gilbert B. Rodman (Routledge, 2003).
34 Richard Dyer, *White: Essays on Race and Culture* (Routledge, 1997).

3

Dazzling Intimacies and the Mirage of Inclusion in *And Just Like That . . .*

STEPHANIE MELISSA PÉREZ

READING NOTE: The reboot of the iconic white postfeminist HBO show *Sex and the City* uncomfortably attempts to bring its racially homogenizing past to a more diverse present moment. However, as Stephanie Pérez documents in her analysis, the more racially diverse revival ultimately continues its celebration of wealthy, white womanhood and conspicuous consumption as a form of feminist power. Because revivals, after all, are beloved by audiences for their nostalgic celebration of idealized white identities, upper-middle-class privilege, and heteronormative values, the inclusion of diverse secondary characters usually exists only in relation to the development of the white main characters. In the case of *And Just Like That . . .* Pérez illustrates that the inclusion of diverse actors and characters reinforces the depiction of race, ethnicity, and queer sexuality as newly discovered and thus ultimately erases the more complicated multiracial present.

Introduction

While conservative and Trumpian politics define the suburban Midwestern milieu in the 2018 reboot of *Roseanne*, New York City's[1] mediated representation as a white cosmopolitan metropolis in *Sex and the City* (*SATC*; 1998–2004, HBO) and its eponymous films (2008, 2010) is interrupted by new ethnoracialized and nonbinary characters featured in the HBO Max[2] reboot series *And Just Like That . . .* (*AJLT*; 2021–). However, *AJLT* renders a sexless parallel version of NYC that otherizes and fetishizes Seema Patel, Nya Wallace, Che Diaz, and Lisa Todd Wexley under the guise of inclusion.[3] These new characters become accessories and vessels through which original characters Carrie Bradshaw,

Miranda Hobbes, and Charlotte York reconstruct their hang-ups about sexuality, gender, race, and class. Situated among several rebooted series that responded to the Black Lives Matter protests, the 2016 and 2020 elections, and the resulting corporatization of DEI (diversity, equity, and inclusion) initiatives, *AJLT*'s characterization of Carrie, Miranda, and Charlotte ultimately exposes the franchise's rebooting of conservative understandings of liberal whiteness through the girlification of white women entering Third Age.

Although the *SATC* series and films culminate in Carrie's romantic reunions with Big and NYC, the platonic reunions between Carrie, Miranda, Charlotte, and Samantha solidify their soulmate status beyond their romantic pairings over two decades later in *AJLT*. By extension, these intimacies open a space for white women to self-correct or preserve their knowledge about gender and sexuality, while incubating anxiety about their ideological obsolescence when confronted by their loved ones, new friends, and the next generation. *AJLT* brings three of the four original leads into 2021 while sprinkling in new ethnoracialized, queer, and nonbinary adults and teenagers who signify the vibrance of multiculturalism in a neoliberal and postfeminist NYC, simultaneously disguising subtle forms of racism by marginally including diverse characters as vessels for white women's growth. Though the younger generation challenges the core characters' self-understanding, Seema, Nya, Lisa, Che, Lily, Rock, and Luisa turn into ethnoracialized and LGBTQIA+ accessories for the core white women, legitimizing Carrie, Miranda, and Charlotte's softened makeover journeys into semi-permanent self-actualization.

The Erotics of Romantic-Platonic Intimacy and Third Age

I define romantic-platonic intimacies as a prioritization of women's intense friendships and body knowledge in community, instead of centering heterosexual romantic fulfillment as a determinant of love. Instead of competing for male attention, the women seek equality in casual dating by mimicking the impersonal nature of casual sex attributed to men,[4] while consistently reaffirming their emotional commitment to each other as soulmates. For Carrie and her friends, dating men as a "narrative of [heterosexual] romantic adventure" serves as a

Figure 3.1. The all-white and heteronormative cast of the original. From left to right: Miranda Hobbes (Cynthia Nixon), Charlotte York (Kristin Davis), Carrie Bradshaw (Sarah Jessica Parker), Samantha Jones (Kim Cattrall). *Source*: Promotional image photographed by Norman Jean Roy for HBO.

"'mere pre-text' for the more important narrative of women-bonding,"[5] and they cultivate self-empowerment, emotional growth, and a physical and emotional understanding of their own and each other's bodies. Narratively and visually, this happens in *SATC* in the beginning and finale of the series and when all four white women leads are framed together.

Carrie, Charlotte, Miranda, and Samantha are white, cisheterosexual, professional New Yorkers who are individual, yet symmetrical, archetypes of white postfeminist womanhood. The women explore sex, friendship, love, and intimacy in NYC, a neoliberal postfeminist "women's world"[6] where their lives revolve around socioeconomic mobility via heterosexual romantic relationships and friendship between women rather than career aspirations. They express agency with a consumerist ethos via fashion and real estate, transitioning into the individual search for fulfillment via cisheterosexual romantic love and marriage with constant platonic intimacies established between all four women.

Racialized, queer, trans, and poor people are nonexistent in this fictionalized women's world except where they are tokenized or fetishized and are often backgrounded, disappeared, or made into sidekicks. *SATC* occasionally accessorizes the women with ethnoracialized sexual conquests whose interiorities are flattened; the only ethnoracialized pairings in *SATC* are Latine/x and Black and endowed with sexual prowess and anger issues, furthering media tropes of violent or rakish Black men and spitfire Latina women. Queerness is almost completely backgrounded, with the two gay best friend characters, Stanford Blatch and Anthony Marentino, acting as sidekicks,[7] recurring characters who accessorize and confirm the context of the series' production, but are not part of the core and are rendered two-dimensionally.

In *AJLT*, the romantic-platonic intimacies between Carrie, Charlotte, and Miranda are born from the frank cosmopolitan conversations about sex and sexuality that shaped *SATC* yet are colored by shame attributed to age and maturity. Now, they try to make sense of loss and aging instead of reveling in romance and sex, a different kind of intimacy with jarring outcomes. Carrie, Miranda, and Charlotte uneasily arrive at the juncture of midlife crises and retirement as they contemplate their futures in light of bereavement, atrophied marriage, and their children's maturation. As the women enter Third Age, the period between raising a family and the fragility entailed by later years, their continuous movement and an entrepreneurial sense of productivity reflect its luminosity,[8] but produce an anxiety that hasn't caught up—and may never catch up— to contemporary values, especially those socially constructed by youth. With unambiguous financial security, the women invest in their own bodies, expand their interiorities, and revive their neoliberal investment in fashion and housing, entailing agency and choice.

While *SATC* celebrated the passage of time, the women and their spouses struggle through aging in *AJLT* by way of graying hair, hearing aids, hip surgery, Botox, uncoolness, and learning to grieve. Third Age also requires Carrie, Miranda, and Charlotte to get used to modern social vernacular lest they be labeled Boomers. Rock's gender-questioning, Miranda's affair, and Lily's body confidence particularly challenge Charlotte. Miranda's affair with Che becomes metonymic for her unhappiness at home, where her sexual repulsion to her husband, Steve, juxtaposes with her teen son, Brady, having loud and frequent sex with his girlfriend, Luisa. Carrie, primed for readjustment, gets her hip surgically fixed and accompanies Anthony to an appointment with a plastic surgeon, but chooses not to aesthetically erase the fine lines of aging and the memories she shared with her husband and friends. Rather, Carrie declares that some people "'don't have [the] luxury' of staying the same," and nervously dives back into the romantic (and platonic) dating scene that propelled her career. Still, after a decades-long career as a sex columnist and acclaimed author, she views being called a "sex writer" a reductive trivialization of her work. Carrie's heteronormative turn away from frank discussions of sex on her cohosted podcast about gender and sexuality pivots her away from writing on the core women's adventures in dating while rendering a sexless and nearly suburbanized vision of NYC. The women might be aging, but whether they are maturing and evolving beyond their nostalgia for their single-girl pasts to expand their own universes is the central question of the reboot.

In *AJLT*, the girlification of Third Age isn't always cosmetic or plastic. While Charlotte assures Carrie that there's nothing wrong with a little Botox, Carrie recognizes that returning to her past self comes at a price. In the neoliberal market of individual choice and self-actualization, one can achieve youth in Third Age with pulls, tucks, and injectables while preserving the knowledge of experience. The opportunities to evolve while embracing newness and their loved ones' transformations become the stakes upon which *AJLT* is built, informed by spontaneity and an entrepreneurial spirit. Such is the nebulousness of artificiality in this rebooted series.

"Alternative Types? Alternative to What?"

AJLT's inclusion of ethnoracialized, nonbinary, and queer characters, as well as the potential for new romantic-platonic intimacies, appears as a white neoliberal overcorrection to their exclusion in *SATC*. Meanwhile, it confirms the Boomer generation's fears regarding the nuclear family and heterosexual romantic relationships. Carrie, Charlotte, and Miranda meet Seema Patel, Che Diaz, Lisa Todd Wexley, and Nya Wallace via transactional interactions: Seema is Carrie's real estate agent, Che is Carrie's podcast cohost and employer, Charlotte knows Lisa (or LTW) from their children's school parent board, and Miranda takes Nya's class at Columbia. In lieu of Samantha, a model of neoliberal postfeminism whose aesthetic and romantic excesses disrupted cisheteronormative white womanhood, the new ethnic friends supplement the lack of chemistry between the core women and their partners and become cool but inauthentic stand-ins for Samantha. However, rather than reading as a genuine effort at friendship, *AJLT* attempts "'wokeness' and 'diversity'"[9] while tokenizing these new characters it has sprinkled into the fold. Such treatment resembles commodified fetish, mimicking corporate DEI initiatives in the post-Trump era of feminism.

As older women, Carrie, Charlotte, and Miranda can meander in and out of permanence because their footing is secured by wealth, whiteness, and womanhood. *AJLT* rehashes Boomer fears of wokeness by "repackag[ing] some of the show's past problematic moments into modern-day microaggressions."[10] While fellow New Yorkers in the reboot are suddenly diverse in ethnicity, race, gender, and sexuality, the "flagrantly out-of-touch but well-meaning"[11] white girlfriends are nostalgic for their youth and frightened of the future, yet sustain the primary perspective through which *AJLT* is told: the series "[leans] into who these characters are."[12] Meanwhile, Seema, Nya, and Lisa don't experience the same degree of self-actualization as Carrie, Miranda, and Charlotte, but are responsible for their coming of (Third) age. This treatment fosters the girlification of the original characters and turns their new Black and brown friends into goalposts of progressiveness.

In *AJLT*, the ethnoracialized characters express agency by "checking" their new white girlfriends and, in doing so, challenge socialized assumptions steeped in seemingly latent racialized aggression or hostility, which—"whether [we] know it or not—guides [our] choices/and [our] actions."[13] A "self-critical imperative"[14] connecting culture and politics to a broader liberatory movement or correcting assumptions derived from known marginalizations and self-proclaimed boundaries,[15] checking is occasionally written into the dialogue of *AJLT*'s minoritized characters to correct the narrative micro- and macroaggressions of their white friends, filling the fictionalized space with awkward tension and raising the stakes of performative (over)corrections. For example, while Carrie grieves her husband by abstaining from dating, she comments to Seema that she thinks "it's great that [Seema's] still putting herself out

Figure 3.2. The reboot incorporates a more diverse cast and storylines in a nod to contemporary ethnic, racial, and sexual politics. Clockwise from back left: Che Diaz (Sara Ramirez), Carrie Bradshaw (Sarah Jessica Parker), Seema Patel (Sarita Choudhury), Nya Wallace (Kim Pittman), Charlotte York (Kristin Davis), Miranda Hobbes (Cynthia Nixon), Lisa Todd Wexley (Nicole Ari Parker). *Source*: Promotional image by Max, May 17, 2023.

there," making Seema visibly uncomfortable at the allusion to her age. Later, when Carrie snaps at Seema because of a chipped picture frame, Seema checks Carrie's white-woman tantrum, reminding her to think before she speaks insensitively. Seema provides a disciplined mothering and sistering of Carrie that revives Carrie's career. Through checking, Seema, Nya, Lisa, and Che force their white girlfriends to see and feel them.

Carrie, Miranda, and Charlotte's attitudes and resistance toward major life changes contrast with the young people of *AJLT* because of "the possible conceptual disjunction between women growing old and growing up."[16] The girlification of the core white women, who don't have the constraint of typical employment or money worries while approaching Third Age, is another form of rejuvenation, only now, it is a psychosocial investment instead of a bodily one. Youthful postfeminist "luminosity,"[17] which the core women awkwardly attempt to recapture by befriending new ethnoracialized people, might reinscribe expected gender performances by Rock, Lily, Brady, and Luisa if the teens weren't already cognizant of their own generational differences. In turn, each teen acts as a safety net to reaffirm the adult women's evolution into more liberal identities, but not without unabashedly responding to the adults' prudishness about sex, drugs, and aesthetic queerness and challenging their judgment of these "alternative types" of fellow New Yorkers.

AJLT attempts to draw resemblances between the core women and their new friends to suggest they view each other as equals. However, these representations are static, external, and plastic, framed in a "degree of diversity . . . synonymous with the quantity of difference rather than the dimensionality of those performances."[18] The reboot's plasticity is apparent in Seema, LTW, Nya, and Che's peripheralization as sidekicks: although they are otherwise normative characters, their potential complexities are flattened to obsolescence. Further, Carrie, Miranda, and Charlotte perform plasticity when vouching for their diverse new friends, a designation that critics have called the "Diversity Girlfriend . . . we learn just enough about them and their desires for them to exist beyond ugly stereotypes."[19] Every pair inhabits the same economic class, but instead of fully integrating the new characters, the dissonance in each pair is evident in varying degrees of narrativized microaggressions and displays of cultural ignorance deployed by the white women.

I borrow from the notion of a scale of "un/threatening un/ambiguity,"[20] in which ethnoracialization, among other marginalizations, is a determinant for measuring how dangerous or at-risk a person is considered depending on their positionality on the spectrum of race and how ambiguously or unambiguously raced they appear in their given contexts. Coupled with the plasticity of diversity, this scale reveals inequity in *AJLT* and reaffirms the anxious, delicate, and expectant boundaries of cultural capitalism. If liberal multiculturalism is defined as an image of inclusion, in which marginalized people are gathered into the collective majority under the condition that they integrate into and ingratiate the common culture to make it appear diverse,[21] then I classify cultural capitalism in *AJLT* in terms of Black excellence, first-generation hustle, the model minority myth, fetishized brownness, and Latine ingenuity, as well as a consumption of gender *as* sexuality through heterosexual malaise.

Black Excellence

Excellence in the US Black American context recalls a "measure [of one's own] success according to a capitalist system that was reinforced by Jim Crow racial logic and bolstered by anti-Black economic policies."[22] At the intersection of racial capitalism and neoliberalism, Black excellence taps into one's own "magic,"[23] a utilization of busy productivity that generates revenue while exploiting the body, foregrounding resilience narratives to please and produce while precluding liberatory movement.[24] In *AJLT*, Black excellence functions as a framework for including ethnoracialized characters in high-stakes storylines. However, in attempting to position the series as diverse and inclusive, such exceptionalism tokenizes the Black women characters it claims to uplift while enabling a parallel cycle of labor resembling mammification.[25]

As a Black woman who teaches humanitarian law at Columbia, Nya Wallace recognizes that "Black folk and people of color have a permanent second job in navigating the way to [their] dreams in a power structure rooted in whiteness."[26] Nya's Blackness is foregrounded aesthetically through "street fashion and street culture" costuming,[27] building a generational and ethnoracialized contrast that catalyzes Miranda's initial white savior complex and overcorrections. Despite reading antiracism books before the first day of school, Miranda, a former corporate attorney and lifelong New Yorker, walks into Nya's classroom assuming that Nya is a student because of her box braids and casual wardrobe. As a result, Nya and the class check Miranda's anti-Black microaggressions with displeased looks and sarcastic remarks.

Nya's presence as professor, "as a sign that progressive political change is taking place, that the American Dream can indeed be inclusive of difference,"[28] does not preclude her illegibility to a fascinated Miranda. Despite graduating from Harvard Law and being a longtime Brooklyn resident, Miranda seems not to have cultivated empathy or a practical awareness of social inequality and intersectional marginalizations. Her development in *AJLT* partially hinges on her coming of age through her relationship to Nya, who mentors and mothers her by guiding her through contemporary notions of gender and race. Nya's mammification is juxtaposed to Miranda's awkward white-girlishness, which "highlights the threat to identity that age entails."[29]

Black excellence also appears as Nya's professional relationship with Miranda develops into friendship, while Nya's marriage to Andre begins to suffer. Nya and her attractive musician husband try to balance multiple IVF procedures while nurturing passionate romance and sex in their marriage. The fissures are revealed by the tension between Andre's desire to have children and Nya's weariness of invasive bodily procedures and ambivalence toward childrearing. In their budding platonic intimacy, Nya reveals her miscarriages and insecurities about fertility to Miranda, whom she sees as her equal, before discussing it with Andre; conversely, Miranda talks to Nya about her marriage to Steve and affair with Che. Though they were originally written to be paired romantically,[30] *AJLT* settles for a pairing of like minds between Nya and Miranda, where power and the boundaries between professional and personal worlds are made liquid and constantly transgressed. Each woman holds space for the other's secrets without judgment, something Miranda seeks unconditionally in friendship.

However, at the end of *AJLT*'s first season, Nya and Andre separate and she is alone in the city while Miranda ditches her prestigious internship to pursue an uncertain future with Che in California. Nya's exceptionalism as one of two financially and intellectually successful Black lead characters leaves her with "half as much as [the] white people receive,"[31] only affording her tenuous personal success. While

Nya had foregrounded Miranda in her summer plans, she is backgrounded by Miranda's relationship with Che, upending any chance for the women to offer each other the mirrored support that Carrie, Charlotte, Samantha, and Miranda shared in *SATC*. Thus, Nya is a Black woman character without a community, marginalized in the series as Miranda's sidekick. The professional walls between the women dissolve to friendship but the balance of power and empathy between them remains nebulous.

In Lisa Todd Wexley's case, the hyperproductivity and hyperconnectivity of Black excellence manifest in her mothering job and leadership in the school parent group, which compete with her work as a documentary filmmaker. In *AJLT*, Charlotte contrives to increase her cultural and social capital among her mom group and parent school board by developing a friendship with Lisa, introduced as LTW, a trendsetting "documentarian and a humanitarian, [whose] husband Herbert is an investment banker who might run for mayor." While Charlotte has an elite pedigree bolstered by her private-school education and career as an art historian and gallery owner, LTW's allyship could pacify the latent potential for competition between them as Upper East Side PTA moms with kids at the same school. Indeed, Charlotte neither befriends other ethnoracialized women nor thinks of them as equals. Lisa affirms Charlotte's allyship by overriding the decisions of the mothers' group in favor of Charlotte's homemaker expertise and friendship.

Charlotte strategizes to impress LTW at Herbert's birthday party by cursorily researching Black art and ensuring her husband, Harry, knows enough about Black authors to ingratiate the Wexleys' social circle. Nevertheless, as she doesn't often interact with Black people, she mistakes one Black woman for another she knows from the kids' school. Coupled with Charlotte's later confession to LTW that she wanted to *seem* like she had Black friends, Charlotte's microaggression is immediately forgiven and her racial awkwardness becomes part of her peppy quirkiness. After all, Charlotte uses her knowledge and pedigree to name every Black artist whose work hangs in the Wexleys' home.

Charlotte's mission to befriend Lisa and find belonging in Lisa's world reads as plastic, a quest to maintain her place in NYC's social hierarchy. Shortening Lisa's name to the acronym LTW, like LBD for Little Black Dress, further indicates Charlotte's characterization as a woman who seeks validation from acquiring fashionable things like "collecting" a Black friend to show off. Stylistically, LTW is Charlotte's model-esque accessory: Lisa presents a glamorous Barbie-like image whose metonym is Charlotte's collection of antique Madame Alexander dolls, costumed in stereotypical outfits. Likewise, Lisa is someone—and some*thing*—Charlotte can play with, an objectified manifestation of her desire to keep up appearances with her PTA group, friends, family, and with the societal expectation of distance between her circle of wealth and those who aren't (net-)worthy of her friendship.

While Lisa and Nya represent Black women in the affluent echelons of contemporary Manhattan society, with less interiority from their own point of view, their appearance reads as "feminism-weightless."[32] Although LTW can smoothly harness control of executive decisions for her family, friends, and parent group as though she were producing a documentary, *AJLT* converts her girlboss leadership into a valuable trove of social capital Charlotte can aspire to and admire. Likewise, Miranda sees Nya as her social equal, yet her hyperawareness of Nya's race transforms into "colorblindness"[33] that collapses the ethnoracialized differences between the two women and enables Nya's lack of community at the end of the season when Miranda ditches her for her lover. These positive but hollow representations of "Black cool,"[34] a cultural currency of survival and thriving, render a nonconfrontational nature that makes both Nya and LTA safe, cool, and acceptable Black women Charlotte and Miranda can befriend.

First-Generation Hustle

Excellence and exceptionalism are mobilized not only by Lisa and Nya's Black womanhood, but also by Seema and Che. The marginalization of all four ethnoracialized characters signifies that excellence is not inherited but a curated façade masking the interiorities of each ethnoracialized character, mostly through the perspective of their white women friends. Seema and Che must make themselves marketable and consistently productive to prosper in their careers, an unending hustle. They, like Nya and Lisa, are bound to their respective occupations, confirmed by their mutual status as first-generation US Americans without inherited wealth or capital.

For Seema Patel, this means appearing impeccably stylish, powerful, and almost unattainable through a postfeminist interpretation of success in which NYC's real estate market is openly available to glamorous, well-connected, and wealthy women. While conducting a walkthrough of Carrie and Big's professionally decorated apartment, Seema's assertion of what needs to be changed about it to attract potential buyers establishes her as an ethnic girlboss. Seema transforms Carrie's home to a neutral, sellable piece of real estate, prompting Carrie to remark to Miranda, "Maybe that's why I'm so drawn to Seema, my realtor . . . When I'm with her, I can just pretend like none of the terrible stuff has happened . . . It's just lunch and some laughs, which is kinda nice . . . Probably more real estate than real." While Carrie suspects this relationship might be temporary and transactional, Seema's first-generation entrepreneurialism is an indicator of financial success, exceptionalism, and assimilation in the US immigrant context.

Additionally, Carrie depends on Seema to regain her confidence in midlife and Third Age. When she notices Carrie limping downstairs, Seema savvily uses her connections and efficiently schedules an orthopedist appointment for Carrie that heals Carrie's body and allows her to keep wearing high-heeled shoes. While Carrie begins to exhibit traits of nihilism and despair that are placated by Miranda and Charlotte, her optimism resurfaces when she interacts with her Indian American friend who makes her check herself and uplifts her.

The hustle for Che Diaz is manifested through the search for advertising revenue through a strong social media presence and comedy gigs. Although Carrie's career is based on her broad knowledge of sex and dating, Che is depicted as more sexually open than Carrie, who becomes visibly nervous when her podcast cohosts ask her about masturbation. Thus, Che's advice to Carrie "to step [her] pussy up" by expanding her own perspective on gender, sexuality, and the potential ambiguities between both is a personal and professional admonishment, especially given that the podcast encompasses frank conversations about gender and sexuality.

Che's nonbinariness defies the structural violences of the cisheterosexual world of *AJLT*, while their aesthetic framing otherizes them in style and sexuality. Carrie's colorfully accessorized wardrobe with ever-present high-heeled shoes contrasts against Che's black fashion palette, multiple piercings, and vaping. Che's stand-up comedy show is metonymic for the historical representation of queer, nonbinary, LGBTQIA+ people in media, in which they reveal their coming-out story in a meta show-within-a-show as a way to uncover their interiority publicly, as if to say "I want you to hear with me as I write what it's like to be 'large and contain multitudes' . . . yet struggle to record the voices that combine to represent a nonbinary life."[35] Just as their comedy special encompasses performance and authenticity carried into the rest of their storyline, the humor imbued into Che's characterization is an uncomfortable and discomfiting ontology of disobedience that empowers them to live who they are messily and publicly. Che is the minoritized stand-in for a multitudinous identity, checking several boxes in the rocky terrain of televisual representation, and hustling to maintain their career because they have no other choice.

Being a Latine/x nonbinary person inhabiting a universe that historically centers white people while othering non-white characters joins Che to Seema, as well as to Lisa and Nya, in a brown commons "pivotal to various struggles to imagine and enact a particularity that is always only salient as coterminous with plurality."[36] In the age of social media, Seema's hyperconnectivity and Che's savvy public marketing skills resemble new forms of social engagement that foster empathetic connections and community-building, challenging the insularity of the core group's original formation.

Model Minority

The model minority stereotype, "a crafted narrative of successful Asian American assimilation,"[37] does not appear dissimilar to Black excellence or first-generation hustle, yet it is mobilized to create artificial distance between and ascribe worth to Black and Asian American people in terms of value. Indeed, it binds Asian Americans to gendered expectations, surveilled ethnoracialization, and assumptions of innate productivity while increasing their racialized distance from Black people, stereotypically constructed as "lazy, uncaring, unintelligent, educational failures with disciplinary problems."[38] The anti-Black otherizing and stereotyping of Asian Americans arises from their alienation as an eternally foreign threat to white hegemonic normativity, while Orientalist fascination includes and ostracizes Asian Americans from whiteness.

In *AJLT*, this trope is a veneer for Lily Goldenblatt's characterization. As Charlotte's oldest child and a Chinese adoptee, Lily exudes confidence in her book smarts and piano virtuosity and maintains a polished appearance of moral goodness in front of her parents as her family's cultural mediator; these qualities are considered part of her giftedness. *AJLT* juxtaposes Lily with LTW's son, Henry, whose grandmother is a classically trained musician. Although both children are equally wealthy and attend the posh Manhattan School of Music for piano, Lily's Asian American identity is attached to her parents' whiteness and is stereotypically framed against Henry's Blackness in terms of musical and academic skills. Nothing is inherently wrong about Lily's talent; however, she is pitted in competitive comparison against Henry in terms of their labor and assumed giftedness when Henry is unable to find the right note. Compounded by her parents' constant reminders that they have invested large sums in their children,[39] the comparison encumbers Lily with the anxieties of productivity, achievement, and body image issues, precluding any risk of her deviating from lily-whiteness.

As the oldest Goldenblatt child, Lily also bears the burden of quelling her parents' anxieties about childrearing. Because Charlotte treats both of her children like little girls, Lily's coming of age from child prodigy to curious teenager frightens her mother, especially when she almost transgresses delicate girlishness. Charlotte is alarmed at finding Lily's posed selfies in form-fitting athleisure clothing, which she deems sexually suggestive. Although Charlotte fears Lily is in danger of being perceived as promiscuous, Lily transforms her teen body self-consciousness into an "articulation of hope as it arises out of pain and the desire for pleasure and play."[40] On social media, Lily can refashion the neoliberal "can-do girl" image[41] imagined by Charlotte into a space of play not bound by gender and sexuality rules. Still, Lily's burgeoning sexuality frightens Charlotte because she believes the circulation of Lily's photos could threaten her family's social status and how they are perceived by the other school moms. Lily might otherwise be peripheralized for her racialization as an Asian American girl, but by confessing she only uses her "finsta" to share selfies with her close friends, Lily preserves the pristine whiteness of her family's image, aligning her with their orthodox Upper East Side values. She performs a feminized whiteness for her parents while still feeling the pressure of productive girlhood elsewhere.

Similarly, as Carrie's cultural intermediary, Seema is *AJLT*'s representative of exotified South Asia while rejecting a fearful arrested development in favor of a polished and worldly Third Age. Seema is an Indian American woman whose primary signifier is her luxurious brownness: everything from her custom car to her designer purses and chic outfits is colored in neutrals and metallics. Her coolness inextricable from her otherness, Seema is marketable as a friend to Carrie, Miranda, and Charlotte because she brings an exotified, if not fetishized, sexiness to the table, the updated version of an absent Samantha. Seema's business acumen and high-powered connections suggest she has both formal and cultural education, which makes her an appealing and resourceful sidekick for Carrie.

Seema's foregrounded ethnicity as an Indian American woman heightens the tension between Carrie's signature aesthetic and the cultures of the ethnic people around them. She invites Carrie to her parents' Diwali celebration while shopping at an upscale South Asian clothing store. She shops for a sari with Carrie, a moment she calls "cultural appreciation"; however, for the party, Carrie is outfitted in a lehenga. Because the sari represents diverse regional "visual design vocabular[ies], with motifs and techniques whose lineage and origin are steeped in history or mythology . . . representing different cultural sensibilities,"[42] the differentiation between sari and lehenga is important. Instead of mobilizing the lehenga as a touchstone to Seema's Indian roots, the conflation of the garments flattens the clothing's significance[43] to palatable and appropriative costume. It is as though Carrie is trying on Seema for fun.

When Seema's parents ask Carrie about Seema's boyfriend and wonder why he is too busy to attend their Diwali party, Carrie vouches for this invisible man. Seema tells her parents that she is dating a white male doctor to preclude invasive suggestions of arranged marriage. Seema's proclaimed liberation from her parents' wish for her to marry revives tropes of arranged marriage in Indian culture to signify an oppressive past instead of cultural difference, reducing the inclusion of this ancient patriarchal practice to a stereotype. Carrie's vouching for this faux boyfriend resembles "white men . . . saving brown women from brown men"[44] and this prioritization of normativity across both cultures is confirmed when Seema rendezvouses with nondescript white European club owner Zed. *AJLT* presents Seema's interest in dating for love and good sex versus disinterestedly entering an arranged marriage as a binaristic choice between US American culture and Indian heritage.

While the model minority trope entangles both Lily and Seema in expectations of productivity, both characters express a yearning to be seen as more than their labor. As well, Lily's longing to feel desirable is not unlike Seema's quest for cosmopolitan pleasure in middle age. Indeed, both characters covet playful interventions into their parents' orthodox expectations yet remain under the auspices of safe class positionality if they work hard, a neoliberal definition of success by maintenance.

Latine Ingenuity and Desire

Latine/x girls similarly endure a pressure to conform to cultural expectations of Latinidad. However, the Latina ingenues of the 2020s "weaponize their assertive power to combat their othering . . . [and visibilize] a demographic group that is historically marginalized within patriarchy, both as U.S. Americans and descendants of Latin America."[45] As well, Latines/xs in *AJLT* experience desire, but the representation of Latine/x sexual pleasure in *AJLT* continue tropes of sexual objectification that reduce those characters' development to tools for white women's personal growth.

Similar to Lily, the sole East Asian character, Luisa Torres is *AJLT*'s only cisheterosexual Latina. As all the teenagers are largely defined by their budding identities, Luisa and Lily are contrasted by their desire. Whereas Lily's search for a malleable identity results in a self-consciousness shaped by her mother's internalized shame about sexuality, Luisa's relationship with Brady and casualness about sex changes Miranda's perceptions of sex and sexuality overall. As oversexed teenagers who make out in public places, Brady and Luisa rarely appear without each other and, to Miranda's annoyance, have loud sex in Brady's bedroom, which shares a wall with his parents' bedroom. While chatting with her girlfriends, Miranda juxtaposes the amount of sex Brady and Luisa are having with the complete lack of sex she and Steve have shared in years. Although Miranda shares with Carrie and Charlotte that she likes Luisa, Luisa's characterization as a sexually active Latina teen who enables Brady's misbehavior is narrowly defined as existing "in relation to [Miranda's] normative white heterosexuality,"[46] a disruption of the show's focus on the older women's romantic lives.

While Miranda often questions whether letting the teenagers have sex in the family home was a good idea, Luisa's character and constant quips at Miranda's conservative attitudes about weed, sex, and non-normative sociality are important for Miranda's eventual transformation. Miranda at first misrecognizes Luisa's Gen-Z values as a political correctness that annoys her, but later factors Luisa's critique into her own rejuvenation. Given that *AJLT* is largely about women's aging, Luisa is a signal for Miranda's acknowledgment of her marital unhappiness as bound to an existential craving to follow her desires despite the rigidity and seriousness she feels are entailed by aging. While an aesthetic makeover—such as dyeing her naturally aged gray hair back to her classic fiery red again—would make a classic *SATC* narrative arc, Miranda instead upends her static lifestyle and emerges newly rejuvenated. Therefore, as another sidekick ethnic character, Luisa aids Miranda in recovering youthfulness by self-actualization, positioning this Latina teenager as a safety net for Miranda's risky decisions while being adultified[47] in the process.

Luisa's hypersexualization, a classic trope marking Latina women as dangerous and deviant, disrupts Miranda's preconceptions of comfort and safety in marriage. Yet she offers a version of an oppositional gaze that perforates such rigidity[48] and makes Miranda realize she is uncomfortably bored in her own home, which acts as a metonym of her marriage to Steve. Since Miranda and Steve haven't had sex in years, it's unsurprising that she sees Brady and Luisa's constant PDA as excessive, suggesting sex and intimacy are precluded by aging. The teens remain unashamed and Luisa remarks to Miranda that her acceptance of their physical relationship—though reticent—is progressive, given that her Catholic mother isn't open about sex. Still, Luisa embodies continuity with tropes about young Latinas as hypersexualized,[49] morally nebulous,[50] and having precocious knowledge about the world.[51] Luisa may not directly be the catalyst for Miranda's self-actualization, but her progressive attitudes about youth and body become fodder that Miranda ponders on her way to her self-discoveries.

While Carrie, Miranda, and Charlotte enter Third Age, they renegotiate the limits of their heterosexuality by countering "the terrorizing force of the *status quo* that makes identity fixed, static, a condition of containment and death."[52] Miranda is attracted to Che Diaz initially because they exhibit a youthful seductiveness that turns her on more than Steve, now characterized by his age and hearing impediment. As Cynthia Nixon proclaims that "not having to be under a man's thumb"[53] is appealing to both actor and character, what thrills Miranda is deviance from her marriage by pursuing an affair with Che, who is thus deemed dangerous to heteronormativity. Like Luisa, Che's extroverted outspokenness and overt sexuality makes Miranda question her conventional attractions to marriage, domestic life, and her former high-powered career.

Although Miranda claims heterosexuality from the beginning of *SATC*, she becomes fascinated by Che, who represents a liberated deviation from her heteronormativity and meticulously organized life. Like Nya, Che becomes a vessel for Miranda's self-actualization, but as a risky adventure into previously unknown queerness. The first moment of potential intimacy between Che and Miranda is eroticized in slow-motion as Miranda shotguns a puff of marijuana from Che's mouth. Along with Che's wish for nonmonogamy, their outspokenness animates Miranda to have an affair and later leave Steve, Brady, and NYC as she falls in love with Che. Evidently, "Che's main purpose is to trigger Miranda's sexual evolution,"[54] and they become an object Miranda pursues and acquires. Consequently, Miranda angrily refuses criticism of her new relationship—which she calls judgment—from the girlfriends whose advice and wisdom she has always sought.

When Carrie gets hip surgery, Miranda and Che get drunk and stoned in Carrie's kitchen and loudly hook up, resulting in an orgasm that Miranda claims makes her feel the most alive she has felt in years. Miranda hopes the encounter will solve her misery in marriage and motherhood, which she masks by drinking heavily. Pursuing and consuming Che doesn't negate Miranda's marriage, motherhood, or past life as a thirty-something lawyer who dated men in Manhattan. Rather, Miranda sexualizes the *idea* of a queer Latine/x partner by virtue of their badness, heteromasculinizing Che in attempting to blur the distinctions between their gender presentation, racialized ethnicity, and open and brash sexuality. With Che, Miranda is newly attracted to having sex with teen-like innocence and the desire of a grown woman, and such pleasure comes out of a desire to recapture her own personal power, yet

Che's ethnoracialized nonbinary body "can be seen as constituting an alternative playground where members of dominating races, genders, and sexual practices affirm their power-over in intimate relations with the Other."[55]

Echoing the treatment of the ethnoracialized romantic partners the core women had in *SATC*, Che and Luisa are marginalized in the world of *AJLT*, relegated to the stereotypes of Latin lover and Latina spitfire, respectively, and potentially disappeared from the series altogether.[56] While Miranda seems not to think highly of Luisa due to her sexual relationship with Brady, Luisa's edginess prompts Miranda to question her own discomfort with sex, youth, and her future. Indeed, Miranda's attraction to Che is colored by her heterosexuality: She understands Che's butchness as masculinity, a familiar articulation of gender and even queerness she is sexually attracted to, but not as an articulation of transness.[57]

Dancing with Gender

Che's presence as a messy Latine character provides much-needed visibility of nonbinary gender identity and queer sexuality, as such characters are increasingly present[58] but still a minority among all TV series as of 2021.[59] Including their nonbinariness in *AJLT* carves a path for the other nonbinary character in the series, Rock Goldenblatt, to assert their own burgeoning tween identity. In *AJLT*, nonbinary gender identity is an articulation of youth that prompts the core women to transform their trepidation about aging into optimism for the future.

A self-proclaimed "queer nonbinary Mexican-Irish diva," Che initially embodies a humorous liveliness that can be described as shimmering, "a line of escape from thinking in set binary oppositions by grasping the ongoing event of differential becomings."[60] While heteronormativity pervades *SATC* and *AJLT*, Che introduces themself as "both and neither . . . representing everyone else outside of these two boring genders," with their "gender-blending while genre-bending"[61] nodding toward a fluidity of gender and sexuality that has already sprouted ambiguity. Che's combined gender, sexuality, and ethnicity parallels the layered identity of the real Sara Ramirez, alluding to a brown commons that touches both character and actor "because they have been devalued by the world outside their commons . . . [and] smolder with a life and persistence."[62] Although Che recognizes that they can't possibly represent the global diversity of genders, sexualities, and races, the humor with which they circumnavigate gender is "unapologetically itself, and tonally beyond the male-female sonic scale, camp, perhaps, but more clearly epicene."[63]

While the character's name evokes a Marxist revolutionary ethos, Che's articulations of butchness and first-generation mixed-race Latinidad disrupt conservative formulations of gender, sexuality, race, and ethnicity, especially given that Che also has a white parent. However, Che's characterization is limited by the "sexual confidence and borderline promiscuity of the character,"[64] inscribing deviance into this nonbinary queer Latine character. As *AJLT*'s writers' room is entirely staffed by cisgender people, the nonbinary perspective, often found under the umbrella of trans identity, only appears as meta-representation with Che's presence. Because the fluidity of their gender, queerness, and ethnoracialization destabilizes binaristic identity formation in *AJLT*, Che cannot permeate the boundaries of the core cast as anything more than a sidekick or romantic interest for a cisgender white woman. Che is another example of Boomer fears, only now the fear is derived from Che's complex characterization as the fascinating object of a white woman's affections.

Intertwining Che's storyline with Rock's tweenhood, the latter becomes a vessel for Charlotte's personal fears and a catalyst for deconstructing her conservative upbringing. Despite Charlotte's extreme dedication to parenting, Rock's revelation that they "don't feel like a girl" and their new name and pronouns surprise both parents. Charlotte consults her best friend, Anthony, about this aspect of Rock's identity; however, as a cisgender gay man of Charlotte's generation, he insists that Rock doesn't need Charlotte's affirmation because they are too young to know their gender identity. This Boomer understanding of children's agency resurfaces when Charlotte and Harry speak to Rock's teachers about Rock's gender expression. The teachers are protective of Rock, yet Harry and Charlotte center their own discomfort and are reticent to accept professional advice from people who also care about Rock and respect their autonomy. *AJLT* acknowledges that the portrayal of accepting parents "isn't the one usually seen, [and] it's also the road not taken,"[65] framing Rock's coming out as a disruption of Charlotte and Harry's conservative, manicured vision of a normative family.

Rock's coming of age is meant to be confirmed at their Jewish "they mitzvah" celebration, which Charlotte sees as an opportunity for opulent spectacle. However, Rock not only is unenthusiastic, but fails to learn their Torah readings and harbors a refusal to be labeled through gender, religion, and even New Yorker-ness by declaring, "I'm only thirteen. Can't I just be me?" Charlotte absorbs her child's rejection of norms as a personal failure while equating Rock's gender realization to choice. Ultimately, Rock forgoes the traditional Jewish blessing and Charlotte takes their place, allowing Charlotte to confirm her own white Jewish womanhood. In attempting to impose feminized whiteness upon both of her children, Charlotte has enabled Rock's rejection of white cisheteronormativity she has curated for them since birth while Lily supports her sibling. Rock unknowingly becomes the harbinger of Charlotte's personal articulation of womanhood via this coming-of-age ceremony, while Rock's refusals and messy teen angst reflect a rejection of whiteness, gender, and neoliberal social status displayed through their mitzvah party. Feeling seen by their family in this moment, Rock can start to build their own identity from scratch.

Together, Che and Rock form a new understanding of gender for the core women that simultaneously disrupts the heterosexual happy endings expected from the *SATC* universe and forges a future-facing path for nonbinariness in *AJLT*. While Che unsettles the suburban-esque order of the core characters' lives, Rock's youthful refusals to adhere to their parents' religious practices, gender performances, and class rules are indicative of the generational divisions between the core women and these two nonbinary characters. That these characters portray strong feelings about identity that are not always positive or can-do also helps normalize the internal transformations that Carrie, Miranda, and Charlotte endure on the way to their newly actualized Third Age.

I Couldn't Help but Wonder . . . : Concluding Cosmopolitanism

Sex and the City provokes its audiences to reconsider and sometimes reject conclusions of heterosexual romantic fulfillment. The platonic intimacies established between Carrie, Miranda, Charlotte, and

Samantha share space with their individual romantic relationships, at times bleeding into romance and discomfort while being prioritized and trusted. The premise of romantic and sexual fulfillment in *SATC* provides mostly young, middle-class professional women audiences a voyeuristic opportunity to try on the stylish, form-fitting garments of women's interiorities that collapse the distances between desire, pleasure, love, and friendship. In this reboot, *AJLT* nostalgically recalls the voyeuristic, consumerist NYC of *SATC*'s moneyed and vibrant past, only now with a multicultural twist. In doing so, *AJLT* hails 2000s postfeminist television once again, confirming that "culture keeps recycling and returning to the same old well"[66] through reboots of popular series and revivals of their outdated themes instead of investing in the interiorities of minoritized people in a globalized city.

Such is the conundrum of the *SATC* franchise. The ethnic people in *AJLT* are plot devices that spur the core girlfriends' character development and their burgeoning progressiveness. It's difficult to suspend the belief that original characters could live in a sanitized, smoothed, and homogenized NYC. Yet it is more difficult to believe the grittier reality that moneyed white women like Carrie, Miranda, and Charlotte might knowingly choose to surround themselves with those unlike them in terms of gender, race, and class. Indeed, the characters' passive preservation of whiteness is mobilized through sidekicking and fetishizing the new ethnoracialized and non-heterosexual friends and lovers now part of the rebooted storyline.

However, the characters of Rock, Lily, Brady, and Luisa make salient demands of the old white guard. Despite being met with eyerolls and initial refusals, the unruly new generation of new New Yorkers insist on being seen, heard, and understood while provoking the older white women to question their static positionalities. The white, cisheterosexual, middle-aged women don't activate singularly. Rather, ethnoracialization, gender-nonbinariness, and youth function as vehicles of change driven by secondary characters, and the teens especially propel Carrie, Miranda, and Charlotte to "reflexively organize their own self narratives rather than rely upon ones shaped through existing relations of gender, class, or race."[67] Despite the girlboss lens through which the original *SATC* was told, the reboot's narrative and character development imply that changing oneself for the betterment of one's own well-being is something none of these women can do alone without the assistance of youth or racialized others.

Filtering white women's self-discoveries through their relationships with ethnoracialized characters subsumes *SATC*'s preoccupation with heterosexual romantic love and capitalistic success via high-end fashion labels. *And Just Like That . . .* is, thus, trapped by its own surface-level DEI to-do list, including diverse characters without unpacking the intertwined complexities of race and capital in the city. Seema, Lisa, Nya, and Che serve as multicultural sidekicks for Carrie, Charlotte, and Miranda, who each seek to "prove her progressive bona fides"[68] through her new ethnoracialized friend by performing the benign, funny, and cute white woman whose awkwardness is girlified. Through the cast, *AJLT*'s New York City is written and imagined as a site of inclusion and diversity, yet the series indulges in a liberal multiculturalism that mitigates the threat of ethnoracialized, queer, trans, and young people disrupting the aesthetic, socioeconomic, and behavioral rules of white cisheterosexual femininity. Thus, it becomes evident that the undoing of innocence is social conservativism veiled by friendship at a distance, a way to articulate Carrie, Miranda, and Charlotte's maturation through the new characters' backgrounds and sidekick differences, with the goal of merely being on equal footing with white cisheterosexual men.

Discussion Questions

1. According to the author, what is the relationship between cultural capitalism and racial capitalism? What role does cultural capitalism play in the depiction of the ethnic and racial minority characters in the *AJLT* reboot?
2. Identify and discuss three examples that illustrate how the inclusion of the ethnic and racial minority characters in the *AJLT* revival reinforces white womanhood as an idealized norm in Hollywood.
3. Reflect on the tensions between the inclusions of ethnic and racial minority actors and characters in revivals and the continued inequalities in Hollywood reboots that privilege the original white producers and actors. Are there other contemporary revivals that display similar tensions?

NOTES

1 New York City is respectfully shortened to NYC hereafter.

2 Max was known as HBO Max prior to HBO's sale to and consolidation with Time Warner Discovery. As of 2025, they have announced that they are returning to the "HBO Max" branding from just "Max."

3 This chapter was written before the release of the second season.

4 Julie Salamon, "The Relevance of 'Sex' in a City That's Changed," *New York Times*, July 21, 2002.

5 Alexander Doty, "Everyone's Here for Love: Bisexuality and *Gentlemen Prefer Blondes*," in *Flaming Classics: Queering the Film Canon* (Routledge, 2000), 133.

6 Doty, *Flaming Classics*, 149.

7 Ron Buchanan, "'Side by Side': The Role of the Sidekick," *Studies in Popular Culture* 26, no. 1 (2003): 15–26, www.jstor.org/stable/23414984.

8 Shir Shimoni, "'Third Age' Under Neoliberalism: From Risky Subjects to Human Capital," *Journal of Aging Studies* 47 (2018): 39, https://doi.org/10.1016/j.jaging.2018.10.004.

9 Melanie Curry, "Why the Attempts to Diversify *And Just Like That . . .* Fell Flat," *Elle*, February 10, 2022, www.elle.com.

10 Curry, "Why the Attempts to Diversify *And Just Like That . . .* Fell Flat."

11 Aisha Harris, "*And Just Like That . . .* Has a Diversity Girlfriend Problem," *NPR*, Jan 22, 2022, www.npr.org.

12 Kevin Fallon, "'And Just Like That' Is Nothing Like 'Sex and the City'—in the Best Way," *The Daily Beast*, December 9, 2021, www.thedailybeast.com.

13 Karla D. Scott, "Check Yo' Stuff: A Black Feminist Rant to 'Allies' Seeking 'Dialogue' in Precarious Times," *International Review of Qualitative Research* 11, no. 2 (2018): 200, https://doi.org/10.1525/irqr.2018.11.2.198.

14 Todd Boyd, "Check Yo Self, Before You Wreck Yo Self: Variations on a Political Theme in Rap Music and Popular Culture," *Public Culture* 7, no. 1 (1994): 289–312, https://doi.org/10.1215/08992363-7-1-289.

15 Tricia Rose, "Never Trust a Big Butt and a Smile," *Camera Obscura* 8, no. 2 (1990): 125, https://doi.org/10.1215/02705346-8-2_23-108.

16 Sofie Van Bauwel, "Invisible Golden Girls? Post-Feminist Discourses and Female Ageing Bodies in Contemporary Television Fiction," *Feminist Media Studies* 18, no. 1 (2018): 27, https://doi.org/10.1080/14680777.2018.1409969.

17 Angela McRobbie, *The Aftermath of Feminism: Gender, Culture and Social Change* (Sage, 2008), 63.

18 Kristen J. Warner, "In the Time of Plastic Representation," *Film Quarterly* 71, no. 2 (2017): 33, https://filmquarterly.org.

19 Harris, "*And Just Like That . . .* Has a Diversity Girlfriend Problem."

20 Stephanie Melissa Pérez, "Quinceañera Ontologies: (Mediated) Latine Girlhoods . . . and Other Stories," in *Quinceañeras: Mediated Approaches to a Cultural Celebration*, ed. Jillian Báez, Diana Leon-Boys, and Angharad N. Valdivia (University of Illinois Press, forthcoming).

21 Sara Ahmed, "'Liberal Multiculturalism is the Hegemony—It's An Empirical Fact'—A Response to Slavoj Žižek," *darkmatter Journal* (2008), https://tinyurl.com/55tbwvh2.

22 Tanisha C. Ford, "*Bel-Air* and the Flawed Logic of 'Black Excellence,'" *The Atlantic*, April 19, 2022, www.theatlantic.com.

23 Ford, "*Bel-Air* and the Flawed Logic of 'Black Excellence.'"

24 Tricia Hersey, *Rest Is Resistance: A Manifesto* (Little Brown Spark, 2022).

25 Patricia Hill Collins, "Mammies, Matriarchs, and Other Controlling Images," in *Black Feminist Thought: Knowledge, Consciousness and the Politics of Empowerment* (Hyman, 1990), 69–96.

26 Jeneé Osterheldt, "Black Excellence? When You Break a Glass Ceiling, No One Talks About the Scars," *Boston Globe*, November 10, 2021, www.bostonglobe.com.

27 Mary Louise Kelly, Courtney Dorning, and Elena Burnett, "'And Just Like That' Stars Talk Race, Fashion and Whether *That* College Scene Worked," *NPR*, December 16, 2021, www.npr.org.

28 bell hooks, *Black Looks: Race and Representation* (South End Press, 1992), 26.

29 Sadie Wearing, "Subjects of Rejuvenation: Aging in Postfeminist Culture," in *Interrogating Postfeminism: Gender and the Politics of Popular Culture*, ed. Yvonne Tasker and Diane Negra (Duke University Press, 2007), 279.

30 Kate Aurthur, "Cynthia Nixon Thinks Miranda Was Always Queer on 'Sex and the City': She Had 'Lesbianic Qualities,'" *Variety*, June 1, 2022, https://variety.com.

31 Ford, "*Bel-Air* and the Flawed Logic of 'Black Excellence.'"

32 Rosalind Gill, "Post-Postfeminism? New Feminist Visibilities in Postfeminist Times," *Feminist Media Studies* 16, no. 4 (2016): 618, https://doi.org/10.1080/14680777.2016.1193293.

33 Isabel Molina-Guzmán, *Latinas and Latinos on TV: Colorblind Comedy in the Post-Racial Network Era* (University of Arizona Press, 2018), 3–4.

34 Rebecca Walker, ed., *Black Cool: One Thousand Streams of Blackness* (Soft Skull Press, 2022).

35 Mike Perez, "A Nonbinary Letter: From Camp Epicene," in *Beyond Binaries: Trans Identities in Contemporary Culture*, ed. Mike Perez, Rachel Friedman, and John C. Lamothe (Lexington Books, 2021), 178.

36 José Esteban Muñoz, *The Sense of Brown* (Duke University Press, 2020), 4.

37 Wayne Au, "Asian American Racialization, Racial Capitalism, and the Threat of the Model Minority," *Review of Education, Pedagogy, and Cultural Studies* 44, no. 3 (2022): 190, https://doi.org/10.1080/10714413.2022.2084326.

38 Au, "Asian American Racialization, Racial Capitalism, and the Threat of the Model Minority," 192.

39 Robert G. Lee, "Disobedient Citizenship: Deconstructing the Oriental," in *Orientals: Asian Americans in Popular Culture* (Temple University Press, 1999), 223–31.

40 Celine Parreñas Shimizu, *The Hypersexuality of Race: Performing Asian/American Women on Screen and Scene* (Duke University Press, 2007), 273.

41 Amy Shields Dobson and Akane Kanai, "From 'Can-Do' Girls to Insecure and Angry: Affective Dissonances in Young Women's Post-Recessional Media," *Feminist Media Studies* 19, no. 6 (2019): 778, https://doi.org/10.1080/14680777.2018.1546206.

42 Praachi Raniwala, "Saris, Lehengas and Why Carrie Bradshaw Should Know the Difference," *New York Times*, January 20, 2022.

43 Arushi Sinha, "Sex and the Sari: Unpacking *And Just Like That* . . . 's Diwali Episode," *Vogue*, January 12, 2022, www.vogue.com.

44 Gayatri Spivak, "Can the Subaltern Speak?," in *Marxism and the Interpretation of Culture*, ed. Cary Nelson and Lawrence Grossberg (Macmillan, 1988), 296.

45 Stephanie Melissa Pérez, "Queen of the Neighborhood: Monse Finnie Mobilizes and Defies the Ingenue Trope in Netflix's *On My Block*," *FLOW Journal*, October 8, 2021, www.flowjournal.org.

46 Isabel Molina-Guzmán, *Dangerous Curves: Latina Bodies in the Media* (New York University Press, 2010).

47 Linda Burton, "Childhood Adultification in Economically Disadvantaged Families: A Conceptual Model," *Family Relations* 56, no. 4 (2007): 329–45, https://doi.org/10.1111/j.1741-3729.2007.00463.x.

48 hooks, *Black Looks*, 116.

49 Emily S. Mann, "Latina Girls, Sexual Agency, and the Contradictions of Neoliberalism," *Sexuality Research and Social Policy* 13, no. 4 (2016): 330–40, https://doi.org/10.1007/s13178-016-0237-x.

50 Rosa Linda Fregoso, "Homegirls, Cholas, and Pachucas in Cinema: Taking Over the Public Sphere," *California History* 74, no. 3 (1995): 316–27, https://doi.org/10.2307/25177514.

51 Burton, "Childhood Adultification in Economically Disadvantaged Families."

52 hooks, *Black Looks*, 22.

53 Aurthur, "Cynthia Nixon Thinks Miranda Was Always Queer on *Sex and the City*."

54 Curry, "Why the Attempts to Diversify *And Just Like That* . . . Fell Flat."

55 hooks, *Black Looks*, 23.

56 As of publication, neither Sara Ramirez nor Karen Pittman will be reprising their roles as Che Diaz and Nya Wallace, respectively, for the third season of *AJLT*.

57 Notably, the *AJLT* writers' room does not include Latine/x or transgender writers.

58 David Artavia, "Showtime's Foray into Genderless TV," *The Advocate* 1090 (April/May 2017): 36–37; Rachel Shatto, "Innovators in Film & TV," *The Advocate* 1117 (September/October 2021): 34–47; Tracy E. Gilchrist, "To Ser, with Love," *The Advocate* 1104 (August/September 2019): 23–32.

59 Ana-Christina Ramón, Michael Tran, and Darnell Hunt, *Hollywood Diversity Report 2022: A New, Post-Pandemic Normal?* (UCLA Entertainment & Media Research Initiative, 2023).

60 Eliza Steinbock, *Shimmering Images: Trans Cinema, Embodiment, and the Aesthetics of Change* (Duke University Press, 2019), 4.

61 Perez, "A Nonbinary Letter," 196.
62 Muñoz, *The Sense of Brown*, 2.
63 Perez, "A Nonbinary Letter," 197.
64 Emma Flint, "And Just Like That . . . Fails Che Diaz with a Clichéd Take on Non-Binary Representation," *Digital Spy*, January 13, 2022, www.digitalspy.com.
65 Flint, "*And Just Like That* . . . Fails Che Diaz."
66 Harris, "*And Just Like That* . . . Has a Diversity Girlfriend Problem."
67 Shelley Budgeon, "Friendship and Formations of Sociality in Late Modernity: The Challenge of 'Post Traditional Intimacy,'" *Sociological Research Online* 11, no. 3 (2006): 50, https://doi.org/10.5153/sro.1248.
68 Harris, "*And Just Like That*. . . . Has a Diversity Girlfriend Problem."

4

Rebooting Queerness, Re-Privileging Whiteness in the Fantasy World of *She-Ra*

RHIANNON BETTIVIA

READING NOTE: Because animated reboots targeted at children are set in a fantasy world disconnected from lived reality, they hold the possibility of producing a reimagined world free from gender, sexual, ethnic, and racial inequality. However, as this chapter demonstrates, flipped animated reboots, reboots where the sexual, gender, and racial identities of the original characters are changed, remain limited by the dominant flow of heterosexual white girlhood that defines mainstream media production. Specifically, this chapter documents how celebrations of queer and animated diversity in the *She-Ra* reboot still center inequality through white savior and settler colonial narratives that continue to privilege the heterosexuality and whiteness of the original.

> I was a child of the '80s and I grew up watching She-Ra. I was just a huge fan of the property because, honestly, there wasn't that much for girls [on television] at the time . . . because I had that personal connection to the show, it was so important to do it right if we were going to reboot it . . . I think we just started to feel like it was the right time . . . like young girls really needed a new superhero to look up to.
>
> —Beth Cannon, DreamWorks Animation

She-Ra, the superhero character of animation and action figures, embodies the girl power archetype of white feminism.[1] The character originated in the 1980s both as a spin-off of *He-Man and the Masters of the Universe* (1983–1985) and as part of a licensing deal between toy maker Mattel and Lou Scheimer's Filmation studio. The titular character, She-Ra, is the alter ego of Adora, a "princess of power," who leads the fight against evil invaders called the Horde.

The original series *She-Ra: Princess of Power* (1985–1987; hereafter *She-Ra*) ran for two seasons and was a stand-out for being a children's animated superhero show starring a female character. In 2018, DreamWorks Animation and Netflix rebooted *She-Ra* as *She-Ra and the Princesses of Power* (2018–2020; hereafter *Princesses*), under the creative direction of showrunner ND Stevenson. *Princesses* incorporated the original's character and location names and maintained the original property's reputation as a hallmark of girl power in animation. The reboot created characters across a wide spectrum of gender identities, sexual orientations, and racialized identities. On the review amalgamator site Rotten Tomatoes, the reboot has overwhelmingly positive ratings across all five of its seasons.

Princesses is an exemplar of the contemporary reboot moment. The diversity of the characters and representations of difference seek to reenergize the franchise by bringing in new viewers. The reboot was praised for its queer relationships in particular. Vox commented, "The new *She-Ra* is one of the most inclusive and diverse shows on television,"[2] while CNN concluded "'She-Ra' is . . . hands down the best queer representation on television."[3]

In this essay, I analyze narratives of girl power in both versions of the show with a focus on queer and animated diversity in the reboot. As discussed in this book's introduction, the push to diversify television narratives and audiences ultimately obscures the show's privileging of whiteness through the storyline of colonization that pervades both the original and its reboot. Both shows make explicit references to the "First Ones," ancient beings who first colonized the shows' planet of Etheria. References to the First Ones' colonization of Etheria are largely unexplored in the original.

The 2018 reboot portrays Etheria as a post-identity world. A post-identity world is one that imagines that cultural identity formations, such as race, class, and gender, do not impact social relationships. In *Princesses*, a range of bodies, genders, and races exist largely without background or intentional references as to how a character's difference plays a role in the narrative development. The reboot's producers acknowledge this as a fantastical representation, speaking about the joy of working in and with a fantasy world without misogyny or body-shaming. Within this intentionally post-identity world, the racialized and gendered conflict surrounding the dominant colonization storyline that drives the narrative remains in the background. The post-identity world formation is necessarily colorblind: racial differences between the characters are unremarked upon, despite the overwhelming presence of race in a fantasy space.[4] The main character, She-Ra, is begrudgingly motivated by others' expectation that she will be the universe's white savior, an established trope in film and television in which a white character liberates or rescues non-white characters while facing alienation from their own community. In *Princesses*, She-Ra and the significance of her role as a settler colonizer after the successful defeat of the bad guys remain underexplored in the face of the progressive, post-identity world that ND Stevenson built on the strong female protagonist and camp, queer sensibility of the original.

She-Ra: Princess of Power, 1985–1987

> SKELETOR: What brings you to Eternia after all this time?
> HORDAK: I'm only here to capture the traitor I told you about.
> SKELETOR: This traitor, who is he?
> HORDAK: It isn't a he. It's a she.[5]

The character She-Ra was introduced in 1985 as the twin sister of He-Man, the popular Mattel action figure turned comic and television cartoon character. The *She-Ra* television show and associated action figures were designed to appeal to girls as a superhero-style alternative to Mattel's Barbie figures. The show began with a multi-part pilot that portrayed He-Man searching for She-Ra, a previously unknown twin sister kidnapped at birth. The sister, known as Adora when not in superhero mode, was living as a magically brainwashed captain working for the Evil Horde on the planet Etheria, a pastel and ethereal fairyland that contrasts with He-Man's stony gray planet of Eternia. Driving the storyline is the battle between the Evil Horde and the Great Rebellion, consisting of human and non-human native Etherian characters led by magical princesses.

The transmedia relationship between the toy and the show anchors early research in childhood studies about *She-Ra*. Toy and show were literally developed together: Mattel created the injection molds but left the design details to Filmation. Filmation developed characters and stories, and Mattel produced the figures to Filmation's color and accessory specifications.[6] Literature about *She-Ra* focused on gender politics of the female action hero: her appeal to both girls and boys, and her embodiment of the 1980s trope of the white Superwoman who can have it all.[7] The action figures enabled girls to move beyond the televised narratives and to incorporate She-Ra in quotidian spaces of play.[8] Margaret Finders encountered a *She-Ra* fan who saw herself as a leader among the other students and described herself as She-Ra-like at a center for children of teenaged mothers excluded from mainstream learning environments.[9] David Buckingham interviewed children in the UK about gender and race in relation to television shows of the 1980s.[10] Children in Buckingham's focus group acknowledged the dearth of Black representation and, in terms of gender, described She-Ra as a woman who can be as strong as He-Man. The children also notice that while He-Man "guest stars" on *She-Ra* frequently, the reverse is not true: The female protagonist is not welcome in the world of *He-Man*. In sum, the literature about early *She-Ra* focuses predominantly on the gendered aspects of the show, the strong female characters, the relatively femme male characters, and the role of the toys.[11] Missing from the analysis is the consideration of race; the races of the characters; the racialized politics of She-Ra as a white savior; discussions of the relationship between white feminism and the emergence of the "superwoman" trope of the 1980s; and the racial politics of settler colonialism, when colonizers invade and occupy a territory and replace existing cultural, social, and legal systems with their own.

In *She-Ra*, most humanoid characters are white. Non-human characters frequently exhibit saturated colors, like purples, blues, and greens, for the sprite-like Twiggets, evil Harpies, and mountain trolls. This is not to say that no non-white racial signifiers exist in the original *She-Ra* but rather that only two characters in the original show are explicitly coded as non-white humanoids, and both are implied to be Black.[12] The first, Huntara, appears in only one episode. Huntara, like many characters in *She-Ra*, is a pastel purple color. She wears less clothing than many female protagonists: Her costume features a skirt so small it doesn't cover the briefs underneath, and her top is cropped to reveal her six-pack. With white hair, worn in a long ponytail with shaved sides, Huntara is humanoid, yet not human. Similarly, that ambiguity applies to her race. She is not Black, yet signifiers for her Blackness include her costuming and lip shape that differ from the homogeneity of the other female characters. According to Filmation staff, she was drawn to echo Jamaican model Grace Jones, with her hair style and the rasp to her voice,[13] suggesting some racial consciousness from the producers.[14]

The other non-white character is Netossa, drawn with more humanistic brown skin. She first appears in "When Whispering Woods Last Bloomed" (S2, E13) and she appears in a further three episodes as a minor character. *She-Ra* characters look basically the same because they are drawn to match the dolls, or action figures, produced by Mattel. Each character starts as a blank slate of "unmarked whiteness," with race and ethnicity essentialized down to the color of the plastic injected into a mold.[15] There is one body type for women and another for men. The only deviations are reserved for minor characters presented as comic sidekicks or villains who appear in a single episode, and thus not in the doll product line. The women all have Barbie-like proportions marked by tiny waists, ample breasts, and disproportionately long legs in high-heeled boots, plus the chiseled muscles of action figures. Netossa appears as the lone character who is explicitly brown skinned.

Netossa's and Huntara's animation serves to tokenize them as lone non-white characters, which further highlights the overwhelming whiteness of the main characters in the original and rebooted *She-Ras*.[16] For example, Netossa's racialized characterization is further enhanced by her accent, a nonspecific but decidedly non–US American fictionalized pronunciation that marks her as other. The girl power message of *She-Ra* is racialized as white girl power: She-Ra is a literal white savior who comes from another planet to free Etheria from the Evil Horde.[17] Her collaborators are largely white women: allies with fantastical magical or superpowers who battle against the hyper-technical gadgets of the Horde, mirroring the fantasy trope of the fight between the preindustrial natural world and modern science-fiction machines.

Underlying the white savior narrative in both the original and the reboot is the settler colonialism of planet Etheria. Eve Tuck and K. Wayne Yang[18] define settler colonialism as "settlers com[ing] with the intention of making a new home on the land, a homemaking that insists on settler sovereignty over all things in their new domain." Whiteness and Eurocentrism are implied by settler colonialism, given the historical colonialization of the global South by European states. In *She-Ra*, Adora is an outsider: She is revealed to be a princess from the planet Eternia, the home world of He-Man. She arrives to Etheria, whereupon she instantly becomes the de facto leader of the Great Rebellion. As leader, she supersedes the authority of the native Queen Angella. She is expected to save the native population from subjugation by the Evil Horde, a rival colonizing power, who are occupying Etheria to expropriate goods and control "people, land, flora and fauna."[19]

Settler colonialism is explicit in *She-Ra*. Multiple episodes reference the First Ones, who in the script are described as the "original settlers of Etheria." Using the term *settlers* establishes them as colonizers, rather than native inhabitants of Etheria. They are presented as a past people, in keeping with the dominant narrative that colonization is a historical moment that has passed.[20] While the First Ones are mentioned in multiple episodes, they are only animated in "The Stone in the Sword" (S1, E21), where they appear as fiery spirits who help She-Ra. They are a superior race of creatures because they possess the knowledge to repair She-Ra's magical sword, as native Etherians do not, representing the colonial sensibility that native populations are primitive while the white colonizer is responsible for invention and technology.[21]

References to the First Ones spell out their role as Euro-colonizers with visual references to Greco-Roman art and architecture.[22] In "Treasures of the First Ones" (S1, E39), She-Ra saves First Ones treasures from the Horde. The treasures consist of art, including gladiator and white marble statues, gilded picture frames, and vases. She-Ra extols the value and virtue of the aesthetically Western-like collection. She says, "The greatest treasures of the First Ones are love, freedom, truth," and the Horde responds by calling her a sentimental fool, contrasting She-Ra's traditional concern for history and cultural artifacts with the Horde's modern focus on space-age technology.

She-Ra and her Great Rebellion colleagues are feminized in their visual representation: They are largely female, colored in pastels, and occupy pastel castles full of round, sweeping shapes. The Horde, on the other hand, appears in shades of gray, blue, and red, occupying a region of factory-like infrastructure known as the Fright Zone, brimming with mechanical technology. She-Ra's sentimentality for art is part and parcel of the characterization of the female hero: Her superpowers are to talk to animals, to heal, and to care. She-Ra's privileging of Western, and more specifically Greco-Roman, cultural foundations and the settler colonial undertones of the show are overshadowed by the gentle feminine characters and landscapes.

She-Ra episodes conclude with a moral or public service announcement, explained by a rainbow-colored anthropomorphic animal named Loo-Kee. In "Treasure of the First Ones" (S1, E40), Loo-Kee ends by saying, "The works of the great artists both here and on your planet are indeed among our most beautiful and valuable possessions. Take a trip to your local art museum, and you'll see with your own eyes just what I mean. Bye now!" The lesson reinforces the First Ones as arbiters of value and the way they imbue She-Ra with power and authority.

Colonialism employs language of feminism and gender equality to speak to the emancipation of white women.[23] She-Ra, the savior of the native Etherians, embodies this colonizing fantasy through her liberatory actions on behalf of her female co-fighters. She rescues native Queen Angella from an evil harpy; in "Just the Way You Are" (S2, E16), Princess Glimmer is kidnapped to be the bride of a "Bubba" stereotype of an uneducated white male from the US south.[24] These stories underscore the overarching narrative of *She-Ra*'s girl power adventures as the emancipation of magical white princesses. The storyline around the emancipation of the white princesses reinforces notions that this leads towards the betterment of all native subjects of Etheria.

The original *She-Ra* represented a groundbreaking approach with its emphasis on female superheroes and the gender role reversals for helpless male characters like sidekick Bow. Yet, lost in conversations about female empowerment is a critical examination of the politics of whiteness. In the Netflix reboot, the racial and colonial politics are clearer but often obscured by the post-identity characters and narratives. In *Princesses*, the representations of queer bodies of color exist alongside the narrative of She-Ra as the white savior. The next section examines the reboot and the ways in which whiteness manifests in different, but still very present, ways.

She-Ra and the Princesses of Power, 2018–2020

She-Ra was soft rebooted in 2018 with relatively little nostalgia for the original property. Showrunner ND Stevenson, a cartoonist and graphic novelist known for the novel *Nimona* and the series *Lumberjanes*, is several years younger than the original show.[25] *Princesses* borrows the theme of female empowerment and original character and place names. Otherwise, *Princesses* focuses on different narratives, centering deeper character development with redemptive arcs, something largely left out of the rapid-fire, one-off episodes that characterized the original. "Roll with It" (S2, E4) makes a tongue-in-cheek reference to the body proportions and costumes of the original show, highlighting the difference in those depictions versus the diverse, body-positive models and more practical clothing of the 2018 reboot. The updated princesses wear sturdy high-tops and biker shorts instead of high-heeled boots and miniskirts.

Updating *She-Ra* required shedding of many of the original show's premises. *Princesses* jettisons the Mattel action figure body, in which the vast preponderance of characters, including prisoners starving in dungeons, are depicted with six-pack abs and where all women wear high heels and eye shadow, even in battle. Kathleen Loock explains that reboots must speak to "televisual aesthetics, cultural environment, and representational norms of the moment in ways that are still consistent with the show's past."[26] *Princesses* maintains the central themes of girl power and love, but adopts a queer, body-positive multiculturalism in both its characterization and its visual styling. The subtle name change signifies the unifying conceptual arc of the show. *She-Ra: Princess of Power* becomes *She-Ra and the Princesses of Power*, conveying a message about the importance of collectivity and a friend squad.

She-Ra becomes "the She-Ra," acknowledging the separation between the person Adora and the role she takes on with her techno-magic sword. The main characters are aged down from adulthood to adolescence, underscoring growth arcs.[27] In *She-Ra*, She-Ra battles the comically, incompetently bad Horde, ignoring her origin story of having lived and worked with the Horde for two decades before switching sides. In *Princesses*, Adora's ties to Horde members she grew up with form central storylines: Much of the action is about resolving the hurt and betrayal on the part of surrogate mother Shadow Weaver and best friend, later lover, Catra.

The burgeoning friends-to-lovers relationship between Adora and Catra of *Princesses* does not exist in *She-Ra*, although there are queer elements in the original show. Lindsay Mantoan writes about the challenges of queer nostalgia: Reading queer stories in older properties is an exercise in digging for subtext and wading through camp.[28] *She-Ra* is decidedly camp.[29] In *She-Ra*, the male character Bow is cast in the damsel-in-distress role. Despite being a main character, Bow is not deemed important enough to know She-Ra's secret identity. Romantic relationships are largely absent in *She-Ra*, despite the adult ages of the main characters. Spinnerella and Netossa are women who vacation together and who are emotionally so close that Spinnerella begins to destroy a forest when Netossa is captured. Whether this is sufficient subtext to understand a lesbian relationship between the two is moot, as Spinnerella only appears in one episode.

Conversely, *Princesses* teems with long-term, neither fraught nor implied, queer relationships. Here, Princesses Spinnerella and Netossa are stated to be married. Showrunner ND Stevenson posted a message on social media that Princesses Scorpia and Perfuma get together after the show ends, and Bow's two dads live in homo-domestic bliss where they maintain a library and conduct historical research.[30] *Princesses* rejects queerbaiting and "bury your gays" narratives, narratives that end before queer characters can resolve romantic tension or that end by killing off a queer character.[31] *Princesses* instead provides the ultimate happy ending for Adora and Catra: The female leads share a kiss that imbues Adora with sufficient strength to defeat the enemies and bring both balance and magic back to the universe. This queerness is all the brighter in the face of continual queer erasure on the part of rival animation studios like Disney.[32]

Beyond romantic relationships, the show represents a spectrum of gender identities. Princess Perfuma, the boho-chic princess who wields flowers and nature as her special powers, is described as a transwoman by creator Rae Geiger, according to Geiger's Twitter account.[33] The show also features transmale character Jewelstar, voiced by trans actor Alex Blue Davis, and nonbinary character Double Trouble, voiced by nonbinary actor Jacob Tobia. This casting was intentional on the part of the showrunners and mirrors the gender diversity of the producers: For example, Ray Geiger is nonbinary and ND Stevenson is a transman.[34] Characters are presented without commentary on their gender identities.[35] Etheria is post-identity: In *Princesses*, gender and sexuality are non-issues.

Figure 4.1. Perfuma brings Scorpia salad. *Source*: DreamWorks/Mattel.

Yet the representation of gender and sexual preference in *Princesses* is itself a form of essentialism, with fixed traits associated with males and females. Like in many multispecies space operas before it, gender needs no explanation. The characters are still largely male or female presenting, and engaged in long-term domestic pairings.[36] Gender identities remain less ambiguous than the racial identities of characters who are often not human and are usually animated in colored pastel shades rather than human skin tones. Adora remains the blond-haired, blue-eyed white savior in *Princesses*, while other characters take on new racialized identities either through their visual design or through the voice cast used to portray them.

The show's focus on bodily diversity and the animated fantasy world of skin coloring and non-humanness means a racial analysis of the reboot requires an exploration of the voice actors and racialized tropes that enable audiences to code non-human characters as Black, Asian, or white. In *She-Ra*, Catra is a complicatedly racialized character: She is animated as white while her voice actor, Melendy Britt, describes Catra's signature voice, replete with purrs and trilled r's to highlight her cat-ness, as influenced by the 1960s Catwoman African American actress Eartha Kitt.[37] Thus, while 1985 Catra is literally white, she is aurally implied to be Black by her voice characteristics, in much the same way white voice actor Erika Scheimer rasps her voice to play Grace Jones–inspired Huntara: Cross-voicing is as queer as cross dressing. In this case, cross-voicing further complicates the racial identities of characters who are drawn as white (original Catra) or lavender (Huntara), while being voiced by white actors impersonating the vocal trademarks of Black female icons of the 1960s and 1970s. In *Princesses*, Catra is covered in light brown fur that makes her body appear ambiguously Brown, if not necessarily Black. She-Ra and Catra cross literal species and implied racial boundaries in the concluding episode of the series when they kiss. The show uses visual tropes and voice actors to convey race in a post-racial, rainbow, pan-ethnic fantasy world.

Race isn't mentioned in *Princesses*. Although the borderland narratives between the occupied Horde lands and the flowering utopic Rebel lands echo earlier animated representations, such as the demarcation between the fertile pride lands and bleak bone gardens of Disney's 1998 *Lion King*, the fantasy setting in *Princesses* also obscures geographical signifiers of race.[38]

Instead, racial tropes are constructed from the interplay of visual and aural signifiers.[39] In *She-Ra*, the visual aesthetic is clear: The bad guys are brightly colored in reds, blues, and yellows and are non-human hybrid animals or robots. They are subhuman. Race in this case can be read as a distinctly human issue, which explains in part the racial ambiguity of the human-ish main characters: If they are only kind of human, they can only be kind of racialized. The two female Horde members, Catra and Scorpia, are represented as white women and animated to convey their proximity to animals: Catra purrs and turns into a cat, while Scorpia has a stinging tail and pincers instead of hands. The voice cast of the original show are all racially white, each actor portraying many characters. The whiteness of the original *She-Ra* is overwhelming in its visual and aural signifiers, and this whiteness is strategic: It provides acceptability for the female lead and her camp entourage. Because She-Ra is racially uncomplicated, she can embody other traits not traditionally associated with female cartoon characters of the era.

Figure 4.2. A publicity photo released on Twitter of the voice cast of the reboot. *Source*: Cartoon Brew Animation News.

The reboot's animation and casting contrasts with the overwhelming whiteness and homogeneity of the original. Racial diversity comes from human voice actors. This is intentional: the producers teased the coming of the reboot on Twitter with a "class photo" of the voice actors (figure 4.2). Several main characters in *Princesses* can be read as non-white. Catra's fur coloring renders her racially ambiguous. Glimmer is coded as Asian, not through visual markers but through her association with her voice actor, Karen Fukuhara (an American actor born to Japanese parents) and through her on-screen relatives. Her father and paternal aunt, King Micah and Castaspella, are voiced by actors Daniel Dae Kim and Sandra Oh to connote Asianness. Bow is drawn as Black and voiced by Black actor Marcus Scribner. The character Princess Frosta is drawn with facial features and costuming evocative of Inuit or other northern Indigenous peoples.

Casting choices fall between a race-conscious approach and a colorblind casting approach: The consciousness exists to employ a diverse set of actors, while at the same time the aesthetic design of the characters means people of color do not appear in the stories they tell.[40]

Latinx actress Aimee Carrero plays a blond, white Adora/She-Ra. Black actor Vella Lovell voices Mermista, whose style is evocative of *Aladdin*'s Princess Jasmine, with flat affect and Kardashian-like vocal fry. British-American actress Reshma Shetty, who has Hindu Indian parents, plays white-presenting Queen Angella, an angelic immortal being, who speaks with a British accent to convey unambiguous whiteness as well as superiority in terms of rank and generation.

By making post-racial decisions in hiring non-white actors to voice both white and non-white characters, the show's producers reiterate whiteness as the desirable default against which people of color are represented and compared. The She-Ra is the white savior to which her entourage of colorful sidekicks is contrasted. In addition to the character development of Adora as the white savior, two additional characters highlight the pervasive whiteness of *Princesses*: Princess Entrapta and Shadow Weaver.

The techno-princess Entrapta may or may not have magical powers, in contrast to the other explicitly magical princesses: Her anthropomorphic, prehensile pink-purple hair is the only marker of a potential physical superpower. Her technological triumphs are tempered by the harm of her experimental failures. In response to these failures, Entrapta is depicted as motivated by logic and scientific progress, traits usually associated with a modernity characterized as white and masculine. She says, "I'm on the side of science!" (S2, E2, "Ties That Bind") and "I should leave, but I have to stay. For science!" (S2, E3, "Signals"). Entrapta is part zany STEM girl, part amoral scientist.[41] Megan Crouse on the blog *Den of Geek* argues that Entrapta is an example of progressive gender representation because the tech role is usually open only to males.[42]

Showrunner ND Stevenson stated on Twitter that Entrapta's preoccupation with her gadgets is the result of her neurodivergence.[43] Entrapta's character typifies the high-functioning autistic person in popular media, often associated with whiteness and high socioeconomic status.[44] In addition to being white, she is rich: She is a Silicon Valley–esque tech worker princess, served by robot and human staff that cater to her every need. This status enables her to operate in a moral gray zone, as a member of both the princess group and, later, the Horde. She is equally happy on the side of the native Rebels and colonizing Horde as long as she has "science" to do.

Shadow Weaver is another racially ambiguous character. In the *She-Ra* episode "The Price of Power" (S1, E47), Shadow Weaver is revealed to have been a white, blonde woman with a pink Renaissance dress, cone hat, and veil. Her magical corruption leads to literal physical corruption, replacing her white skin with greenish-gray skin and her princess gown with a hooded red cloak that erases her blond hair. Shadow Weaver's transformation from white to non-white, literally gray, is a metaphor for her fall from good to bad. It is a transformation that also occurs to a lesser extent with Shadow Weaver in *Princesses*. *Princesses*' Shadow Weaver includes magic hair that moves, giving it the appearance of naturally textured Black hair. Her ears and fingers have gray skin tone and a mask obscures her face. While her visual signifiers are ambiguous, her sonic signifiers are clearer.[45] Shadow Weaver is voiced by Black and Trinidadian American actor Lorraine Toussaint. The aural signifier of Toussaint and her non-white appearance render her race ambiguous to audiences of the show.

The five seasons of *Princesses*, which ended less abruptly than Filmation's original show, entail more detailed character arcs for virtually all the characters. While Shadow Weaver's backstory is told in both the original and the reboot, in *Princesses* her role as surrogate mother to Adora is foregrounded. The development of the character centers on her desire to bring Adora back to the Horde, while she is depicted as having a fraught relationship with her other adopted daughter, Catra. Shadow Weaver favors the literal golden child and subjugates the non-white daughter. During the show's final season, Shadow Weaver is partially redeemed by the writers when she embraces the ultimate role for any postfeminist female character: motherhood.[46] After Glimmer's mother dies, Shadow Weaver takes on that role, and she eventually gives up her own life to save both her adopted daughters, Adora and Catra. This sacrifice ultimately allows Adora to save the world.

She-Ra was built on homogeneity through the whiteness of the voice actors, the characters' animation, and the homogeneity of body types shaped by the commercial relationship between the show and the marketing of the action figures. *Princesses* consciously embraces a raceless gender fluidity and body positivity and attempts to present both visual and aural diversity. Still, whiteness remains central to the story, privileging white characters like Entrapta and Adora and serving as a symbolic marker of good and evil in the case of Shadow Weaver. The final section of this article returns to the issue of settler colonialism and its relationship to the whiteness of the reboot.

Settler Colonialism: Princesses and the First Ones

> ADORA: What's a First one?
> GLIMMER: You've never heard of the First Ones?
> BOW: The First Ones are the original settlers of Etheria. They disappeared a thousand years ago, but they left behind a lot of old ruins and technology . . .
> ADORA: So what happened to them?
> BOW: No one knows. They just disappeared.[47]

The First Ones are an underexplored narrative concept in *She-Ra*, mentioned in a handful of episodes as a people of days gone by. Yet their wisdom dominates the mythological landscape of the planet Etheria, a name that stems from the Greek root denoting airiness and spirituality: The spirits of the First Ones have the power to repair She-Ra's magical sword when it breaks. In *Princesses*, the First Ones are given a much larger role. They are a seemingly extinct and superior species who arrived to settle Etheria and left behind powerful technology used in the fight against the Horde. In both versions of the show, the First Ones have left behind treasures sought by heroes and villains alike. These treasures are relegated to art stereotypes in the original *She-Ra*; in *Princesses*, the First Ones' legacy includes the technology that turns Adora into the She-Ra.

Settler language of colonization shapes both shows: First Ones are literally described as settling on Etheria. However, *Princesses* explicitly grapples with the colonial legacy of the First Ones. In early episodes of *Princesses*, many characters seek First Ones technologies for their power. Reminiscent of *Ancient Aliens*, *Princesses* literally posits technologically advanced superbeings as the source of ancient machinery on Etheria.[48] The First Ones made the She-Ra sword that transforms Adora into a superhero, while characters like Queen Angella and Perfuma reference mythology that states that First Ones technology will return to help them win against the Horde. Adora returning as the She-Ra is seen as the coming of a savior, and *Princesses* depicts Adora struggling with the weight of this responsibility.

As the show progresses, the role of the First Ones as benevolent colonizers comes into question. Typical of colonial projects, the actual process of colonization is depicted as something that occurred in the distant past, like Disney's construction of the Pocahontas story: Colonization was a thing that happened then and does not retain any bearing on the now.[49] Relegating colonial activities to the past, particularly the violent displacement and expropriation of people, serves to remove culpability from current populations. The First Ones caused the violent moving of Etheria, not Adora and her comrades. The relationship between the native inhabitants and the First Ones is not explored at all in *She-Ra*; yet in *Princesses*, Great Rebellion members are implied to be the native inhabitants. While the natives fight to remove the Horde, there is no evidence that they fought the First Ones. This reinforces the notion that the First Ones, from whom Adora is descended, were benevolent in their colonization of the natives, transforming rustic savages who rely on magic into a progressive techno-centric people.[50]

In season 3, it is revealed that Adora is a First One, consequently troubling the project of colonial storytelling that often relegates colonization to the past by bringing colonization into the fictionalized present. Adora learns of a previous She-Ra, a First One named Mara, who arrived with the settlers to study native magic on Etheria. This is shown in an encounter between Mara, who represents the techno-colonizers, and Razz, the magic. In the episode "Hero" (S4, E9), Razz enters Mara's interdimensional spaceship in search of sugar for pies. Razz's domestic project contrasts with the techno-scientific mission of Mara. In a series of flashbacks, Mara and Razz form a relationship that impacts Mara's approach to colonization.

Mara is depicted as a gentle form of colonization in contrast to the other First Ones, who represent a destructive and extractive form of colonization.[51] Mara embodies the "benevolent ideology of good will, proto-environmentalism, proto-feminism, and cross-cultural tolerance," the idea that colonization is not inherently bad, but that there are good forms of colonization and bad forms.[52] When Mara discovers that the colonial project is designed to use Etheria's magic to power a superweapon capable of destroying worlds, she transports the entire planet to a distant empty dimension so the weaponry cannot hurt others: This move is a literal expropriation of an entire planet.[53] As a result, the natives are depicted as coping with the loss of the stars because the new dimension has an empty night sky.

In the series finale of *Princesses*, Adora releases Etheria's magic, bringing magic back to the universe and stars back to the sky, partially rectifying some of the colonial violence. Her character occupies a place of double resistance against two colonizing powers: She must resist the long-term plans of the First Ones to extract the magic of Etheria, while also fighting against the current colonization attempts by the Horde. When the narrative heads to outer space, Adora encounter other planets where the First Ones and the Horde have fought, where the cannibalization of rival colonizing powers leaves behind destroyed and uninhabitable worlds. The First Ones and the Horde travel the universe, settling planets to harness magic toward their expansionist projects. The head of the Horde explains this long-running contest in "An Ill Wind" (S5, E9), saying, "The First Ones sought a new source of power on ancient worlds. Why bend themselves to the whims of magic and myth? The fools took their secrets with them when they died, but I will find another way." While Adora fights against the Horde and the First Ones, she cannot shake her origins as a member of the First Ones. When Adora frees a town from a Horde occupation in "An Ill Wind," she replaces the Bat-Signal-like Horde beacon shining over the town with a She-Ra sword beacon. The She-Ra sword is a First One technology, a symbol of recolonization, by a rival colonial power, rather than one of liberation and decolonization.

The post-identity ethos of *Princesses* downplays the racialized aspects of the underlying settler colonialism narrative. Attempts to grapple with this by both Adora/the She-Ra and Mara/the previous She-Ra only further entrench the centrality of the white savior and casting of the She-Ras in the role of benevolent colonizers as central to the show.[54] Ultimately, the white settler Adora, the whitest and blondest of the fighting princesses, saves the day. Not only does she release the native magic of the planet, but she also harnesses all of the native magic into herself, which she then uses to cover the war zone with greenery and put a permanent end to the Horde. What is left unclear by the storyline is what happens to the First Ones, who ostensibly still exist somewhere, given that teenage Adora is acknowledged to be a First One: One set of colonizers, the benevolent ones, are left standing.

Conclusion

The original *She-Ra* stood as a cultural lodestone in the 1980s in its depiction of a female protagonist and its explicit marketing of a superhero for girls. Its emphasis on girl power and the 1980s superwoman made it the focus of gender analysis scholarship and popular criticism. The hegemonic whiteness of the show enabled the acceptance of a female action hero lead and her comparably feminized, camp male sidekicks: Her whiteness gave physical cover to her transgression of traditional gendered power relations. If *She-Ra* embodies tropes of white second-wave feminism with its adult princesses, *Princesses* embodies the postfeminist ideal in its aging down of the characters and portraying the heroes as girls represented as family units in relationship to motherhood.[55] The 2018 reconceptualization of *She-Ra* creates a post-identity fantasy realm that stands in explicit contrast to a non-post-identity reality, the Trump era that followed the progressively cast Obama years. The representation of non-white and queer characters potentially troubles the traditional princess narrative and the homogeneity of the original property. Indeed, the reboot has achieved popular acclaim for its portrayal of queer relationships and a diversity of body types. Because it is a fantasy space opera rife with not-quite humans, science-fiction tropes are employed to convey race and ethnicity. The irony is that gender is so essentialized, seen as absolute, even in the multi-dimensional world of *She-Ra* and *Princesses*.

Princesses also attempts to grapple with the She-Ra's complicated role as a white savior and a settler colonizer, characterizations carried over from the original when they were posited by the writers as unproblematic. The queerness of the show as headed by showrunner ND Stevenson is used to soften settler colonialism in the reboot released in the era of *posts*: the diversity of voice actors and character portrayals stands as liberatory in the face of the colonization narrative that remains at the root of the storyline. Colonization fits neatly in this *post*-space because it too is nearly always cast as part of the past. *Princesses* struggles to address the role of the First Ones' expansionist goals and Adora's origins as a First One. These concerns are obscured by Adora's queer happy ending with her lover Catra, where the damage done by successive colonizers is seemingly erased by an alliance between the white colonizer and her queer, non-white, colonized native "best friend squad." The series finale embodies settler fragility, or the inability to talk about the privilege afforded to Adora in her role as the hero of the rebellion.[56] Adora liberates the natives yet takes most of their resources in the form of Etheria's planetary magic and is celebrated as a white savior by her squad. The show ends not with a non-metaphorical plan for decolonization following the destruction wrought by wars raged by rival colonizers,[57] but instead with rainbow squad goals to export the native resources, magic, across the universe. In a show that is so conscientious of its representations of gender, queerness, and race, the inability to decolonize Etheria demonstrates the persistence of settler colonialism and its dependency on whiteness.

Discussion Questions

1. Define settler colonialism. What role does settler colonialism play in the original and the reboot in maintaining racially white identity as the norm?
2. What possibilities and limitations do reboots of animated shows create for producers to challenge the whiteness and heterosexuality of the majority of Hollywood television programming?
3. Do you think the producers of *Princesses* succeed in challenging Hollywood's norms around race, gender, and sexuality? Why or why not?

NOTES

Epigraph: "Netflix's She-Ra Reboot Looks to Empower a New Generation of Kids," *Today*, March 6, 2019, video, 5:42, www.today.com.

1 Jessie Daniels, "The Trouble with White Feminism: Whiteness, Digital Feminism and the Intersectional Internet," pre-print version (*The Intersectional Internet, Section Two: Cultural Values in the Machine*, CUNY Academic Works, February 16, 2015).

2 Alex Abad-Santos, "Netflix's *She-Ra* is a Terrific Reboot—and a Huge Step for LGBTQ Representation on TV," *Vox*, November 21, 2018, www.vox.com.

3 Lindsay Mantoan, "'She-Ra and the Princesses of Power' Is the Rarest of Television Feats," *CNN*, May 22, 2020, www.cnn.com.

4 Lisa Nakamura, "Don't Hate the Player, Hate the Game: The Racialization of Labor in World of Warcraft," *Critical Studies in Media Communication* 26, no. 2 (2009): 128–44.

5 *She-Ra: Princess of Power*, season 1, episode 4, "Reunions," written by Larry DiTillio, directed by Marsh Lamore, aired September 12, 1985.
6 Marsha Kinder, *Playing with Power in Movies, Television, and Video Games: From "Muppet Babies" to "Teenage Mutant Ninja Turtles"* (University of California Press, 2023); Norma Odom Pecora, *The Business of Children's Entertainment* (Guilford Press, 1998); Angharad N. Valdivia, *The Gender of Latinidad: Uses and Abuses of Hybridity* (Wiley-Blackwell, 2020).
7 Peggy A. Bulger, "The Princess of Power: Socializing Our Daughters Through TV, Toys, and Tradition," *The Lion and the Unicorn* 12, no. 2 (1988): 178–92, https://doi.org/10.1353/uni.0.0131; Christine LaFia, "'Superwoman' in Television Situation Comedies of the 1980s," *Studies in Popular Culture* 11, no. 2 (1988): 78–90; Margaret J. Finders, "'Gotta Be Worse': Negotiating the Pleasurable and the Popular," *Journal of Adolescent & Adult Literacy* 44, no. 2 (2000): 146, www.jstor.org/stable/40013533.
8 Bulger, "The Princess of Power."
9 Finders, "'Gotta Be Worse.'"
10 David Buckingham, "What Are Words Worth? Interpreting Children's Talk About Television," *Cultural Studies* 5, no. 2 (1991): 228–45, https://doi.org/10.1080/09502389100490181.
11 Kinder (2023) notes the ubiquity of *She-Ra* toys in the toy aisle years after the show concluded its original run in 1987.
12 Jennifer Barker, "Hollywood, Black Animation, and the Problem of Representation in *Little Ol' Bosko* and *The Princess and the Frog*," *Journal of African American Studies* 14 (2010): 482–98, https://doi.org/10.1007/s12111-010-9136-z; Sarita McCoy Gregory, "Disney's Second Line: New Orleans, Racial Masquerade, and the Reproduction of Whiteness in *The Princess and the Frog*," *Journal of African American Studies* 14 (2010): 432–49, https://doi.org/10.1007/s12111-010-9138-x.
13 The voice cast of the 1985 *She-Ra* series was very small, with most actors voicing several roles. Huntara was voiced by Erika Scheimer, daughter of Filmation co-founder Lou Scheimer.
14 Dale Henrickson, "Remembering 'She-Ra' and 'He-Man': Interview with Lou Scheimer," *Animation World Network*, November 7, 2006, www.awn.com.
15 Mary Thompson, "'Learn Something from This!' The Problem of Optional Ethnicity on *America's Next Top Model*," *Feminist Media Studies* 10, no. 3 (2010): 335–52, https://doi.org/10.1080/14680777.2010.493656.
16 Sarah Projansky and Kent A. Ono, "Strategic Whiteness as Cinematic Racial Politics," in *Whiteness: The Communication of Social Identity*, ed. Thomas K. Nakayama and Judith N. Martin (Sage, 1999): 149–74.
17 Michelle S. Bae, "Interrogating Girl Power: Girlhood, Popular Media, and Postfeminism," *Visual Arts Research* 37, no. 2 (2011): 28–40, https://doi.org/10.5406/visuartsrese.37.2.0028.
18 Eve Tuck and K. Wayne Yang, "Decolonization Is Not a Metaphor," *Decolonization: Indigeneity, Education & Society* 1, no. 1 (2012): 1–40.
19 Tuck and Yang, "Decolonization Is Not a Metaphor."

20 Derek T. Buescher and Kent A. Ono, "Civilized Colonialism: *Pocahontas* as Neocolonial Rhetoric," *Women's Studies in Communication* 19, no. 2 (1996): 127–53.

21 Ella Shohat and Robert Stam, *Unthinking Eurocentrism: Multiculturalism and the Media* (Routledge, 2014).

22 Shohat and Stam, *Unthinking Eurocentrism*.

23 Jenny Sharpe, *Allegories of Empire: The Figure of Woman in the Colonial Text* (University of Minnesota Press, 1993).

24 Michael A. Chaney, "Coloring Whiteness and Blackvoice Minstrelsy: Representations of Race and Place in *Static Shock*, *King of the Hill*, and *South Park*," *Journal of Popular Film and Television* 31, no. 4 (2004): 167–84, https://doi.org/10.3200/JPFT.31.4.167-184; Shohat and Stam, *Unthinking Eurocentrism*, 156–161.

25 *Today*, "Netflix's She-Ra Reboot Looks to Empower a New Generation of Kids."

26 Kathleen Loock, "'Whatever Happened to Predictability?': *Fuller House*, (Post) Feminism, and the Revival of Family-Friendly Viewing," *Television & New Media* 19, no. 4 (2018): 371, https://doi.org/10.1177/1527476417742.

27 Sarah Projansky, "Mass Magazine Cover Girls: Some Reflections on Postfeminist Girls and Postfeminism's Daughters," in *Interrogating Postfeminism: Gender and the Politics of Popular Culture*, ed. Yvonne Tasker and Diane Negra (Duke University Press, 2007); Diana Leon-Boys and Angharad N. Valdivia, "The Location of U.S. Latinidad: *Stuck in the Middle*, Disney, and the In-Between Ethnicity," *Journal of Children and Media* 15, no. 2 (2021): 218–32, https://doi.org/10.1080/17482798.2020.1753790.

28 Mantoan, "'She-Ra and the Princesses of Power' Is the Rarest of Television Feats."

29 Lisa Duffy, "From the Evil Queen to Elsa: Camp Witches in Disney Films," *Frames Cinema Journal* 16 (2019), https://framescinemajournal.com; Fabio Cleto, ed., *Camp: Queer Aesthetics and the Performing Subject: A Reader* (University of Michigan Press, 1999).

30 Steven Edward Doran, "Housebroken: Homodomesticity and the Normalization of Queerness in *Modern Family*," in *Queer Love in Film and Television: Critical Essays*, ed. Pamela Demory and Christopher Pullen (Palgrave Macmillan, 2013), 95–104.

31 Joseph Brennan, "Queerbaiting: The 'Playful' Possibilities of Homoeroticism," *International Journal of Cultural Studies* 21, no. 2 (2018): 189–206; Elizabeth Bridges, "A Genealogy of Queerbaiting: Legal Codes, Production Codes, 'Bury Your Gays' and '*The 100* Mess,'" *Journal of Fandom Studies* 6, no. 2 (2018): 115–32, https://doi.org/10.1386/jfs.6.2.115_1.

32 Adam Vary and Angelique Jackson, "Disney Censors Same-Sex Affection in Pixar Films, According to Letter from Employees," *Variety*, May 9, 2022, https://variety.com.

33 Alex Dewing, "PRIDE 2020: The Casual Queerness of 'She-Ra and the Princesses of Power' (2018)," *Flipscreened*, June 13, 2020, https://flipscreened.com.

34 Raina Deerwater, "Creator of 'She-Ra and the Princesses of Power' Noelle Stevenson and Actor Jacob Tobia on Season Four's Radical Inclusion," GLAAD Blog, November 4, 2019, www.glaad.org/blog/.

35 Tracy Brown, "In Netflix's 'She-Ra,' Even Villains Respect Nonbinary Pronouns," *Los Angeles Times*, November 5, 2019.

36 Robin Roberts, *Sexual Generations: "Star Trek, the Next Generation" and Gender* (University of Illinois Press, 1999).

37 Melendy Britt and Alan Oppenheimer, "PowerCon 2011: Melendy Britt Alan Oppenheimer Panel," Panel, PowerCon 2011, September 24–25, 2011, Los Angeles, CA, video, 43:20, https://youtu.be/luI-PwIZU-k.

38 Manuel Martin-Rodriguez, "Hyenas in the Pride Lands: Latinos/as and Immigration in Disney's *The Lion King*," *Aztlán: A Journal of Chicano Studies* 25, no. 1 (2000): 47–66, https://doi.org/10.1525/azt.2000.25.1.47.

39 C. Richard King et al., "Animated Representations of Blackness," *Journal of African American Studies* 14, no. 4 (2010): 395–97, https://doi.org/10.1007/s12111-010-9141-2.

40 Lyra D. Monteiro, "Review Essay: Race-Conscious Casting and the Erasure of the Black Past in Lin-Manuel Miranda's Hamilton," *Public Historian* 38, no. 1 (February 2016): 89–98, https://doi.org/10.1525/tph.2016.38.1.89.

41 Leon-Boys and Valdivia, "The Location of US Latinidad."

42 Megan Crouse, "*She-Ra*: In Defense of Entrapta," *Den of Geek*, May 20, 2020, www.denofgeek.com.

43 Michele Kirichanskaya, "Brain Power: Cartoons Diversify the Face of Neurodivergence," *Bitch Media*, August 19, 2021, www.bitchmedia.org.

44 John Aspler, Kelly D. Harding, and M. Ariel Cascio, "Representation Matters: Race, Gender, Class, and Intersectional Representations of Autistic and Disabled Characters on Television," *Studies in Social Justice* 16, no. 2 (2022): 323–48, https://doi.org/10.26522/ssj.v16i2.2702.

45 Meina Yates-Richard, "'Hell You Talmbout': Janelle Monáe's Black Cyberfeminist Sonic Aesthetics," *Feminist Review* 127, no. 1 (2021): 35–51, https://doi.org/10.1177/0141778920973648.

46 Projansky, "Mass Magazine Cover Girls."

47 *She-Ra and the Princesses of Power*, season 1, episode 2, "The Sword Part II," written by ND Stevenson, directed by Jen Bennett, released November 13, 2018, on Netflix.

48 Shohat and Stam, *Unthinking Eurocentrism*; Derek D. Turner and Michelle I. Turner, "'I'm Not Saying It Was Aliens': An Archaeological and Philosophical Analysis of a Conspiracy Theory," in *Explorations in Archaeology and Philosophy*, ed. Anton Killin and Sean Allen-Hermanson (Springer International, 2021), 7–24.

49 Buescher and Ono, "Civilized Colonialism."

50 Ella Shohat, "Gender and Culture of Empire: Toward a Feminist Ethnography of the Cinema," *Quarterly Review of Film & Video* 13, no. 1–3 (1991): 45–84, https://doi.org/10.1080/10509209109361370.

51 Jodi A Byrd, *The Transit of Empire: Indigenous Critiques of Colonialism* (University of Minnesota Press, 2011).

52 Buescher and Ono, "Civilized Colonialism," 254.

53 Tuck and Yang, "Decolonization Is Not a Metaphor."

54 Buescher and Ono, "Civilized Colonialism"; Nicole Maurantonio, "'Reason to Hope?': The White Savior Myth and Progress in 'Post-Racial' America," *Journalism & Mass Communication Quarterly* 94, no. 4 (2017): 1130–45, https://doi.org/10.1177/1077699017691248.

55 Projansky, "Mass Magazine Cover Girls"; Kathleen Loock, "American TV Series Revivals: Introduction," *Television & New Media* 19, no. 4 (2018): 299–309, https://doi.org/10.1177/1527476417742971; Leon-Boys and Valdivia, "The Location of US Latinidad."

56 Dina Gilio-Whitaker, "Settler Fragility: Why Settler Privilege Is So Hard to Talk About," *Beacon Broadside* 14 (2018), www.beaconbroadside.com.

57 Tuck and Yang, "Decolonization Is Not a Metaphor."

PART II

(E)-Racing Whiteness in Reboots

5

Rebooting Latinidad

Differential Visibilization of Latinx in the Recent Reboot Craze

ANGHARAD N. VALDIVIA

Reading Note: This chapter explores three television reboots that include Latinx: the *Gilmore Girls: A Year in the Life* (*GG*) revival (2016, Netflix), the *One Day at a Time* (*ODAAT*) remake (2017–2019 Netflix; 2020 Pop/CBS), and the *Party of Five* (*POF*) reboot (2020, Freeform/Disney).[1] These shows represent three approaches to the inclusion of Latinx[2] in the contemporary reboot moment, which is the major element they all have in common—they are all reboots that add Latinx who were not in the original. The three shows originally aired on post-network television as well, *GG* and *ODAAT* on streaming giant Netflix and *POF* on Freeform/Disney. Other than that, these shows differ in substantial ways. To begin, the shows represent three television genres: *GG* is a dramedy, combination of drama and romantic comedy; *ODAAT* is a traditional family sitcom; and *POF* is a young adult family drama. As well, the shows range from a subtle, almost imperceptible inclusion of Latinidad in *GG*, to a focus on Latinx through contemporary social issues, some of which are Latinx specific but most of which are generalizable to the majority of the population in *ODAAT*, to a focus on one of the most pressing issues for underprivileged Latinx, the specter and experience of deportation in *POF*—creating an arc of visibility and presence from symbolic annihilation to commodification of deportation.

"The minimal yet increased visibility of Latina/o characters on TV comedies across all platforms (broadcast, subscription, and streaming) is ultimately an economic strategy . . . that creates the market appearance of progressive inclusion while still ignoring the ethnic and racial structural inequalities of TV production and everyday life in the United States."[3]

"What is at stake when Latinx representations are part of a project of nostalgia?"[4]

Introduction

In the latest wave of reboots, remakes, and revivals, Latinidad appears in a range of visibilities, from a confusing subtlety and as a background detail in *Gilmore Girls: A Year in the Life*, to a focus on a Latina/o family of Cuban Americans specifically in *One Day at a Time*, to a Latina/o Mexican American family dealing with one of the major Latina/o issues of contemporary politics, Latina/o immigration and deportation, in *Party of Five*. Reboots, revivals, and remakes are the stuff of media ecology. Indeed, as Henry Jenkins reminds us,[5] transmedia content dates back more than a century, and thus cannot be attributed to the recent deployment of digital media. Similarly, the production of Latinidad, the state or process of being or becoming Latinx, dates back to the creation of the US, and thus cannot be attributed to the recent redeployment of nostalgic reboots. Neither the presence of Latinx nor the quality of that presence in the latest wave of transmediated post-network television comes as a surprise. While television has not readily included Latinx beyond very circumscribed roles and genres,[6] the latest wave of digitally streamed reboots, revivals, and remakes, as the introduction to this book suggests, appears to be consistent in this marginalization as its nostalgic dimensions work through re-centering whiteness. Kathryn Pallister,[7] writing specifically about Netflix, notes that nostalgic media ignores the challenges faced by marginalized groups. Manuel G. Avilés-Santiago urges media scholars to explore "what is at stake when Latinx representations are part of a project of nostalgia."[8] Nostalgia, as a form of retroactive utopia, looks back to the original television shows as a fountain of productive creativity to inform and infuse the diverse present with ethnic sensibility. The original shows themselves were nostalgic visions of that present wherein they were created and distributed. Accordingly, the inclusion of Latinx in the latest wave of reboot can be classified as *nostalgia 2.0*.

This chapter explores three recent television reboots that included Latinx, none of which are still being produced: the *Gilmore Girls: A Year in the Life* (*GG*) revival (2016, Netflix), the *One Day at a Time* (*ODAAT*) remake (2017–2019, Netflix; 2020, Pop/CBS), and the *Party of Five* (*POF*) reboot (2020, Freeform/Disney). These shows represent three approaches to the inclusion of Latinx in the contemporary reboot moment, which is the major element they all have in common: They are all reboots that add Latinx who were not in the original. The three shows originally aired on post-network television as well, with *GG* and *ODAAT* on streaming giant Netflix and *POF* on Freeform/Disney. Other than that, these shows differ in substantial ways. To begin, the shows represent three television genres: *GG* is a dramedy, combination of drama and romantic comedy; *ODAAT* is a traditional family sitcom; and *POF* is a young adult family drama. As well, the shows range from a subtle, almost imperceptible inclusion of Latinidad in *GG*, to a focus on Latinx through contemporary social issues in *ODAAT*—some of which are Latinx specific but most of which are generalizable to the majority of the population—to a focus on one of the most pressing issues for underprivileged Latinx in the specter and experience of deportation in *POF*, creating an arc of visibility and presence from symbolic annihilation to commodification of deportation. Another major difference is the length of the reboot: The *GG* revival was a limited four-episode mini-series, with enough of an open ending to suggest the possibility of yet another revival; *ODAAT* managed a bumpy survival into its fourth season; and *POF* only made it through the first season. Finally, Sony Television Productions produced two of the shows (*ODAAT* and *POF*), which have aired across three different channels. In terms of scholarly attention, the original *GG* has been analyzed in many articles and entire books, but there is very little scholarship in relation to its (lack of) diversity. The original *ODAAT* has received relatively little attention, being one of the least written-about shows from the Norman Lear corpus, but its reboot has already generated much scholarly attention from Latinx media studies scholars. *POF* is the latest show and therefore it is too early for scholarly articles to be published, but the original was largely discussed in terms of some of the progressive youth issues the show tackled. Thus, the three shows represent a range of productive forces and scholarly analysis with some overlaps and different outcomes.

This chapter explores the presence of Latinidad in the latest wave of reboots, focusing on the relative deployment of Latinidad rather than a deep textual analysis. Using production studies as the prism of analysis, this chapter aims to "offer a window into how media content is made, circulated, and engaged throughout a series of moments and a process of articulations."[9] The moment for the release of these shows was squarely within the political maelstrom following the election of the forty-fifth US president. We are no longer dealing with the hipster racism present during Obama's second presidential term,[10] but have transitioned through comedic escapism into subtle or full confrontation with unavoidable political turmoil. Looking at the forces that impel the recycling of old programs, and the reasons given by producers and other involved players for these shows at this time, this chapter provides a modified production analysis. Relating the original shows in terms of what they sought to represent to their reboots, this chapter investigates three different strategies of Latinx representation and the resulting visibility, in terms of acknowledgment of Latinidad and endurance of the show.

The Shows

Gilmore Girls: A Year in the Life

The *Gilmore Girls: A Year in the Life* revival (2016) represents a low measure of Latinx inclusion in this wave of reboots. Production-wise, the series is heavily identified with Amy Sherman-Palladino, the writer, director, and producer who created, directed, and produced the first six seasons and the Netflix mini-series. Sherman-Palladino specializes in white middle-class women-centered shows, with *The Marvelous Mrs. Maisel* (2017–2023, Amazon Prime) being her latest hit show. The original *GG*, set in fictional Stars Hollow, ran for seven seasons from 2000 to 2007, with six seasons on The WB and the seventh season on The CW. Following the lives of three generations of Gilmore "girls,"[11] grandmother Emily Gilmore, mother Lorelai Gilmore, and daughter Rory Gilmore, the original series wasn't exactly a hotbed of racial inclusion.[12] True to form with series set in nostalgic and pastoral Northeast towns, Stars Hollow's cast of quirky characters included only one recurring Latina/Puerto Rican actress, Miss Patty (Liz Torres), whose Latinidad was not part of the narrative—she was the ballet instructor, cast against type as she was a plus-sized actor. Miss Patty appears briefly in the revival, and in the ten intervening years she has lost quite a bit of weight, something that was repeatedly mentioned in celebrity press coverage about the revival. Other racialized characters in the original included Rory's Korean American best friend Lane Kim (Keiko Agena) and her mom, Mrs. Kim (Emily Kuroda), a classic dragon lady stereotype of the

Figure 5.1. The *Gilmore Girls* revival continues privileging the whiteness of the original. In this scene the patrician grandmother Emily Gilmore (Kelly Bishop) asks her granddaughter Rory Gilmore (Alexis Bledel) what language her Latina maid Berta (Rose Abdoo), seen in the background, speaks. *Source*: Netflix. Screen capture by the author.

hyper-controlling, hyper-religious, asexual, humorless mom, and Lorelai's inn manager, Michel Gerard (Yanic Truesdale), who provided comic relief and thinly veiled homophobic humor. The original show garnered much attention because of its postfeminist politics[13] and frequent references to popular culture. Many books, academic articles, and book chapters have analyzed the show,[14] but there has been little attention to issues of race and ethnicity in the series. For example, while Lara C. Stache and Rachel D. Davidson[15] include chapters on feminism and class, they include none on ethnicity. Similarly, none of the chapters in Ritch Calvin's volume[16] explored intersectionality, and Hye Seung Chung's[17] is the sole chapter on issues of race in David Scott Diffrient and David Lavery's volume,[18] focusing on Rory's best friend, Lane.

Eagerly awaited by *GG* fans, the revival in 2016, which was released on the Thanksgiving holiday weekend, consisted of four episodes: "Winter," "Spring," "Summer," and "Fall." Nearly the entire original cast returned, without patriarch Richard Gilmore (Edward Herrmann) because Herrmann passed away in 2014. Sookie St. James (Melissa McCarthy), Lorelai's best friend and business partner, also barely appeared, as McCarthy had become a major star in the intervening years and had difficulty fitting the revival into her schedule. Anecdotal evidence suggests that many viewers, especially fans, binged the four-season episodes at once. Given that Netflix does not release ratings, we have no hard comparative data.

True to the first six seasons[19] of the original show, the revival focused on the three Gilmore women/girls. However, there was a befuddling inclusion of Latinidad in the Gilmore universe of 2018. In the "Winter" episode,[20] as she deals with grief after losing her husband, Emily Gilmore, one of whose running gags in the original show was the revolving door of maids she hired and fired, hires not just a maid, but apparently an entire extended family of ambiguous Latinx. Lorelai greets Berta, who opens the door for her, when visiting her mother and begins to understand that Berta's husband Alejandro and their two children are also living with Emily. During dinner, which includes rice and beans, a clear departure from Emily's usual Eurocentric upscale menus, they can hear children playing soccer in the patio. The inclusion of this family becomes more confusing to all who know Emily's exacting standards for help, when she admits she does not understand their language and, furthermore, does not even know what language they speak! As Emily prepares to downsize and move, it appears an entire community of Latinx moves in with her. She gives away her clothing and other things to them. But Emily still can't figure out what language they speak, claiming in "Winter" that her friend's daughter, who works at the UN, came over and could not figure out what language they speak either. In "Fall,"[21] the Latinx family moves with Emily to her new seaside place in Nantucket, where her male friend Mr. Smith addresses Berta in Spanish: "Gracias, Berta." Meanwhile, in New York City, where Rory stays at her friend Paris's flat, the nanny to Paris's children is a Latina named Clementina. Also, at his diner, Luke Danes, Lorelai's partner, has a cook named Cesar who asks for higher pay as he receives greater responsibility. Thus, the *GG* revival increases its Latinx presence from Miss Patty to a group of stereotypically employed and curiously represented Latinx.

One Day at a Time

Of the three television shows, the oldest original is *One Day at a Time*, which ran on CBS from 1975 to 1984. The show featured a divorced

Figure 5.2. The Norman Lear reboot flipped the ethnicity of the cast and the storylines. The characters were played by an all-Latinx cast of actors. From left to right: Alex Alvarez (Marcel Ruiz), Elena Alvarez (Isabella Gomez), Penelope Alvarez (Justina Machado), Lydia Riera (Rita Moreno). *Source*: Promotional image from CBS.

single mom raising her two teen daughters in Indianapolis. The original *ODAAT* was part of a wave of socially relevant shows developed by Norman Lear and is now considered a classic example of second-wave feminism. The single female parent of the original *ODAAT* was aspirational middle-class, and the urban setting was populated by whites and white ethnics—specifically, Italian Americans. The show was part of a successful Sunday night lineup in the early '80s of shows produced by Norman Lear. Lear foregrounded race relations rather than gender,[22] in contrast to shows produced by MTM, the other successful production firm of the era, which generated such hits as *Mary Tyler Moore* and *Rhoda*. *ODAAT* stood out as one of two "gender" shows, alongside *Maude*, in the Lear lineup. Kirsten Marthe Lentz[23] makes a highly persuasive argument that code words of the era equated "relevance" with race and "quality" with gender, as CBS successfully sought to update its prime-time television lineup partly in response to Newton Minow's "wasteland" speech[24] and previously declining ratings. Lear specialized in setting his shows in a working-class situation, in comparison to MTM's bourgeois upwardly mobile characters, so that race was further coded as working class and gender issues as middle class. *Maude*,

Lear's other effort to deal with feminism, coded the lead character as excessive especially in relation to her racial politics: Feminism was situated within white liberalism and its race-blindness, or rather, its racism. *Maude* receives more attention than *ODAAT* in academic literature,[25] partly because it was one of the few television shows to tackle the issue of abortion.

As with *Gilmore Girls*, the *ODAAT* reboot was produced by some of the same creative team as the original; in this case, Norman Lear was one of two producers. Norman Lear proposed the reboot with a "Hispanic" cast[26] and hired Gloria Calderón Kellett as cultural translator[27] to co-showrun with Mike Royce. Calderón Kellett's previous credits included writing and/or producing stints in a range of shows such as *How I Met Your Mother*, *Devious Maids*, and *Jane the Virgin*. A West Coast Cuban American Latina, Calderón Kellett intentionally wrote in Cuban American specificity rather than a pan-Latinx approach. Mike Royce's background included being a stand-up comic, crossing over as a writer in *Everybody Loves Raymond*, and moving up to the position of executive producer in that show, as well as in Louis CK's HBO show *Lucky Louie*, then co-producing, with Ray Romano, *Men of a Certain Age*. One wonders whether Royce's experience in highly masculinist shows was supposed to balance Calderón Kellett's gender and ethnic skills. Lear also prevailed on the sitcom genre and the multi-camera, live-audience format, which some critics[28] praised as "new and crucial again," thus reiterating narrative, genre, and production nostalgia. *ODAAT*'s reboot, partly with Lear's input, reproduces his approach to a notion of authenticity, adjudicating racial representations in terms of good and bad—telling a "truth" about race.[29] This measure and approach to relevance/race remains a factor in the reboot of *ODAAT*. Lear's previous effort to launch a Latinx show dated back to *a.k.a. Pablo*, which was produced for ABC in 1984 and was not renewed, although Mary Beltrán's analysis shows that even the episode entitled "The Whole Enchilada"[30] was full of subtlety and specificity.[31] The show's "struggling Mexican American family faced audience protests over offensive stereotypes,"[32] even as its production team included Latinx trying to construct a sophisticated narrative arc, and the series was canceled after six episodes. Calderón Kellett praised Lear upon his passing and reminds viewers that he was a supporter of Latinx actors and stories, dating back to *a.k.a. Pablo*.[33]

Lear's nearly mythical status strongly influenced the reboot, which bore the marks of a 1970s approach to production. Additionally, the sitcom genre filmed before a live audience with multiple cameras has proven to be a useful vehicle for defusing difficult political and cultural issues through the use of laughter.

Unsurprisingly, the tensions within Latinidad linger within *ODAAT*, partly due to its Norman Lear–inspired Hispanicization. Calderón Kellett was hired to provide not only the cultural translation into Latinidad but also a Cuban American specificity, which did not extend to the cast, who were primarily Puerto Rican actors.[34] Grandmother/Abuela Lydia is played by EGOT-winning Puerto Rican actress Rita Moreno, the most awarded Latina actress in Hollywood, while the theme song "This Is It" is performed by Cuban American crossover star Gloria Estefan, whose anti-Castro politics are part of her brand. Accordingly, Avilés-Santiago finds that the Cubanidad in the show, especially as embodied by Abuela Lydia, harks back to a pre-revolutionary Cuban nostalgia, and avoids the multiple Cuban identities and politics now present in the US.[35] Similarly, Stephanie Melissa Pérez finds the exclusion of Afro- and indigenous Cubanidades to be a gap in the show.[36] Moving the setting to the Echo Park neighborhood of Los Angeles instead of Miami, where Estefan and many waves of Cubans actually reside, was a fresh approach, and probably influenced by Calderón Kellett, who identifies as a West Coast Cuban American.

Los Angeles neighborhoods are the latest locations of Latinx authenticity: *ODAAT* is located in Echo Park; *Party of Five* in some unnamed East Los Angeles location; *East Los High* and *Vida* in Boyle Heights; and *On My Block* in Freeridge, a mixture of the San Fernando Valley and South Central Los Angeles.[37] Most relevant for this chapter, the location change for *ODAAT* coincides with the protagonists being Latinx. This rebooted aspirational Latina/o family, like the original, is also headed by a single mom. The original mom, Ann Romano (Bonnie Franklin), was an Italian American, upwardly mobile, high school–educated advertising industry worker[38] raising two teenage daughters and marked the first time a divorced woman had been protagonist in mainstream US television show. In the rebooted *ODAAT*, Cuban American single mom Penelope Alvarez (Justina Machado) is a nurse and an army veteran raising her two children and living with her mother. Pérez succinctly outlines the story arcs for each of the three female protagonists: coming out for daughter Elena, immigration issues for grandmother Lydia, and single parenthood plus mental health issues for mother Penelope.[39] The first season indulges in the stereotypical trope of a mom planning a quinceañera for a daughter who does not want one, but presents it with a twist: daughter Elena's coming out, her father's rejection, and her chosen family's support.

Despite being a darling in critic circles, *ODAAT* experienced existential threats, in the form of non-renewal, beginning in its second season. Twitter campaigns such as #SaveODAAT, abetted by talk shows, Lin-Manuel Miranda and Busy Phillips, and Rotten Tomatoes perfect 100 ratings for the second and third season could not persuade Netflix to renew beyond the third season. One of the issues is that Netflix does not reveal ratings, so that showrunners, such as Gloria Calderón Kellett, do not really know what their numbers are, what they are aiming for, and what they failed to reach.[40] Thus, although Netflix claims low ratings killed the show, it can't be confirmed; however, Bradley suggests that the cancellation might very well be due to Sony Pictures Television producing the series[41]—Netflix prefers to stream its own productions.

Commentators and reviewers repeatedly mention the old-school production of the first three seasons of *ODAAT*, using multiple cameras and filmed in front of a live studio audience. As well, both producers said they valued the generic freedom of producing for Netflix, which not only provides a flexible time for each episode but also allows for development of a story arc, all without the pressure of appealing to advertisers. Ethnicity-wise, Calderón Kellett infuses the narratives with her own background as a Cuban American, explicitly wanting that ethnic specificity rather than a flattened-out Latinidad. Surprisingly enough, some of the struggles represented by daughter Elena's character, especially her journey in coming out, are based on co-producer Mike Royce's daughter. As a result, the show is a hybrid of the producers' ethnic and family histories that cohere to create the *ODAAT* universe wherein Cuban American characters living in the US, in a Latinx neighborhood, deal with Latina/o as well as contemporary issues affecting women and people regardless of gender across a range of generations. Pérez affirms that *ODAAT* aims for a hybrid audience.[42] Via a "Hispanic" family, Lear sought to reboot one of his old properties through a prism of Latinidad, but to reach a broad "universal" audience.

Indeed—and a bit sadly from today's perspective—Esteban del Río and Kristin Moran end their 2020 article with the rosy conclusion that *ODAAT*'s "complex notion of Latinidad rooted in cultural specificity in the show and in the mind of the producers that is enabled by digital delivery" operates "outside of the audience-centric creative process," which in turn "portends profound changes to television in general and Latina/o representation in particular."[43] Echoing Isabel Molina-Guzmán's assessment of *East Los High* as only possible in the post-network era,[44] most of this utopian conclusion, written after the second season, needs to be amended after Netflix canceled the show following the third season, and Pop/CBS picked up distribution and then canceled as well. *ODAAT* returned as a post-network streamed reboot to legacy TV, perhaps the first time in TV history that such a reverse distribution setup had been arranged. In effect, much of what Calderón Kellett has publicly celebrated about the previous Sony production/Netflix distribution arrangement, and what del Río and Moran had identified as a promising trend for Latinx representation,[45] was reversed by the show being picked up by one of the major legacy networks, CBS, through their cable channel Pop, with advertisers and the fixed half-hour time slots minus commercials. Adding the global pandemic as yet another wrinkle to the bumpy history of *ODAAT*'s production, this reboot did not survive.

Party of Five

Sony Television Productions also produced the now-canceled reboot of *Party of Five*. The original ran from 1994 to 2000 on the Fox network. Set in an upscale neighborhood in San Francisco,[46] *POF* followed five children orphaned after their parents died in an automobile accident. Despite low ratings in the first two seasons, critics' support and a Best Series Golden Globe at the end of the second season boosted its ratings for the remaining three seasons. The original *POF* remains a favorite for young adult drama and is endlessly available in reruns; scholarly attention focuses on some of the progressive social issues tackled in the show[47] that were nonetheless resolved through centralizing whiteness,

Figure 5.3. The Acosta siblings, from left to right: Emilio (Brandon Larracuente), Valentina (Elle Paris Legaspi), Beto (Niko Guardado), baby Rafa (played by various actors), and Lucia (Emily Tosta). The cast of *Party of Five*. *Source*: Nino Munoz/ Freeform, *Us* magazine.

such as the end of an interracial romance due to differences about having children.

The *POF* reboot aired on Disney's cable network, Freeform, and retained the trope of five children living alone, adhering to elements of the original such as basic personality types of the children and even particular stories such as the house party in first episode.[48] The Latinx theme moves the family from San Francisco to the Echo Park neighborhood in Los Angeles and changes the reason for them being alone to their parents' deportation. In the series' first episode, a celebratory dinner at the parents' restaurant turns tragic when, during an ICE raid that the Acosta parents originally interpret as targeted at their kitchen staff, ICE actually arrests the parents, who lack documents, despite their two-decade residence in the neighborhood and ownership of an establishment. Unlike the original series, in the reboot the children stay parentless in Los Angeles and communicate with their parents on the other side of the border via digital technology. They are not orphaned.

Indeed, the family reunites briefly in Mexico in episode 9.[49] Their constant digital tether becomes one of the narrative arcs in the one season of the show.

POF premiered on January 8, 2020, and was eagerly awaited in Latinx media circles. For instance, Remezcla.com had four separate articles about its release. Viewership dropped from the debut to the season/series finale, and *POF* wrapped its run with an average of 250,000 live same-day viewers. Unfortunately, the series concluded with its tenth and final episode on March 4, 2020, as it was not renewed. Given that the series was produced by an outside studio, the numbers made it hard to justify a second season, as Disney-backed Freeform had to pay a licensing fee to air the show.[50] Goldberg also attributed the show's cancellation to its changing cast of managers, as the Freeform head who aired *POF* departed to head Cartoon Network. Indeed, Freeform leadership changed between the time the show was ordered and when it was produced, and between when it was produced and when it aired. Thorne adds that the series had very low ratings; only two other shows had lower ratings.[51]

Unlike *GG*'s non-inclusive inclusion of ambiguous Latinx, and *ODAAT*'s universalization of the Cuban American family experience, the rebooted *POF* specifically sets out to tackle one of the major issues of the day, namely, President Trump's policies against immigration, which target primarily Latinx, resulting in widespread deportation, separation of families, and fear of rollback of DACA status. The oldest son, Emilio Acosta, has DACA status, and the rest of the Acosta children are citizens. Producers acknowledge this purpose yet also insist that rather than politics, they seek to represent the human and individual lived experiences of those directly affected by these policies.[52] Zebede, co-executive producer and writer, added that it was important to tell the story from a human as well as a political perspective, asserting, "This is an opportunity to really get into the perspective of a group of people in this country that has been marginalized—and on many occasions villainized—and just show they are people, too."[53] Producers claimed a loftier goal for this reboot, beyond the profit from risk averse profit maximization, since this "urgent . . . story was literally ripped from the headlines."[54]

Most of the published material available on the *POF* reboot draws on critics who assessed the first three episodes made available to them for the purposes of review, yet that did not stop some reviewers from declaring the characters undeveloped.[55] Brian Lowry compared *POF* to the reboot of *One Day at a Time*, because both included a "Hispanic family."[56] Other reviewers see *POF*, like *ODAAT*, as a "throw back" to a simpler time of teen issues, despite it being focused on deportation.[57] Jen Chaney gushed over the "sweetly nostalgic and bracingly current" reboot: "The underlying message of this lovely series enables the audience to hold nostalgia and a bracing sense of reality in their heads and hearts all at once, and that's a rare and special thing."[58] Imagine that, nostalgia and reality all at once—this could be the definition of reboots—and indeed it is. Caroline Framke praised *POF*'s "granular" approach to issue of deportation, rather than "lofty philosophizing."[59] This everyday lived-experience approach to the consequences of deportation and threats on DACA status set the teen drama against an unavoidable specter of contemporary politics, which is why Chaney proposed the internally contradictory assessment that *POF* is "not overtly political . . . It is political."[60] Scholars have begun assessing the reboot, with early research finding the reboot transgressive in that it succeeded in "problematizing dominant ideologies, complicating gender roles, offering nuanced constructions of Mexican immigrants, and depicting experiences of racialization and acculturation."[61]

Created by Chris Keyser and Amy Lippman, who created the original, the reboot hired Michal Zebede, of Costa Rican and Panamanian background, as co-executive producer with Rodrigo García Barcha, who also wrote and directed the first two episodes. García Barcha is a famous Colombian filmmaker and son of the Nobel Literature Prize–winning Colombian novelist Gabriel García Márquez.[62] Zebede has previously written episodes of *Devious Maids*. You have here immense talent grounded in a transnational Latine experience, something that Beltrán notes occasionally happens in the production of Latino TV, but it is not always enough to result in long-lasting production of an ethnically sensitive show.[63] While the main characters, the four Acosta children, are played by Latinx actors, the supporting cast includes many Latin Americans who, like García Barcha, hail from different countries in South America: father Javier (Bruno Bichir Nájera) is Mexican; mother Gloria (Fernanda Urrejola Arroyo) is Chilean; babysitter Natalia (Sol Rodríguez) is Argentinian; et cetera. Actors and producers exerted considerable effort to make sure this show was not "trauma porn." Unlike

ODAAT, *POF* did not garner a social media campaign or support from talk shows and famous actors actively calling for its renewal.

Conclusion

This chapter identified three television reboots in terms of their visibilization of Latinx. Other than Miss Patty (Liz Torres) in the original *Gilmore Girls* series, the shows had no discernible presence of Latinidad in their original versions. All three reboots were released during the turbulent binary political moment of the forty-fifth US presidency, though *GG* was produced prior to Trump assuming power. As such, the three shows provide an arc of visibility that is instructive in terms of the presence of Latinidad in contemporary mainstream television. To begin with, mainstream television includes the streaming platforms such as Netflix plus cable television channels of the big five media corporations such as CBS and Disney and enduring production houses such as Sony. There are no minor players in this effort to represent Latinidad, as Latinx are an inescapable component of the population. Yet, as media studies scholars know, presence does not equal improved representation.

The three original shows represented a utopian narrative. Pastoral Stars Hollow provided a family and community of support for the younger two Gilmore Girls with the wealthy Gilmore parents as financial backup; in *ODAAT*, mother Ann Romano eventually came to own her own advertising company and moved for a job in London, all the while navigating single parenthood and raising two headstrong teenage girls; and in *POF*, five young people managed to survive and thrive despite their parents abruptly and prematurely passing away. The reboots stage these utopian impulses in nostalgic overdrive, something noted by reviewers. Stars Hollow reappears a decade later barely changed: There has been no suburban growth or gentrification, though there is a group of unemployed Millennials. The *ODAAT* Alvarez family perseveres despite economic and cultural challenges, some of them related to their Latinx ethnicity. However, the Acosta children face myriad obstacles, many of them similar to what thousands of Latinx families are enduring in real time.[64] We do not find out if the Acostas persevere, as the show did not get to develop narrative arcs in its brief existence. Despite the sweetness of four of the siblings, *POF* may have been too close to currently traumatic policies and outcomes to garner audience support.

The arc from inclusion, as spice in a white utopia, to immensely dated utopian narratives, to the depiction of deportation and its emotional drama suggests that Latinx have achieved a representational status. We have to be included. However, the inclusion in *GG* was highly stereotypical and offensive. Aside from a cook and a nanny, the Latinx family living with Emily Gilmore was treated as a running gag. Emily's inability to recognize the Spanish language amounts to explicit insult and outright marginalization. The Alvarez family represents an effort toward Latinx specificity through universal themes, through the inclusion of a cultural translator (Calderón Kellett), the impetus of a liberal icon (Norman Lear), and the focus on a Latinx family in a Latinx neighborhood. The show had to fight for existence, despite having the support of a hashtag movement, talk shows, and major Hollywood stars.[65] The Acosta family arrived to "humanize" the trauma of deportation, separated families, and DACA status uncertainty. Ratings were not sufficient to merit renewal. However, ratings may have been influenced by elements beyond the quality of the show. This remains to be seen in future research.

At the level of production, creators and industry forces function to provide a context wherein Latinidad appears in a range of properties. The whiteness of the creative team behind *Gilmore Girls* produced a symbolic annihilation that was utterly unsurprising. What was astounding was that the near-erasure of the original was made worse by the offensive presence in the reboot. Norman Lear's desire to "Hispanicize" *ODAAT* pretty much sums up his old-school approach. Latinx do not use the word "Hispanic" other than in a historical sense to refer to outside labels imposed on a pan-Latinx community. In addition to Calderón Kellett, the writers' room at *ODAAT* was gender, ethnicity, and LGBTQ diverse. This diversity generated inclusion of progressive issues such as coming out, immigration documentation, elderly sexuality, and mental health. Yet Lear's unmistakable influence also prevailed with issues such as veterans' rights, as "universally" relevant. Moreover, even though the quinceañera episode highlights coming out, it stereotypically reiterates one of the "authentic" ways that mainstream US popular culture represents Latinidad. *POF* did not have a quinceañera episode, though we might surmise that if future seasons had been produced, they would have included one (or two). In focusing on DACA and deportation and the uneasy and unresolvable agony of digital connectivity against physical distance, *POF* foregrounded a major issue that many Latinx are currently facing. It may have been too much for audiences—both the specificity for general audiences and the trauma for Latinx audiences.

Continuities and ruptures can be seen in these reboots, as within all nostalgic media. Like Pérez, Molina-Guzmán finds that producers roll out "universally familiar and relatable situations without . . . social edge."[66] The offensive stereotyping in *GG* was an unfortunate and present continuity. As a recurring element of Latinx authenticity, location in Echo Park seems to have become de rigueur, despite specificity within Latinidad. The deported parents in *POF* were restaurant owners, both a continuity and a rupture: Restaurant work is a continuity and ownership a rupture. Seventh-grader Valentina in *POF*, a precocious math whiz, represents yet another example of the new Latina STEM girl trope.[67] All Latinx in the three reboots are working class and light brown, reproducing narratives of class and race within Latinidad. Our ever-expanding archive of representations remains firmly framed by continuities with small ruptures in the margins.

Production-wise we have the continuity that all of these shows were produced by the majors for the majors. This is the mainstream. A cultural translator for *ODAAT* makes a difference, but she must function in relation to a co-executive producer whose experience resides in masculinist shows and an iconic creator who specializes in liberal politics. Furthermore, and dating back to Dávila,[68] there is still a reliance on creative talent from Latin America, most extensively in the *POF* reboot.

In the digital age, within which all of these reboots were produced and circulated, we have Leon-Boys's finding of "repromotion."[69] This can be most explicitly seen in *ODAAT*, when a Latinx audience's labor was recruited toward a social media movement to save the show. Similarly, actors in the show and other Latinx actors and cultural creators expended considerable labor in highlighting and circulating demands for renewal of the show. Analogously, *POF* actors circulated to assert that their show was not trauma porn. This suggests that Latinx actor and creator labor is routinely recruited to boost Latinx shows, yet another form of Latinx labor exploitation. Nonetheless, these three reboots illustrate the visibility of Latinx—especially in relation to the original shows. We still are living through a moment bearing the weight of underrepresentation. The narratives, characters, and shows fall short of textured inclusion. Yet we are beyond total exclusion, through an overlap of tropes and ruptures. We are no longer in the lily-white universes of their originals. As well, we continue to advocate for more textured and respectful inclusion, within a mainstream whose structural formation, while resistant to change, has begun to include some producers and narratives of Latinx visibility.

Discussion Questions

1. Compare and contrast the representations of Latinidad and reproduction of Hollywood inequality across the three case studies.
2. Do you think the flipped reboots *One Day at Time* and *Party of Five* failed because the programs featured Latina/o/x characters and storylines? Why or why not? What other reasons contributed to the non-renewals of the shows?

NOTES

1 This chapter draws on research assistance from Sienna Gudino and extensive conversations with Stephanie Pérez, who not only wrote a master's thesis on *One Day at a Time*, but also attended tapings of the show when it was produced for Netflix and Pop/CBS.

2 I use the suffix of x to signify singular and plural as well as non-binary possibilities.

3 Isabel Molina-Guzmán, *Latinas and Latinos on TV: Colorblind Comedy in the Post-Racial Network Era* (University of Arizona Press, 2018), 114, referencing Mari Castañeda, "The Role of Media Policy in Shaping the U.S. Latino Radio Industry," in *Contemporary Latina/o Media: Production, Circulation, Politics*, ed. Arlene Davila and Yeidy Rivero (New York University Press, 2014), 186–205.

4 Manuel G. Avilés-Santiago, "'This is It!' [Is It?]: The Marketing of Nostalgia on Netflix's *One Day at a Time*," *Journal of Latin American Communication Research* 7, no. 1–2 (2019): 64.

5 Henry Jenkins, *Convergence Culture: Where Old and New Media Collide* (New York University Press, 2008).

6 See, e.g., Molina-Guzmán, *Latinas and Latinos on TV*.

7 Kathryn Pallister, ed., *Netflix Nostalgia: Streaming the Past on Demand* (Lexington Books, 2019).

8 Avilés-Santiago, "'This is It!' [Is It?]," 64.

9 Derek Johnson, "Production," in *Keywords for Media Studies*, ed. Laurie Oullette and Jonathan Gray (New York University Press, 2017), 152.

10 Molina-Guzmán, *Latinas and Latinos on TV*, 113.
11 The fact that only Rory was actually a "girl" reiterates the postfeminist approach to the girling of femininity, regardless of actual age.
12 Jennifer Maas, "'Gilmore Girls: A Year in the Life'—15 Things That Still Bother Fans About Revival of CW Series," *The Wrap*, November 25, 2017, www.thewrap.com.
13 See, e.g., Francesca Gamber, "Riding the Third Wave: The Multiple Feminisms of *Gilmore Girls*," in *Teen Television: Essays on Programming and Fandom*, ed. Sharon Marie Ross and Luisa Ellen Stein (McFarland & Company, 2008), 114–31.
14 See, e.g. Ritch Calvin, ed., *Gilmore Girls and the Politics of Identity: Essays on Family and Feminism in the Television Series* (McFarland & Company, 2008); Lara C. Stache and Rachel D. Davidson, *Gilmore Girls: A Cultural History* (Rowman & Littlefield, 2019); David Scott Diffrient and David Lavery, eds., *Screwball Television: Critical Perspectives on Gilmore Girls* (Syracuse University Press, 2010).
15 Diffrient and Lavery, *Screwball Television*.
16 Calvin, *Gilmore Girls and the Politics of Identity*.
17 Hye Seung Chung, "Escaping from Korea: Cultural Authenticity and Asian American identities in *Gilmore Girls*," in Diffrient and Lavery, *Screwball Television*, 165–85.
18 Diffrient and Lavery, *Screwball Television*.
19 Between the sixth and seventh season the show moved from The WB to The CW and its writer, Amy Sherman-Palladino, resigned. Fans of the show reacted strongly against the plotline of the seventh and final season.
20 *Gilmore Girls: A Year in the Life*, season 1, episode 1, "Winter," written by Amy Sherman-Palladino, featuring Lauren Graham, Alexis Bledel, and Kelly Bishop, directed by Amy Sherman-Palladino, aired November 25, 2016, Netflix.
21 *Gilmore Girls: A Year in the Life*, season 1, episode 4, "Fall," written by Amy Sherman-Palladino, featuring Lauren Graham, Alexis Bledel, and Kelly Bishop, directed by Amy Sherman-Palladino, aired November 25, 2016, on Netflix.
22 Kirsten Marthe Lentz, "Quality Versus Relevance: Feminism, Race, and the Politics of the Sign in 1970s Television," *Camera Obscura* 15, no. 1 (2000): 44–93, https://muse.jhu.edu/article/7943/pdf.
23 Lenz, "Quality Versus Relevance."
24 Newton N. Minow, "Television and the Public Interest," presentation, National Association of Broadcasters, May 9, 1961, Washington, DC, www.americanrhetoric.com/speeches/newtonminow.htm.
25 See, e.g., Nicole S. Kypker, "One Right-on Sister: Gender Politics in *Maude*," *Comedy Studies* 3, no. 2 (2012): 139–49, https://doi.org/10.1386/cost.3.2.139_1; Kathryn C. Montgomery, *Target: Prime Time: Advocacy Groups and the Struggle Over Entertainment Television* (Oxford University Press, 1989).
26 Maria Elena Fernandez, "After Two Decades Away, Norman Lear Has a New TV Show," *Vulture*, December 2016, www.vulture.com.
27 Litzy Galarza and Paulina A. Rodríguez Burciaga, "Un Puente a la Mesa: The Role of Cultural Translators in the Production of Disney/Pixar's *Coco*," in *Immigrant*

Generations, Media Representations, and Audiences, ed. Omotayo O. Banjo (Palgrave Macmillan, 2021), 155–182, https://doi.org/10.1007/978-3-030-75311-5_8; Juan Piñón, "*Ugly Betty* and the Emergence of the Latina/o Producers as Cultural Translators," *Communication Theory* 21, no. 4 (2011): 392–412, https://doi.org/10.1111/j.1468-2885.2011.01389.x.

28 See, e.g., Caroline Framke, "5 Reasons One Day at a Time Is One of the Best, Most Empathetic Shows on TV," *Vox*, January 27, 2018, www.vox.com.

29 Lenz, "Quality Versus Relevance," 58.

30 *a.k.a. Pablo*, season 1, episode 5, "The Whole Enchilada," written by Norman Lear, Rick Mintz, and Seth Greenland, directed by Hector Elizondo and Thomas McConnell, aired April 3, 1984, on ABC.

31 Mary Beltrán, *Latino TV: A History* (New York University Press, 2022), 119.

32 Angharad N. Valdivia, *The Gender of Latinidad: Uses and Abuses of Hybridity* (Wiley-Blackwell, 2020), 136.

33 Raul A. Reyes, "Norman Lear Remembered as a Champion of Latino Actors and Content Before Representation Was a Buzzword," *NBC News*, December 6, 2023, www.nbcnews.com.

34 Daniel Fienberg, "'*One Day at a Time*': TV Review," *Hollywood Reporter*, January 3, 2017, www.hollywoodreporter.com.

35 Avilés-Santiago, "'This is It!' [Is It?]," 60–78.

36 Stephanie Melissa Pérez, "'I Got You': The Modern American Family and Latinx Reconfigurations in Netflix's *One Day at a Time*" (master's thesis, California State University, 2019), https://doi.org/10.13140/RG.2.2.29144.32001.

37 I thank Stephanie Pérez for providing the specific locations of these shows through her careful research.

38 It is very difficult to find Ann Romano's profession, as most websites and articles just say "divorcée" as if that were her job. Actually, she was a high school graduate, without a college degree, who moves up the ladder in the advertising industry (Museum of Broadcast Communications, n.d.).

39 Pérez, "'I Got You,'" 14.

40 Lauren Alvarez, "Was Netflix Justified in Cancelling 'One Day at a Time'?," *Forbes*, March 14, 2019, www.forbes.com.

41 Laura Bradley, "Why *One Day at a Time*'s Cancellation Is So Disappointing," *Vanity Fair*, March 14, 2019, www.vanityfair.com.

42 Pérez, "'I Got You.'"

43 Esteban del Río and Kristen C. Moran, "Remaking Television: *One Day at a Time*'s Digital Delivery and Latina/o Cultural Specificity," *Journal of Communication Inquiry* 44, no. 1 (January 2020): 21–22, https://doi.org/10.1177/0196859918825332.

44 Isabel Molina-Guzmán, "#OscarsSoWhite: How Stuart Hall Explains Why Nothing Changes in Hollywood and Everything Is Changing," *Critical Studies in Media Communication* 33, no. 5 (2016): 438–54, https://doi.org/10.1080/15295036.2016.1227864.

45 del Río and Moran, "Remaking Television," 5–25.

46 In today's real estate market, there are virtually nothing but "upscale" neighborhoods in San Francisco. However, in 1994, Pacific Heights already signified gentrified housing.

47 Kirstie M. Farrar, "Sexual Intercourse on Television: Do Safe Sex Messages Matter?," *Journal of Broadcasting & Electronic Media* 50, no. 4 (2006): 635–50, https://doi.org/10.1207/s15506878jobem5004_4; Christina Slade, "Why Not Lie?: Television Talk and Moral Debate," *Television & New Media* 1, no. 4 (2000): 419–30, https://doi.org/10.1177/152747640000100404; Kylo-Patrick R. Hart, "Representing Gay Men on American Television," *Journal of Men's Studies* 9, no. 1 (2000): 59–79, https://doi.org/10.3149/jms.0901.59.

48 Jen Chaney, "*Party of Five* Is Both Sweetly Nostalgic and Bracingly Current," *Vulture*, January 7, 2020, www.vulture.com.

49 *Party of Five*, season 1, episode 9, "Mexico," written by Amy Lippman and Christopher Keyser, directed by Edward Ornelas, aired February 26, 2020, on Freeform.

50 Lesley Goldberg, "'Party of Five' Reboot Canceled at Freeform," *Hollywood Reporter*, April 17, 2020, www.hollywoodreporter.com.

51 Will Thorne, "Party of Five Reboot Canceled After One Season at Freeform," *Variety*, April 17, 2020, www.variety.com.

52 Anna Rumer, "'Party of Five' Reboot Canceled at Freeform After First Season," *Popculture*, April 17, 2020, https://popculture.com.

53 Rumer, "'Party of Five' Reboot."

54 Lauren Sarner, "How the 'Party of Five' Reboot Was Ripped from the Headlines," *New York Post*, December 31, 2019.

55 Kelly Lawler, "Review: A Deportation-Focused 'Party of Five' Remake Is Timely but Shallow," *USA Today*, January 8, 2020, www.usatoday.com.

56 Brian Lowry, "'Party of Five' Brings an Urgent Immigration-Related Hook to Freeform Reboot," *CNN Entertainment*, January 8, 2020, www.cnn.com.

57 Willa Paskin, "Party of Five Still Promises a Good Cry, but the Reboot Has a Political Edge," Slate, January 7, 2020, www.slate.com.

58 Chaney, "*Party of Five* Is Both Sweetly Nostalgic and Bracingly Current."

59 Caroline Framke, "Freeform's 'Party of Five': TV Review," *Variety*, January 8, 2020, www.variety.com.

60 Chaney, "*Party of Five* Is Both Sweetly Nostalgic and Bracingly Current."

61 Sonya M. Alemán and Jillian M. Báez, "More Than Tortillas: The Transgressive Possibilities of the Chicano-Centric *Party of Five* Reboot in a Racially Dissonant Television Landscape," *Aztlán* 49, no. 1 (2024): 47–78, https://doi.org/10.1525/azt.2024.49.1.47.

62 I must admit that I was amazed at this lineage, which was not mentioned in any of the US articles.

63 Beltrán, *Latino TV*.

64 Colleagues told me their Latina/o/x students found this show to be the most accurate and heart-wrenching—as so many of them were personally going through

this trauma or knew somebody who was experiencing these difficulties. "Enjoying" the show would not be a way of describing this affinity and recognition.

65 Was anyone hotter than Lin-Manuel Miranda?

66 Molina-Guzmán, *Latinas and Latinos on TV*, 114.

67 Diana Leon-Boys and Angharad N. Valdivia, "The Location of U.S. Latinidad: *Stuck in the Middle*, Disney, and the In-Between Ethnicity," *Journal of Children and Media* 15, no. 2 (2020): 218–32, https://doi.org/10.1080/17482798.2020.1753790; Diana Leon-Boys and Claudia Bucciferro, "The Teenage Latina Genius on Television: Netflix's *Ashley Garcia*," *Women's Studies in Communication* 46, no. 1 (2023): 87–107, https://doi.org/10.1080/07491409.2022.2147676.

68 Arlene Dávila, *Latinos, Inc.: The Marketing and Making of a People* (University of California Press, 2001).

69 Leon-Boys and Valdivia, "The Location of U.S. Latinidad"; Leon-Boys and Bucciferro, "The Teenage Latina Genius on Television."

6

Shining, Shimmering, Splendid

The Nostalgia Factor in Disney's Live-Action Aladdin *Remake and Beyond*

ZHUI NING CHANG AND SHYAMALA PARTHASARATHY

READING NOTE: Analyzing a live-action remake of *Aladdin*, the authors illustrate the limits of Disney's ability or desire to update the narrative within a more contemporary understanding of ethnicity, race, and gender. Because Disney Corporation's economic success depends on the recirculation of nostalgia grounded in childhood emotions, its creative producers are unable to stray far from the original's Orientalist, racist, and sexist narratives and characters. Contemporary diversity in Disney's live-action remakes is constrained by the representational politics of inequality in the original animated texts.

Introduction

Since the success of Tim Burton's 2010 *Alice in Wonderland*, Walt Disney Pictures has been generating a slew of live-action remakes based on their repertoire of classic animated movies. In 2019 alone, five live-action CGI remakes of Disney animated movies were released—*Dumbo, Aladdin, The Lion King, Maleficent: Mistress of Evil*, and *Lady and the Tramp*—contributing to a staggering US$11.1 billion global box office revenue for the House of Mouse.[1] Disney entertainment now "exerts a greater influence on our line of vision than any of its competitors" due to its ubiquitous reach,[2] and it continues to play an important cultural role in the representation of race and ethnicity in Anglophone on-screen media. As is well documented by media studies and popular culture scholars, generations have learned about the world from their favorite Disney films, which have overwritten the source fairytales and folklore, with the House of Mouse instead imposing conservative US values.[3] In the live-action remakes, Disney attempts to update classic narratives for a twenty-first-century audience. Sean Bailey, president of Walt Disney Studios from 2010 to 2024, claimed that "inclusivity is not only a priority but an imperative for us, and it's top of mind on every single project."[4] Responding to motions such as #OscarsSoWhite and growing mainstream criticism about the failure to diversify Hollywood,[5] Disney's changes to the animated source material include a feminist Belle in *Beauty and the Beast* (2017) and Halle Bailey's casting as a Black Ariel in *The Little Mermaid* (2023). However, scholars such as Ida Yoshinaga and Richard M. Breux[6] have criticized the commodification and exploitation of Polynesian and Black communities, among other marginalized groups, as part of Disney's attempt to sustain and grow its consumer base. Works like *Pocahontas* (1995), with the original's appropriation and conflation of Native American cultures entirely unaddressed by the House of Mouse, are not among the slate of films planned for remakes.

The move to remake Disney's animated films, a short handful of decades after release, is an appeal to the audience's sense of nostalgia. Sara Ahmed's framework of affective economies, where the driving force of affect (emotion) as a circulating network of objects acting as "a form of capital,"[7] is a useful tool to examine the ways in which Disney's marketing and merchandising works, particularly when political identity has become a market demographic. For Ahmed, feelings appear as an object; the more they circulate, the more affective they become, shaped by histories of production, circulation, and exchange. In a market-driven media industry,[8] Disney makes full use of both the affect and the history through its call to nostalgia—live-action remakes are bankable intellectual properties; do not require extensive research and development as would original, untested films, thus minimizing the creative risks and effort required to entice an audience; and act as a relatively stable source of profit generation. Hence, the object is not the (re)made film but the nostalgia that is sold to audiences: the nostalgia of childhood, now relived by the financially independent child-turned-adult, who will (re)introduce it to their own children. Disney had recognized and cultivated this demand, as at least eleven more remakes are in development for future release, as at the time of writing this.[9]

Figure 6.1. Agrabah's Royal Palace. *Source*: *Aladdin* (Disney, 1992).

In this chapter, we investigate Disney's current approach to representation and inclusive storytelling via a comparative case study of the 1992 animated film *Aladdin* and its 2019 reboot.[10] Loosely inspired by one of the narratives in *One Thousand and One Nights*,[11] originally a collection of West and South Asian folktales, *Alf Laylah wa-Laylah*, Disney appropriated and westernized *Aladdin* into a major animated film, produced and directed by Ron Clements and John Musker. Arab Americans, including the American Arab Anti-Discrimination Committee, have long criticized the film for its Orientalist inaccuracies, offensive music, and anglicized hero and princess characters.[12] Remade by Guy Ritchie, the 2019 *Aladdin* acts as a callback to the original animated film while attempting to revise its Orientalist roots.

Agrabah: A Fantasy of the Orient

In the animated *Aladdin*, the setting of the city Agrabah paints a wealthy and decadent Arabia, a fantasy Islamic land assembled from various real-life locations, ranging from West Asia to South Asia. Situated in the middle of a desert with camel caravans and a searing sun, Agrabah's design draws visual inspiration from a broad mishmash of classical Islamic architecture, with curving arches, sandstone buildings, and a towering royal palace bearing a stylized likeness to the Taj Mahal (figure 6.1). These elements variously trace back to Persian architecture, Assyrian design, common cross-country West Asian motifs, and Indo-Islamic Mughal tastes. While drawing inspiration from multiple sources is perfectly normal, the blurring of so many visual elements from across West Asia, North Africa, and the Indian subcontinent speaks of an absence in aesthetic care and cultural focus, and an assumption that these multiple locations and cultures can be conflated into a single monolith, flattening the difference and erasing contexts specific to each community. This process of conflating visual and aural ethnic stereotypes strips away the specific references to local and time-bound geographies and allows them to be co-opted into ahistorical sites located in the Western imaginary,[13] replicated for capitalist consumption in Disneyland theme parks.[14] As *Aladdin* is the only major work in the Disney princess line to feature an Arab-inspired setting and story, Agrabah becomes representative of such cultures, defined and perceived through Disney's lens.

Moreover, Disney has long been known for what Paul Wells dubs a "hyper-realist" animation house style, whereby it "approximates live-action film's representation of reality" to naturalize its animated depictions of life.[15] The opening number, "Arabian Nights," plays over shots of the city, with a storyteller singing out "it's barbaric, but hey, it's home,"[16] and shots of a fire-eater, a snake-charmer, and a ware-seller, all speaking with heavy, stereotypical "Arab" accents. The prevailing aesthetic and lyrics reinforce the view of Agrabah and its inhabitants as objects seen as exotic, dangerous, and alien to the US viewer. Further, in locating Agrabah as a fantastical place with flying carpets and magic lanterns, the film blurs the transplant of ethnic stereotypes into imaginary settings with the reimagination of Arab folklore. The magical elements of the film demand a suspension of disbelief from the audience, making it more difficult to perceive the stereotypes as a deliberate construct born of a US perspective, further reducing it an essentialist ethnic trait.[17] Thus, within the context of a hyper-realistic visual approach, the lack of a specific real-world aesthetic for Agrabah underlines that its US animators draw from a fictional Orient, which Edward Said describes as "less a place than a topos, a set of references, a congeries of characteristics, that seems to have its origin in . . . some bit of previous imagining"[18]—Agrabah is an imaginary construct of what the US American viewer expects to be Oriental and Other.

In rebooting the animated representation into a live-action format, Disney retains the general flavor and flow of the introduction to Agrabah, preserving the nostalgic element for the audience. The 2019 *Aladdin*'s close adherence to the audio-visual spectacle of the animated text allows the knowing audience to (re)create and reinforce their memory of the original film through an active, deliberate evocation of nostalgia, further limiting the idea of alternate approaches outside of remembrance. The film repackages the opening number with an initial scene of a traveler and his family—later revealed to be the Genie as a free human—singing "Arabian Nights," then sweeps through a view of Agrabah. The color palette is darker and favors a dusty beige, as compared to the bright reds and purples of the animated film, but much of the visual design remains the same. The remake retains the melody of "Arabian Nights" but rewrites the lyrics as "it's chaotic, but hey, it's home,"[19] removing the overt association with barbarism. Although human actors embody the ensemble on screen, the heavy use of CGI to recreate Agrabah's setting enhances a sense of the hyperreal, amplifying the fantastical veneer of the city and rendering it less believable as a real-world location.

The film revises some key scenes, such as Jasmine and Aladdin's first meeting at the marketplace, when she takes some bread off a stall to give to a street child. In the animated text, the shopkeeper—selling apples instead of bread—takes out a blade and threatens to cut off Jasmine's hand for being unable to pay for it, referencing an extreme variant of sharia law that decrees theft should be punished by cutting off the perpetrator's hands. However, in the remake, Aladdin intervenes earlier and deescalates the situation before there is any hint of violence. Such creative decisions remove specific mentions of brutal and uncivilized behavior, no longer illustrating a dark and dangerous Islam to be feared.

However, the visuals and music do not demonstrate any textured, progressive depiction of Arab Muslim cultures or communities, still shrouding Agrabah in a veil of mystery and intrigue. There is a generic, celebratory lyric "where you wander among every culture and tongue" in "Arabian Nights," rewritten over the original line pointing out sand dunes and the sun. While the new lyric gestures toward the region's diversity of languages and localities, the film exists independent of a locale and recalls a specific narrative of neoliberal multiculturalism in the US. Despite the original folktale's Islamic roots, the animated film had been devoid of meaningful representations of Islam and the live-action remake persists in a similar hollow secularization. John Wills suggests that *Aladdin* promotes "an ethos of harmony, happiness, and social progress conducive to better race relations,"[20] but instead, the remake of *Aladdin* plays on nostalgia to erase the nuances of various West Asian and North African cultures that may seem alien and othering, making Agrabah a safe and digestible setting for US audiences. Most tellingly, the film opens with a wide shot of the sea with a large European sailing ship that slides away to reveal a much more modestly sized Arab vessel—a moment that foreshadows Disney's perception of the inferiority and otherness of the Arab Muslim world as compared to the might of European exploration, and one that underlines the US and therefore Disney's place in the cultural sphere.

Princess Jasmine: The Strong Woman

The performance of supposedly empowered princesses has been Disney's approach to the princess line in the twenty-first century. Whether Disney achieves this is debatable; some scholars argue that it has, while others disagree.[21] *Aladdin*'s live action falls somewhere in between, with Princess Jasmine's character receiving an upgrade from the animation but falling into the trap of postfeminist ideals.

In a study of Arab portrayals in more than 900 Hollywood films, Jack Shaheen notes that a majority of Arab characters are misrepresented as bombers, belly dancers, and billionaires, with only around fifty characters not overtly cast as the antagonist, or otherwise eroticized or without agency.[22] Within this terrain Erin Addison argues that Oriental femininity is weaponized into a terrain that is both muted and dangerous; where the hijab is meant to be an ornament of "veiling," it becomes a "coquetry" that "signals beauty and promises to reveal, not cover."[23] In the animated film, the women follow classic Orientalist iconography, from the voluptuous women at the marketplace who appear as Aladdin is trying to escape, to the scantily clad girls that the Genie magically conjures up in his song, to the dancing girls who introduce Prince Ali at the palace, acting not just as sexualized fantasies for the Occidental viewer, but also invoking the fantasy of the harem. Jasmine is produced via this optic, associated with a motif of Oriental seduction, in "harem-esque" costuming that "accentuates the physical" and thereby evokes "exotic, sexual stereotypes."[24] She first appears dressed in the same manner as the dancers of the bazaar, serves as the protagonist's love interest throughout, and seduces Jafar at the end of the film. Addison identifies her as the manner in which "the colonial catalysis occurs, through whom the narratives of naive individualism, romance, and secularism pass into and unravel the fabric of Islamic culture."[25] Jasmine represents the Western understanding of Islamic/Arab women (conflated here as the Orient) and is synonymous with Agrabah, the symbolic key to accessing a fertile Orient waiting to be consumed. Taken in conjunction with the hyper-sexualized harem-girl imagery, Jasmine's character becomes a passive object of Western consumption, waiting for someone to come and rescue her.[26]

In comparison, the live-action film reduces the effect of seduction—in Jasmine as well as in Agrabah. Amy M. Davis notes that the mainstream entry of feminist discourse in US popular culture has led to Disney's attempts to create more dynamic and dimensional female characters,[27] constructing an image of women and femininity that is not perfect but seems positive as a whole—though this too has its limitations. Here, Jasmine is allowed to have desires other than romance. She is given a brand-new "I Want" song, "Speechless," where Naomi Scott's voice soars through Jasmine's declaration that she will not be "unheard." Although the law that a princess can marry only a prince who will then rule the kingdom is left untouched from the 1992 film, Jasmine's ambition this time around is not just to marry the man she chooses, but to rule Agrabah as sultan after her father. She stresses the fact that she "has been training for this [her] whole life." The film makes her well suited to this role of aspiring ruler by focusing on her intelligence as well as her beauty—she peppers Aladdin with questions about Ababwa with far more intensity than her animated counterpart.

While the film aims to foreground women's ambition, it falls flat in execution. For all that Jasmine insists she knows her people better than any foreign prince possibly could, she is still a princess, with all that her class implies. Her interactions are entirely with the nobility except the protagonist Aladdin, the antagonist Jafar, and several commoners she meets at the marketplace—mostly angry men who chase after her and Aladdin. The narrative centers Jasmine's struggle for individual power against the backdrop of a patriarchal society; not only does this add to US media's propagation of an oppressive Islamic system, it also reeks of a neoliberal, individualist postfeminist attitude,[28] where Jasmine's objective is not to change the law for greater class mobility or more equitable access across genders, but only to access power for herself. By the end of the film, when Jasmine becomes the first female sultan, the status granted to her is less about empowering women and more about Jasmine's individual worth as a ruler. Her power as sultan is enabled not by her own active pursuit of the change of law, but by the defeat of Jafar at the hands of Aladdin.

Furthermore, the Americanization of Jasmine stands in for the neocolonialist project of using feminism as a way of civilizing "barbaric" lands.[29] The very lyrics of "Speechless" are problematic: "Written in stone / Every rule, every word / Centuries old and unbending / Stay in your place / Better seen and not heard"—entrenching the idea that Jasmine is competent, but the barbaric lands she lives in do not allow her to attain individual power. Add to this the paratextual racism of Naomi Scott's clothing and much of the set design being drawn from Bollywood,[30] the live-action makes distinctly different cultures—West Asian, North African, and South Asian—interchangeable, flattened into a singular, homogenous Oriental landscape. Disney's representation of empowerment lasts only as long as Jasmine conforms to a version of feminine ambition that abides by a US ideal of consumerist, domesticated feminism.

Jafar and Aladdin: Design and Backstory

As with Jasmine, Jafar is also allocated more backstory. The lechery of the original vizier is now dampened, and the film also attempts to tackle some form of class politics with his character. He only decides to marry Jasmine when it becomes clear that he needs to in order to consolidate his own power. There is a brief mention that he was once a street urchin like Aladdin, now risen through the ranks to become the sultan's vizier and his second-in-command. Those nostalgic for the villainy of the animated Jafar will be pleasantly surprised by some nuance now given to the character—in a clearly classist system, he hates being second to anyone, and longs for power and control.

In terms of design, Jafar's character remains faithful to the original animation. Dressed in dark robes and carrying a snake-staff of power, live-action Jafar shares with his animated counterpart a similar beard, accented English, and costume. His parrot, Iago, continuously taunts him by repeating phrases that he hates hearing from others, such as "Remember your place, Jafar," or "Second place!"—a fine turn from the comedic bird that acted as Jafar's irritating but definite co-conspirator in the animation. The implication that Jafar's status is a hard-earned one, and the hints at an invisibilized class system of Agrabah, expand his role from the animated film. Yet we never truly see why Jafar is so angry, or what his story is outside of the quest for power. It is strongly implied that he might have assassinated Jasmine's mother, the queen, who hailed from Shirabad, but the narrative does not follow through with a confirmation. His hatred for Shirabad, his need to conquer and control, the brutality of his anger—all remain unexplained, thus diluting any nuance he is attributed. It does, however, play into the rhetoric of the violent, angry immigrant—in an Americanized setting, the narrative conditions the viewer that a turbaned, bearded, dark-robed man is to be feared.

Meanwhile, the design, casting, and characterization of Aladdin the protagonist play into stereotypical notions of colorism and rhetoric of the model minority. An impoverished and mischievous street urchin, Aladdin wants to climb the social ladder and find a better life for himself and his monkey companion Abu. Aladdin is clean-shaven and wears light-colored clothes and a cap for most of the film. Played by Egyptian-Canadian actor Mena Massoud, a light-skinned man who speaks with an anglicized accent, he functions in stark contrast to Jafar, who is angry, speaks accented English, and works from the shadows.[31]

Aladdin's primary occupation as a thief is also reduced in screen time, as the number introducing him, "One Jump Ahead," now takes place after he rescues Jasmine from the shopkeeper instead of before. This shift in scene sequence recontextualizes the musical number as two partners in crime moving through the city on a thrilling adventure. The remake emphasizes desirable heroic qualities such as his streetwise charm, innovation in constructing the machinery that operates his rooftop home, and burgeoning romantic connection with Jasmine—the audience is invited to forget that Aladdin is first introduced on-screen pawning stolen jewelry. Aladdin is quite literally the "diamond in the rough," an ambiguous "chosen one" status that grants him entry to the Cave of Wonders, where he discovers the magical lamp that precipitates all his fortune afterward. Aladdin then performs an assimilationist narrative where he first tries by false pretenses to become the wealthy and noble man Jasmine can marry, then redeems himself by saving the kingdom and accesses the privilege of marrying incoming Sultan Jasmine. Thus, he is "liberated" from the poverty and barbarism of the streets and welcomed into the halls of decadence and power.

Both Jafar and Aladdin are contrasted by the narrative in their personal quests. Aladdin's journey is romanticized, as he is only looking to be with the woman he loves. Viewers are encouraged to sympathize with him, his hard work, and the circumstances of his birth. In direct contrast, Jafar's quest is rooted in selfishness and an unexplained anger and insecurity constantly driving his need for power. The narrative thus sets up the binary of a "good" and "bad" immigrant mold in these two characters against the backdrop of an Oriental Agrabah where colonialist fantasies play out.

Aladdin and the Genie: Master, Slave, Friend, Foe

A key relationship in *Aladdin* is between the eponymous protagonist and the Genie, played in the remake by Black American actor Will Smith, who takes over the iconic role from Robin Williams. Linda Hutcheon suggests that audiences who experience a remake with the awareness of the original feel a multi-layered pleasure in viewing the film, "a conceptual flipping back and forth between the work [they] know and the work [they] are experiencing."[32] The nostalgia factor cannot be entirely preserved here, as Williams's brand of comedy was unique and any attempts at replicating it would only result in inferior imitation. So, Will Smith, an actor with global star power and a track record of comedic timing and singing, steps in to make the role his own. This plays into what Rebecca-Anne C. Do Rozario calls "Disney's creation of a sense of timelessness."[33] Disney does not shy away from the nostalgia of Williams's Genie—the music, the lyrics and the magic all remain the same, if now enhanced by CGI. However, as Do Rozario points out, it is necessary to cut through the nostalgic poses to arrive at the original conditions. Where Williams's Genie was one of exuberance, Smith's Genie evokes a different affect—from nostalgia and grief for the late Williams, to the pointed character dynamics of this racebent casting choice.

Aladdin and the Genie already explore a master-and-slave relationship in the original animated text, explicitly illustrated with the master's ability to exercise control over all aspects of the Genie's existence, including his materialization from the lamp, his inability to disobey a given order, and the gold cuffs on his arms that are literal chains of service. The Genie is the secret central power behind Agrabah and the Arabian lands, yet, as Alan Nadel describes, despite the Genie's limitless ability to transform and grant wishes, he still "cannot escape the role of slave,"[34] reinforcing the existing hierarchy of power. The Genie tells Aladdin that his greatest wish is to be free and human, the phrasing emphasizing his inhuman (superhuman) status and encouraging the audience to hold him to a different standard from the rest of the characters. The Genie himself is a trope drawn from Islamic and Arab folklore, with complicated histories both oral and written.[35] In Disney, much of that history is sanitized, focused more on the individual narrative of freedom for this genie, who is far from the trickster jinn and ifrits of traditional folklore,[36] and serving the merchandised role of the humorous creature sidekick.

Smith describes the Genie character as a trickster and mentor figure, whose role is "to guide Aladdin to the truth of the greatness that's already within him." Embodied by a Black actor, this casts the character in a new light as a "Magical Negro" figure,[37] a stereotype emerging out of US cinematic tradition. The fact that Aladdin is a light-skinned man with westernized traits of heroism and the Genie is in a Magical Negro role sets up a charged space where a character from one minority community is performing a master-and-slave dynamic with a character from another minority community, where the "unconscious assumption in design production" is the white US audience as primary consumer.[38] Further, as a Hollywood star and representative of US cultural hegemony, Smith hijacks the Genie's narrative and Americanizes it, revising its appeal toward Disney's consumer base and denying another opportunity for deeper engagement with the source folklore.

Aladdin in Production: Paratextual Racism Behind the Scenes

The problem with (re)making a premise that is inherently racist in its original conception is that it is difficult for the new product to sidestep those flaws without a deep reimagining and rewriting of the material. However, since Disney sells the affect of nostalgia through its remakes, it must represent a sanitized past that allows white and Western audiences to see themselves (re)inscribed onto Disney narratives, no matter where they are set. In this economy of affect,[39] Disney taps into nostalgia for the knowing viewer—the iconography of the film, the familiar characters and setting—and then capitalizes on the language of inclusion and diversity to draw in new viewers.

Disney's processes of production and distribution attempt to disorient the animated film's racism but instead embed it further. Disney reportedly had trouble looking for actors of Arab and Indian descent who could also sing and dance, only to end up casting Egyptian-Canadian actor Mena Massoud as Aladdin, British-Indian actress Naomi Scott as Jasmine, and Dutch-Tunisian actor Marwan Kenzari as Jafar.[40] Though British-born Dev Patel and Bollywood actress Tara Sutaria were reportedly considered,[41] the studio sought new, rising actors not previously affiliated with prominent films, seeking to "discover" them. Additionally, in the production phase, accusations of brownface were hurled at Disney,[42] with many of the extras cast as white, except the singular Black woman in the song "One Jump Ahead," who calls Aladdin "tasty." Forgoing the overt racism of this particular act, Disney creates a white male character for the remake, a Prince Anders, who is neither required for the story to progress nor was present in the original animation. Similar to the character of Everett Ross in *Black Panther* (2018), Disney demonstrates an anxiety to shoehorn white characters into narratives that primarily feature people of color, spending extra resources on such characters to appease white viewers and to reinforce a view of white presence and proliferation.

Moreover, in a film that is touted as diverse, many of the creative leads are white. From director Guy Ritchie to one of the screenplay writers, Terry Rosario (who has faced previous allegations of racism),[43] Disney apparently could not or would not hire creatives of color. Though this has been a common critique of Disney as well as of the wider Hollywood corpus, we reiterate that a mainly white creative team not only takes space from potential writers and producers of color, it also does not prioritize meaningful representation of lived experiences, focusing instead on market capitalization through its consistent use of nostalgia to appeal to an audience that is already familiar with and fond of the animated original. As Yoshinaga observed in relation to *Moana* (2016), Disney's first and only princess narrative drawing on Indigenous Polynesian culture, the studio did not recognize writing talent from the relevant communities at the highest employment level of screenplay and story credit, yet continues to profit from their histories, cultures, and folklore.[44]

All these particular creative and production choices build a narrative of paratextual racism, where the white gaze struggles to differentiate between different ethnicities and the Oriental is a mishmash of many cultures, where all difference is flattened. In such a case, the film as a response to diverse representation becomes a superficial, tokenistic gesture. In order to profit from a narrow evocation of nostalgia, *Aladdin*'s (2019) notion of diversity and inclusion can only be gestured toward in minimal elaborations and editorial changes such as Jasmine's solo number and sultanship. Nevertheless, that a studio of Disney's reach and dominance was compelled to do so is notable as a reflection of the slow, structural shifts occurring in wider media.

Conclusion: Not a Whole New World

The live-action *Aladdin* may be considered as using a framework of the affective economy system, wherein emotions act as a driving force for marketing products and experiences and consumer purchasing decisions,[45] to appeal to audiences—calling back to the nostalgia of the older, Orientalist animation with a familiar narrative and iconography, now made new and exciting in a live-action remake, with associated changes to the screenplay and casting to draw in new consumers of color and racially sensitive audiences, casting as large a net for the film as possible. It expands on a world already familiar to its audiences, provides updated versions of Jasmine and Jafar with some degree of nuance, and allows for some truly fantastical musical scores and performances to shine through the entirety of the film. The older viewer, who once watched the animated version, is drawn back, invited not only to reexperience the story in live action but also to contrast the two versions. The racebent Genie, ambitious Jasmine, and revised Jafar serve as both continuities and ruptures of their original versions.[46]

However, a deeper analysis of the film's representation of race and ethnicity show that Disney still performs dominant race-scripts,[47] where portrayals of non-Western minority cultures contain stereotypical Orientalist discourses because they assume the centrality of a white, Western gaze.[48] Given its billion-dollar revenue, *Aladdin* falls into the legion of (re)produced Disney films that act as "raw materials to be extracted and reconstructed, with the most profitable selected, hyperinflated, packaged, and sold back to the customers in an incomplete but adequately efficient process."[49] In this case, the 2019 *Aladdin* takes the raw material of the extremely profitable 1992 animation, (re)packages it, and then inflates it through the callback to the previous film through its sales. The live-action remake may have made an attempt to address overt stereotypes in its narrative, but a closer look at the film's creative and production choices reveals that this is the extent to which the Mouse is willing and able to traverse—as Henry Giroux argued, Disney's core mission is to transform audiences "from a democracy of citizens to a democracy of consumers,"[50] and that aim has held fast even as the studio's messaging on race, gender, and childhood shifted with the times. As such, *Aladdin* (2019) only temporarily disorients the hetero-white patriarchy of the West, and its (re)iteration becomes a cog in the profit-driven Hollywood capitalist machine that remains white and patriarchal.

Discussion Questions

1. What is the relationship between Orientalism, racial nostalgia, and paratextual racism in the animated film and live-action remake of *Aladdin*?
2. What economic and cultural role do reboots, remakes, and revivals play in the economic success of the Walt Disney Corporation?
3. Identify three examples of how the *Aladdin* case study illustrates the reproduction of inequality in Hollywood production.

NOTES

1 Adam B. Vary, "Disney Explodes Box Office Records with $11.1 Billion Worldwide for 2019," *Variety*, January 2, 2020, https://variety.com.

2 Douglas Brode, *Multiculturalism and the Mouse: Race and Sex in Disney Entertainment* (University of Texas Press, 2005), 5.

3 Annalee R. Ward, *Mouse Morality: The Rhetoric of Disney Animated Film* (University of Texas Press, 2002), 2.

4 Rebecca Ford, "Black Santa and Hip-Hop 'Oliver Twist': Disney's Diversity Push," *Hollywood Reporter*, November 2, 2016, www.hollywoodreporter.com.

5 Michael Schulman, "Is the Era of #OscarsSoWhite Over?," *New Yorker*, January 23, 2018, www.newyorker.com; Reggie Ugwu, "The Hashtag That Changed the Oscars: An Oral History," *New York Times*, February 6, 2020.

6 Ida Yoshinaga, "Disney's *Moana*, the Colonial Screenplay, and Indigenous Labor Extraction in Hollywood Fantasy Films," *Narrative Culture* 6, no. 2 (Fall 2019): 188–215, https://doi.org/10.13110/narrcult.6.2.0188; Richard M. Breaux, "After 75 Years of Magic: Disney Answers Its Critics, Rewrites African American History, and Cashes In on Its Racist Past," *Journal of African American Studies* 14, no. 4 (December 2010): 398–416, https://doi.org/10.1007/s12111-010-9139-9.

7 Sara Ahmed, "Affective Economies," *Social Text* 22, no. 2 (Summer 2004): 120, https://doi.org/10.1215/01642472-22-2_79-117.

8 Sarah Banet-Weiser, "What's Your Flava? Race and Postfeminism in Media Culture," in *Interrogating Postfeminism: Gender and the Politics of Popular Culture*, ed. Yvonne Tasker and Diane Negra (Duke University Press, 2007), 214. Banet-Weiser discusses how empowerment is discursively figured as media visibility and market demographics; empowerment thus becomes a market strategy to appeal to a broader consumer audience.

9 Kirsten Acuna, "Disney has 14 More Live-Action Movies of Its Animated Classics Planned—Here They All Are," *Business Insider*, June 21, 2023, www.businessinsider.com.

10 John Musker and Ron Clements, dirs., *Aladdin* (1992; Walt Disney Pictures, 2015), DVD; Guy Ritchie, dir., *Aladdin* (2019; Walt Disney Pictures, 2019), Blue-Ray Disc, 1080p HD.

11 Michael Cooper, "The Monstrous Births of Aladdin," in *The Arabian Nights Reader*, ed. Ulrich Marzolph (Wayne State University Press, 2006): 265–82; Heinz Grotzfeld, "The Age of the Galland Manuscript of the Nights: Numismatic Evidence for Dating a Manuscript?," in *The Arabian Nights Reader*, 105–21; Musin Mahdi, "The Sources of Galland's Nuits," in *The Arabian Nights Reader*, 113–26. The folktale "Aladdin and the Wonderful Lamp," on which the Disney version is loosely based, was first translated for European audiences by French translator Antoine Galland; there has been some debate on whether it was indeed part of the original Arabic collection or if it was incorporated from a different oral source into Galland's translation.

12 Katherine Bullock and Steven Zhou, "Entertainment or Blackface? Decoding Orientalism in a Post-9/11 Era: Audience Views on *Aladdin*," *Review of Education, Pedagogy and Cultural Studies* 39, no. 5 (July 2017): 446–69, https://doi.org/10.1080/10714413.2017.1344512; Sarita McCoy Gregory, "Disney's Second Line: New Orleans, Racial Masquerade, and the Reproduction of Whiteness in *The Princess and the Frog*," *Journal of African American Studies* 14 (2010): 432–49, https://doi.org/10.1007/s12111-010-9138-x; Jack Shaheen, "Aladdin: Animated Racism," *Cinéaste* 20, no. 1 (1993): 49, www.jstor.org/stable/41687300; Breaux, "After 75 Years of Magic," 398–416.

13 Bullock and Zhou ("Entertainment or Blackface?," 455) examine how the Disney filmmakers compiled over 1,800 photographs of Isfahan, a city in Iran, to serve as general reference photos for the film, thereby assuming that "1990s Iran can stand in for the mythical fifteenth-century city of 'Agrabah' and Arabia in general."

14 Scott Schaffer, "Disney and the Imagineering of Histories," *Postmodern Culture* 6, no. 3 (1996), https://doi.org/10.1353/pmc.1996.0028.

15 Paul Wells, *Understanding Animation* (Routledge, 1998), 25.

16 Musker and Clements, *Aladdin*.

17 David Gillota, *Ethnic Humor in Multiethnic America* (Rutgers University Press, 2013), 109.

18 Edward Said, *Orientalism* (Pantheon Books, 1978), 176.

19 Ritchie, *Aladdin*.

20 John Wills, *Disney Culture* (Rutgers University Press, 2017), 121.

21 Scholarship on whether representations of the Disney princesses have progressed is split; some argue that it has, while others oppose this notion. For more on the former, see Amy M. Davis, *Good Girls and Wicked Witches: Women in Disney's Feature Animation* (John Libbey Publishing, 2006) and Tracey L. Mollet, *A Cultural History of the Disney Fairy Tale: Once Upon an American Dream* (Palgrave Macmillan, 2020). Scholars like Cassandra Stover (referenced below) disagree, drawing on theories of postfeminism to demonstrate how Disney uses the rhetoric of feminism to peddle the same tropes while drawing in newer audiences.

22 Jack G. Shaheen, "Reel Bad Arabs: How Hollywood Vilifies a People," *Annals of the American Academy of Political and Social Science* 588 (July 2003): 171–93, www.jstor.org/stable/1049860.

23 Erin Addison, "Saving Other Women from Other Men: Disney's *Aladdin*," *Camera Obscura* 31, vol. 11, no. 1 (May 1993): 4–25, https://doi.org/10.1215/02705346-11-1_31-4.

24 Celeste Lacroix, "Images of Animated Others: The Orientalization of Disney's Cartoon Heroines from The Little Mermaid to The Hunchback of Notre Dame," *Popular Communication* 2, no. 4 (2009): 221, https://doi.org/10.1207/s15405710pc0204_2.

25 Addison, "Saving Other Women from Other Men," 6.

26 Katherine Bullock, "Orientalism on Television: A Case Study of *I Dream of Jeannie*," *ReOrient* 4, no. 1 (Autumn 2018): 8–9, https://doi.org/10.13169/reorient.4.1.0004. For more on harem and harem girls, see Leila Ahmed, "Western Ethnocentrism

and Perceptions of the Harem," *Feminist Studies* 8, no. 3 (Autumn 1982): 521–34, https://doi.org/10.2307/3177710; Katherine Bullock, *Rethinking Muslim Women and the Veil: Challenging Historical and Modern Stereotypes* (Institute of Islamic Thought, 2002).

27 Davis, *Good Girls and Wicked Witches*, 52.

28 Angela McRobbie, "Post-Feminism and Popular Culture," *Feminist Media Studies* 4, no. 3 (2004): 255–64, https://doi.org/10.1080/1468077042000309937; Cassandra Stover, "Damsels and Heroines: The Conundrum of the Post-Feminist Disney Princess," *Lux* 2, no. 1 (2013): 1–10, http://dx.doi.org/10.5642/lux.201301.29.

29 Addison, "Saving Other Women from Other Men."

30 Haroon Rashid, "Naomi Scott on Aladdin's Bollywood connection," *BBC Asian Network*, May 6, 2019, video, 4:33, https://youtu.be/_Z2Q7gYaR-4.

31 Joao "Jota" Rosa, "Discourse, Linguistic Production, and Subjectivity: Disney-fying Language," *Taboo: The Journal of Culture and Education* 10, no. 2 (2006): 121, https://doi.org/10.31390/taboo.10.2.14. Rosa dissects the way in which Disney uses language and accents to construct character subjectivity, and the material implications of such constructions.

32 Linda Hutcheon, *A Theory of Adaptation* (Routledge, 2006), 139.

33 Rebecca-Anne C. Do Rozario, "The Princess and the Magic Kingdom: Beyond Nostalgia, the Function of the Disney Princess," *Women's Studies in Communication* 27, no. 1 (Spring 2004): 37, https://doi.org/10.1080/07491409.2004.10162465.

34 Alan Nadel, "A Whole New (Disney) World Order: Aladdin, Atomic Power, and the Muslim Middle East," in *Visions of the East: Orientalism in Film*, ed. Matthew Bernstein and Gaylyn Studlar (Rutgers University Press, 1997), 191.

35 Mark Allen Peterson, "From Jinn to Genies: Intertexuality, Media, and the Making of Global Folklore," in *Folklore/Cinema: Popular Film as Vernacular Culture*, ed. Sharon R. Sherman and Mikel J. Koven (Utah State University Press, 2007), 93–112, https://doi.org/10.2307/j.ctt4cgnbm.8. Peterson traces the way in which the Arab jinn becomes the recognizable, domesticated Western genie in media.

36 Anne E. Duggan, "From Genie to Efreet: Fantastic Apparitions in the Tales of 'The Arabian Nights,'" *Journal of the Fantastic in the Arts* 92, vol. 26, no. 1 (2015): 113–35, www.jstor.org/stable/26321083. Duggan examines how the genie shifts from an folkloric figure to racialized Other in Western media.

37 Cerise L. Glenn and Landra J. Cunningham, "The Power of Black Magic: The Magical Negro and White Salvation in Film," *Journal of Black Studies* 40, no. 2 (November 2009): 135, https://doi.org/10.1177/0021934707307831.

38 Caroline Ferris Leader, "Magical Manes and Untamable Tresses: (En)coding Computer-Animated Hair for the Post-Feminist Disney Princess," *Feminist Media Studies* 18, no. 6 (2018): 1095, https://doi.org/10.1080/14680777.2017.1390688.

39 Sara Ahmed, "Affective Economies," 117–39; Henry Jenkins, *Convergence Culture: Where Old and New Media Collide* (New York University Press, 2006), 20.

40 Doha Madani, "Disney Has Trouble Casting 'Aladdin,' So People on Twitter are Doing it Instead," *HuffPost*, July 12, 2017, www.huffpost.com.

41 Rebecca Ford and Mia Galuppo, "'Aladdin': Disney Struggles to Find Stars for Its Live-Action Movie," *Hollywood Reporter*, July 11, 2017, www.hollywoodreporter .com.

42 Kimberly Yam, "Disney Admits to Darkening White Actors' Skin For 'Aladdin,' Sparking Outrage," *HuffPost*, January 9, 2018, www.huffpost.com.

43 Lee Moran, "'Shrek' Writer Terry Rossio Likens Being Called 'Anti-Vax' to Being Called Racial Slur," *HuffPost*, November 24, 2018, www.huffpost.com; Lauren Huff, "'Pirates' Screenwriter Terry Rossio Sparks Controversy With N-Word Tweet," *Hollywood Reporter*, November 23, 2018, www.hollywoodreporter.com.

44 Yoshinaga, "Disney's *Moana*," 199.

45 Ahmed, "Affective Economies," 117–39; Jenkins, *Convergence Culture*, 20.

46 Stuart Hall, "Cultural Identity and Diaspora," in *Identity: Community, Culture and Difference*, ed. Jonathan Rutherford (Lawrence & Wishart, 1990), 226.

47 Leader, "Magical Manes and Untamable Tresses," 1086–1101.

48 Emilie Snedevig Hoffman, "Diversity Dissected: Intersectional Socialization in Disney's *Aladdin*, *Mulan*, and *The Princess and the Frog*," *Leviathan: Interdisciplinary Journal in English*, no. 5 (2019): 114.

49 Mike Budd, "Introduction: Private Disney, Public Disney," in *Rethinking Disney: Private Control, Public Dimensions*, ed. Mike Budd and Max Kirsch (Wesleyan University Press, 2005), 10–11.

50 Henry Giroux and Grace Pollock, *The Mouse That Roared: Disney and the End of Innocence* (Rowman & Littlefield, 2010), 211.

7

Not So Charming

Continuities and Ruptures in the Latina-Centric Charmed *Reboot*

JILLIAN M. BÁEZ AND SONYA M. ALEMÁN

CHAPTER NOTES: The fantasy series *Charmed* was first released in 1998; the reboot aired in 2018. The authors compare the original *Charmed* to the reboot as important feminist television shows that illustrate key shifts in representations of race, ethnicity, and gender. In particular, the reboot's reworking of the Charmed sisters as Latina, along with intersectional dialogue and themes, points to contemporary television industry's newer strategies to attract younger and more educated viewers.

Introduction

The original *Charmed* (1998–2006) television series aired on The WB, a broadcast network emerging from the multichannel era that targeted adolescents and young adults. The show featured three sister witches, the "Charmed Ones," who use their powers in concert to save the world from evil. Following the original series' high ratings and cult popularity, a reboot of *Charmed* (2018–2022) was in the works since 2013.[1] In 2017, the CW reboot was announced, reworking the Charmed sisters as Latinas—Mel and Maggie Vera and their half-sister Macy Vaughn—and featuring a multiracial cast. *Jane the Virgin*'s (2014–2019) showrunner Jennie Snyder Urman envisioned this retelling and served as its executive producer. Urman explained her interest in creating the reboot: "The original was so much about female empowerment and sisterhood and strong women taking over the world and I feel like that's what we need right now. It felt like a good time to get back to that and show women kicking ass."[2] In addition to the re-envisioned Latina leads, the new *Charmed* series also hired Latina talent behind the screen, including writer Natalia Fernandez and story editor Emmylou Diaz, who also wrote for *Jane the Virgin*. Reimagining *Charmed* through Latina characters pivoted the original series from its liberal and postfeminist themes[3] to broach some radical and intersectional strands of televisual feminism, if not completely embrace them.

In this essay, we use a Latina feminist theoretical framework to analyze the first seasons of the original and reboot *Charmed*. The original *Charmed* made significant progress in feminist television history.[4] While Isabel Molina-Guzmán's chapter in this collection focuses on anti-fan response to the reboot grounded in nostalgia for postfeminist values, in this essay on *Charmed* we explore the representational absences of race, ethnicity, gender, and sexuality in the original and how the reboot producers and actresses address the erasure of difference. We map the *Charmed* reboot shift from white liberal feminist and postfeminist themes to a nascent intersectional approach to feminism that addresses inequality in television representation. In particular, our analysis reveals a larger trend in television remakes whereby Latina/o/x characters are deployed to stand in for more diverse and edgy programming sometimes successfully and other times, as Angharad Valdivia notes in this collection, with limited success. Similarly to Valdivia's conclusion, we find that both *Charmed* versions fall short of centering women-of-color feminist perspectives and building a larger Latino-centric world for their main characters.

The CW's *Charmed* reboot casting of the sisters as Latinas is significant. The Latina/o/x characters in this show make up part of the paltry 5.7 percent Latina/o/x characters featured on broadcast television and 4.9 percent on cable television in 2022[5]—a proportion that has only slightly increased over the past four decades.[6] Indeed, in the first season of the original, only two Latino characters were introduced over its first twenty-two episodes, and both of these were killed off. To address such long-standing underrepresentation, reboots with a distinctive Latina/o focus have evolved as a recent strategy for inclusion, as do the multicultural ensembles that emerged in the 1990s.[7] *One Day at a Time* (2017–2020, Netflix/Pop), *Party of Five* (2020, Freeform), and *Roswell, New Mexico* (2019–2022, The CW) are examples of such remakes. These shortcuts hope to tap into existing fan bases, tend to be rooted in nostalgia,[8] and often rely on Hollywood templates to tell stories about Latinas/os/xs, rather than anchoring narratives through a Latina/o/x worldview.[9]

With Latina bodies functioning as a key cultural signifier for Latinidad in media,[10] strategies to diversify the televisual landscape often use Latinas. Molina-Guzmán argues media depictions of Latina identity are sublimated or abstracted from the cultural politics of Latino communities and converted into a form that is palatable and easily disseminated to global audiences.[11] To explore how the reimagined *Charmed* continues or disrupts long-standing negligible or clichéd portrayals of Latinas/xs, we employed race- and gender-based analytical lenses to guide a textual analysis of this reboot. We outline four ways the revamped *Charmed* universe offers unconventional depictions of Latinas. These include (1) non-stereotypical depictions of Latinas; (2) references to ethnic specificity; (3) Latina-centric critiques of dominant ideologies; and (4) increased dimensionality of Latina subjectivities. We conclude that despite these inroads, the reboot of *Charmed* falls short of centering Latina feminist perspectives or building out larger Latino-centric worlds. By not realizing this potential, aspects of the first season uphold a white-centered feminism as well as simplistic binaries that equate whiteness with goodness.

Latina Feminist Media Studies (LFMS) as a subfield has established itself over the past two decades, primarily examining the representations of Latinas from all ethnicities in film, television, social media, and music, but also accounting for the roles—if any—Latinas play in the political economy of production and the ways Latina audiences engage both mainstream and Latino-centric content.[12] Two distinct focal points of this approach are (1) recognizing the fluidity of Latinidad[13] as a category of identity that flattens and disrupts nation-based understandings of identity[14] and (2) problematizing the Latina female body as exoticized, surveilled, commodified, and disciplined.[15] Both approaches resist singular understandings of what it means to be Latina, often relying on hybridity as a useful construct to articulate this malleability. We apply the LFMS framework to analyze the possibilities and limitations of rebooting televisual storytelling formulas with Latina characters.

Reimagining *Charmed* as Latina-Centric

Complicated Gender Roles and Identities

There are some continuities across both the original and the reboot of *Charmed*. First, the series is women-centered, focusing on the sisterhood of the three lead witches. Both series also highlight the Charmed Ones' femininity and non-physical strength.[16] However, the *Charmed* reboot offers more nuanced and radical representations of gender than the original series—which relied on traditional white heteronormative representations of femininity—allowing for non-stereotypical images of Latinas. Depictions of the new set of sisters work against typecasts of Latinas as hypersexual, exotic, and speaking with thick Spanish accents; they eschew the spitfire stereotype so prevalent in film and television.[17] Instead, the new Charmed Ones are dynamic and empowered women who are well educated, exemplifying what Molina-Guzmán terms the "antiexotic Latina character."[18] These characters are counterpoints to prevailing images of heterosexual Latinas as hypersexualized side characters scripted to provide comedic relief. Moreover, one of the Vera sisters is queer, not only disrupting representations of Latinas as objects for male desire, but also altering the heteronormative *Charmed* universe of the original.

In regard to class, the Vera/Vaughn women depart from overrepresentations of Latinas in television as maids, domestic workers, and criminals and differ from the original Halliwell sisters and family line who were not all formally educated, as only Prue is described as having pursued higher education. Marisol Vera, the mother of the Charmed Ones, is a women's studies college professor who dies in the first episode. The eldest sister, Macy, holds a PhD in molecular genetics and works in a lab at the university where Marisol worked. Mel, the middle sister, is a graduate student in women's studies completing her thesis. Maggie, the youngest sister, is a college student. The Vera/Vaughn sisters live together with Harry, their Whitelighter, who is a magical protector, in a large Victorian home. The sisters are fluent English speakers, departing from the perpetual foreign Other trope so often applied to Latina/o characters. Within the first few episodes Harry, who is British, calls Maggie "a typical American Millennial," contesting stereotypic messages that Latina/os are foreigners in the US.

Charmed also rejects the virgin/whore binary—which the first season of the original leaned on with its depictions of sexually reserved Piper and sexually active Phoebe—especially as this dichotomy manifests for Latinas. The men in the reboot do not treat the sisters as exotic sex objects. Instead, the Vera/Vaughn sisters engage in sex-positive dialogue—unlike the more subtle innuendo the Halliwells used to talk about sex—and are depicted as having healthy consensual sexual partnerships and romantic relationships. For instance, Macy is a virgin when the series begins, but she later chooses to engage in a sexual relationship with her boyfriend Gavin. Mel, a lesbian, is depicted as having a healthy sex life with her partner Nico, and Maggie also engages in sexual activity with her boyfriend. The Vera/Vaughn sisters also espouse an explicit feminist critique of rape culture, recuperating the Medusa mythology by scolding fraternity brothers for "slut shaming."[19]

Ethnic Specificity and Multi-Layered Representation

The Halliwell sisters of the original series do not discuss ethnicity but do chart their lineage back to the Salem witches, indicating a White Anglo-Saxon Protestant (WASP) background. The Latina sisters in the *Charmed* reboot are ascribed a specific Latina/o ethnicity rather than a generic pan-Latina/o identity, as is typical when Latina/o/x characters are included.[20] Although ethnic identity is not foregrounded in the larger narrative of the *Charmed* reboot, various visual signifiers and dialogue point to the sisters' Puerto Rican heritage. For example, the sisters mention Puerto Rican foods and drinks such as asopao and coquito. The Puerto Rican flag also hangs on Mel's bedroom wall in the apocalyptic final episode of the season. When Maggie's white sorority sister Lucy asks for help with a Cinco de Mayo party, Mel retorts, "you know we're Puerto Rican, right?"[21] However, by not providing a lineage for the Vera/Vaughn sisters that extends back over seven generations, the reboot misses the opportunity to anchor Latino-descended communities to the continent prior to the arrival of English colonial settlers.

The *Charmed* reboot depicts a well-developed spectrum of multifaceted Latina characters. In addition to the sisters' Puerto Rican heritage, Macy and Maggie also share a Black father, marking them as Afro-Latinas, a segment of the Latino-identified population that is marginalized because of its ties to Blackness and its unsettling of the Black/white dualistic understanding of race in the US. The romantic pairing of Latinas with Black men is also rare in film and television. Latinas are instead depicted as desiring, and sometimes attaining, relationships with white men.[22] Notably, in the first season (and most of the seasons) of the original, there are no depictions of interracial relationships whatsoever. In the single episode that foregrounds non-Western mythology, Piper becomes attracted to a ghost based in San Francisco's Chinatown.[23] At the end of the episode Piper and the ghost, Mark (John Cho), mimic kissing, but do not touch. In this way, interracial relationships, particularly among the Halliwell sisters, are not visible. In contrast, in the reboot, Whitelighter Harry, a British white man, expresses his romantic interest in Macy, a mixed-race black/Puerto Rican woman.

Blackness is centered in the reboot in ways that are absent in the original *Charmed*, which focused on postfeminist whiteness. The only regular non-white character in the original is Darryl (Dorian Gregory), a light-skinned Black detective. In the reboot, although Macy and Maggie are both half Black, they have different relationships to Blackness. Macy grew up with her Black father and has a darker complexion and more textured hair than Maggie. Macy identifies as Black several times in the season and marks herself as racially different from her sisters. For example, Macy tells Maggie "not to touch her hair," evoking hair politics surrounding Black women whereby white women desire to feel tightly coiled and kinky hair.[24] Maggie, on the other hand, finds out she is half Black in episode 10 and struggles with her newfound identity as a mixed Black woman. Creating Latina characters who are also tied to a Black identity adds dimensionality to the flat and pan-ethnic brand of Latinidad seen on the small screen, widening the spectrum of Latino identity to include its African heritage.

Challenges to Dominant Gender Ideologies

The *Charmed* reboot is more transgressive in its representation of feminism in ways missing from the original, which reinscribed traditional notions of marriage and motherhood as ideals for the Halliwell sisters. The original also showcased the sisters forming a bond of sisterhood as a postfeminist stand-in for feminist values, an observation that is further developed in Isabel Molina-Guzmán's chapter in this collection. In contrast, the dialogue in the reboot is littered with critiques of patriarchy often voiced by Mel, who explicitly critiques white male privilege and whiteness. For example, in one of the earliest episodes Mel enters a fraternity house and says, "it smells like beer and white privilege."[25] Mel is also critical when Harry is introduced as the Charmed Ones' Whitelighter. Mel tells Harry that he is "a white man taking credit for my idea" and accuses Harry of being "afraid of powerful women" when she discovers he is surveilling the sisters. In one episode, Macy is literally drawn into a '90s male-dominated TV show, and Mel quips that "even fictional guys are gross."[26] Young white women are also game for critique. The show pokes fun at the way Maggie's white sorority members speak and dress. For example, when villain Alistair places a spell that mesmerizes sorority leader Lucy under his control, he uses a valley accent (or white girl vernacular on television) to make fun of her.

The show also blurs the boundaries of good and evil, a binary that remained firmly intact in the original series. For example, Charity, the white, blonde Elder assigned to the Charmed sisters, is on the surface "good." She is a leader in philanthropy, managing microloans for women. Professionally Charity empowers women, but in her role as an Elder she does not trust the Sarcana women-of-color witches. When the storyline eventually reveals that Charity murdered Marisol and gaslit Macy to cover up her crime, Charity appeals to Harry (a white man) for affirmation that she was well-intentioned. Harry holds Charity accountable for her actions, and Charity is stripped of her Elder status. In this way, the *Charmed* reboot challenges the good/evil dichotomy so firmly tethered in the original series.

The reboot also departs from the female clown roles Latina supporting characters conventionally perform.[27] It is one step further from Sofía Vergara's depiction of Gloria Pritchett on *Modern Family* (2009–2020, ABC), who embodies both the sexualized Latina clown (curvaceous, accented, and feisty) and the Latina straight man, a character who offers critiques of the "racist, xenophobic, or socially inappropriate actions and dialogues of her white family members."[28] Whereas in the original *Charmed* series the main white characters poked fun at the demons, in the reboot white characters are positioned as the fodder for humor. At times, the dialogue and storylines in the original *Charmed* allow the sisters to call attention to and mock white masculinity and white femininity. The infrequency of this type of Latina-centric humor is made evident in Molina-Guzmán's analysis of the character Carla Espinosa (Judy Reyes) on *Scrubs* (2001–2010, NBC).[29] She notes that "ethnic and racial minority characters" like Carla "rarely have the narrative opportunity to symbolically exert power against the white lead characters," especially where "women of color are the rational characters and white characters are the butt of the joke."[30] Similarly, as the exceptionally powerful Charmed Ones, the Vera/Vaughn Latina sisters atypically act as the show's moral compass, offering acerbic critiques of whiteness rather than provide amusement based on cultural, linguistic, ethnic or racial differences.

The *Charmed* reboot also uniquely departs from television genre conventions in science fiction and fantasy. Latinas are rarely the leads in science fiction and fantasy, what Ebony Thomas calls an "imagination gap," where people of color largely remain on the sidelines.[31] Latina characters on *Charmed* upend the regime of representation for Latina women on television, particularly in the realm of fantasy.[32] In sum, the *Charmed* reboot echoes popular forms of feminism currently espoused on social media that are familiar to and likely resonate with The CW's younger and educated viewership. Despite the inroads of both *Charmed* versions, there are limitations. These new images leave little room for narratives that expand beyond trite white feminisms or Black/white racial binaries. As Molina-Guzmán argues about *Scrubs*, *Charmed* is likewise "socially conscious, but not disruptive."[33]

Trite and White Feminism

Mel is the central voice of feminism on the show, and as a woman-of-color lesbian character, she is a stereotypical voice for these concerns. Macy only occasionally agrees with Mel's sharp feminist critiques. Maggie, similar to the original Halliwell sisters, seldom makes mention of gender inequalities. Positioning Mel as the voice of feminism in the series can be read as minimizing the experiences of marginalization rooted in gender and racial oppression. Mel's identification as a lesbian and feminist are constructed as mutually constitutive, thereby reproducing hegemonic tropes that equate lesbianism with feminism.

In addition, while the reboot espouses an overt critique of patriarchy that is more transgressive and intersectional than the original series, it does not draw on Latina-specific feminisms that emerge from the experiences of Latinas and are rooted in intersectional, decolonial, culturally hybrid, and transnational understandings of womanhood. The Vera/Vaughn sisters symbolically challenge the white female Elders, who represent the old guard/generation, but they accomplish this largely through discourses that harken back to first- and second-wave feminisms with the occasional reference to Black feminist thought. While the mere mention of Black feminist ideas is formidable on broadcast television, the sisters' Latinidad is disconnected from their feminism. Mel's dialogue is littered with references to feminism in addition to visuals (books lying around, posters with quotes or images of feminist writers) that define her character. But references to women-of-color feminism are less present, especially in relation to Latina feminist epistemologies. While the show draws on the heightened circulation of the concept of intersectionality on social media (trending at the time of the release of the series), it does so without attention to the specific experiences of Latinas despite featuring three Latina protagonists.

Reinscribing Dichotomies

Latina feminisms work to undo Western binaries and subvert normalized matrices and hierarchies of power.[34] Rather than dismantling hierarchies of white Eurocentricity, the reboot utilizes long-standing tropes, symbols, imagery, metaphors of white, Western civilization and thought as superior to non-Western people. For example, Greco-Roman mythology is centered in the majority of the storylines instead of drawing on Latin American and/or African mythology and folklore. Furthermore, Blackness is signified as dark, evil, monstrous, illegible, impenetrable, and uncivilized. In the original, this was embodied by The Seer (played by Black actress Debbi Morgan), a very powerful demon that is the surrogate mother of the Source of All Evil. In the reboot, the equation of Blackness and evil is most clearly evident when Macy, the darkest complected of the sisters, refers to "the darkness within" once she realizes she is part demon. In the reboot's only wink toward Anzaldúan conceptions of Chicana hybridity,[35] Macy says that she's "too demon for some, not demon enough for others."[36] Macy is viewed as dangerous and uncontrollable by the Elders due to her mixed identity as a witch and demon, Black and Latina, mirroring sentiments historically held about mixed-race individuals. The established council for "white" magic consists of the Elders, who are largely white-Anglo and always dressed in white. The Sarcana, an underground coven that operates outside of the purview of the Elders, are all dressed in black. The members of the Sarcana also appear to be racially ambiguous. In particular, the leader of the Sarcana is Jada, who is half Whitelighter and half witch and also visually appears to be mixed race with light brown skin, light eyes, and long dark hair styled in dreadlocks. We later learn that the Charmed sisters' mother, Marisol, was an ally to the Sarcana, occupying a place in between the Sarcana and the Elders/white magic. Marisol's use of both white and black magic, both racially inflected terms, cements her "in-betweenness," a racialized characterization long reserved for Latina roles in film and television to mark them as different from both Anglo white and African American characters.[37]

In the first season of the original, the supernatural tales rely primarily on Western and Christian worldviews. Only episode 4 draws on Chinese mythology and incorporates Mandarin language and culture as a central storyline. In the reboot, however, good and evil are not only marked by mixed-race or magic identities (e.g., half human, half demon, etc.), but also by language. For the rest of the reboot, English and Latin are positioned as the languages of pure, good magic. For example, after several unsuccessful attempts at "white magic" spells, the Vera/Vaughn sisters learn that Marisol secretly practices Santería, which means they can only undo a very potent spell by employing a spell based on Santería[38] that they must chant in Spanish. Associating non-English languages with black magic happens again in a storyline where the necromancer that resurrects Macy as a baby is an overweight white woman who speaks Russian to perform the spell. It occurs two more times when the Charmed sisters consult with a Haitian priestess who speaks Creole and when Macy's boyfriend Gavin makes contact with his deceased grandmother, who speaks Yoruba.[39] In these ways, non-English languages are used to signify a taboo "black magic" that falls outside the purviews of the "white magic" of the English-speaking Elders.

Figure 7.1. The sisters cast a Santería spell in *Charmed*. *Source*: Remezcla, photo by Robert Falconer. Courtesy of The CW.

Lastly, the *Charmed* reboot only mildly unsettles racial binaries. Instead of identifying as Afro-Latina, Macy identifies herself as Black. She can speak Spanish like her sisters, but she does not use Latina as a racial identity, reinforcing a Black/white dualistic understanding of race. Latina feminisms, on the other hand, interrogate seemingly fixed racial binaries, and this sensibility was not highlighted in the series.

Missing Latino-Centric Narratives

The *Charmed* reboot misses the opportunity to excavate and/or celebrate curanderismo, sets of indigenous- and African-based based spirituality. Given the magical universe of the show, including folk healing practices makes narrative sense, such as a character or storyline incorporating a curandera, or healer. Episode 6 introduces a Yoruba priestess and Black Haitian grandmother who uses Haitian Yoruba "folksy" magic on her grandson Gavin (episode 13), but the reboot did not develop a similar character from a Latina/mestizo/Indigena perspective. Although the

Vera/Vaughn sisters are marked as Puerto Rican, expressions of this identity are limited to food and language. Even so, Spanish is only used as a last resort for a forbidden spell. The sisters do not speak Spanish to each other, listen to music in Spanish, or watch Spanish-language television. They do not engage in Spanglish or use Puerto Rican slang, nor do they refer to Puerto Rican popular culture. Audiences discover that Maggie's actual name is Margarita Emilia Vera when the sisters perform an induction ceremony for her. The sisters' Puerto Rican identity, then, is peripheral to the storyline.

Conclusion

As a representational strategy, rebooting a successful, woman-centered, progressive show like *Charmed* only twelve years after its original series run poses several risks. While the setting and time period for a reboot shifted from a prequel with roots in Salem to present day in order to capitalize on the current racial and gendered climate,[40] the new showrunners always intended to center a multiracial cast. In this way, the *Charmed* reboot draws on several representational strategies for inclusion, including diversifying the writing team. While the gamble has proven successful—as of this writing the *Charmed* reboot has aired its final fourth season—the conceit of an all-Latina-led cast embodying contemporary feminist sensibilities has played out in ways that still continue to center whiteness in its storytelling devices. As such, the racially marked bodies of the Latina Vera/Vaughn witches stand in for diverse and edgy programming, but the storylines still primarily uphold dominant discourses, ideologies, and narratives.

The epistemological touchstones of Latina feminisms helped to highlight this limitation, and they reveal the transgressive ways the *Charmed* reboot complicates depictions of gender roles and expectations of Latinas; avoids pan-ethnic portrayals of Latinas/os/xs; leverages varying degrees of critiques against dominant ideologies, namely white liberal feminisms; and adds depth and dimension to the Latina characters that compose the majority of the nominal images seen on television. Nonetheless, it falls short of centering Latina or woman-of-color feminisms via the perspectives of the Vera/Vaughn sisters. As a result, the reboot reinscribes various problematic dichotomies, particularly those anchored in a Black-and-white racial paradigm that equates whiteness with virtuosity, and Eurocentric ideologies, discourses, and language with enlightenment and intellect. Additionally, it does not build a larger Latina/o/x world for the sisters, one that is replete with additional Latina/o/x characters or culturally relevant story arcs or themes, underutilizing the potentiality of a Latina-centered lead cast.

Despite its shortcomings, the reboot delves deeper into feminist issues than the original series with its overt critiques of patriarchy and foregrounding of women of color. Its non-normative production practices, namely all-Latina characters that include two Black Latina characters, make an important rupture in the visual optic of Latinidad on television. Given the dearth of Latina/o/x representation on primetime television, the *Charmed* reboot offers significant inroads in carving spaces for Latina characters and storylines. At the same time, the reboot works within narrative devices rooted in whiteness due to the original show's format and mythology.[41] The original cast's response to the casting and premise of the reboot illustrates this investment in white feminisms. Lead actresses Shannen Doherty and Holly Marie Combs expressed offense that the reboot was marketed as more "feminist" than the original,[42] an observation analyzed in more depth by Isabel Molina-Guzmán's essay in this collection.

Ultimately, the *Charmed* reboot oscillates between the normative liberal white feminist and postfeminist threads of the original series and a multicultural third-wave feminism that is inclusive of women of color and occasionally offers an intersectional analysis. In this way, the series may create a "dual register"[43] among a potentially bifurcated viewership where some audience members expect the postfeminism of the original series while other non-normative identities prefer more overt and nuanced critique of patriarchy, whiteness, and heteronormativity. Latinas and other women of color may indeed recognize aspects of their physical selves and the glimpses of transgressive storytelling on the small screen, but the main storylines of the reboot are still entrenched in white feminist discourses.

In doing so, the *Charmed* reboot produces a form of "woke capitalism"[44] instead of a more radical envisioning of intersectional feminism, and more specifically Latina feminisms, that many Latina and other women of color may desire. The Latina bodies foregrounded in the

Charmed reboot may satisfy the industry's need to create content that reflects an increasingly racialized and gendered society, as well as mainstream audiences' desire to see a diverse cast of characters, but by relying on familiar narratives, ideologies, and discourses, these bodies ironically uphold the hierarchies that have historically excluded well-rounded representations of Latinas.

Discussion Questions

1. According to the authors, the flipped rebooting of *Charmed* presents an opportunity for breaking representational inequality through new narratives featuring Latina characters. Identify three reasons the authors argue the reboot fails to do so.
2. Reflecting on this case study, why do you think it is difficult for Hollywood representations, even those that feature ethnic and racial minority actors and characters, to break away from Hollywood's legacy of inequality?

NOTES

1 Lesley Goldberg, "'Charmed' Reboot in the Works at CBS," *Hollywood Reporter*, October 25, 2013, www.hollywoodreporter.com.

2 Sydney Bucksbaum, "'Charmed' Producers Vow CW Reboot Will Honor Original," *Hollywood Reporter*, July 19, 2018, www.hollywoodreporter.com.

3 Hannah E. Sanders, "Living a Charmed Life: The Magic of Postfeminist Sisterhood," in *Interrogating Postfeminism: Gender and the Politics of Popular Culture*, ed. Yvonne Tasker and Diane Negra (Duke University Press, 2007), 73–99.

4 See Isabel Molina-Guzmán's chapter in this volume for a discussion of this history.

5 Ana-Christina Ramón, Michael Tran, and Darnell Hunt, *Hollywood Diversity Report 2023* (UCLA Division of Sciences Report, 2023).

6 Frances Negrón-Muntaner et al., *The Latino Media Gap: A Report on the State of Latinos in U.S. Media* (National Association of Latino Independent Producers, The Center for the Study of Ethnicity and Race at Columbia University, and the National Hispanic Foundation for the Arts, 2016).

7 Isabel Molina-Guzmán, *Latinas and Latinos on TV: Colorblind Comedy in the Post-Racial Network Era* (University of Arizona Press, 2018).

8 Manuel G. Avilés-Santiago, "'This is It!' [Is it?]" The Marketing of Nostalgia on Netflix's *One Day at a Time*," *Journal of Latin American Communication Research* 7, no. 1–2 (2019): 60–78.

9 Carolina A. Miranda, "Stuck in a Reboot Vacuum; Original Shows like 'Gentefied' and 'Vida' Reflect a Wider Worldview than the Rehashed Narratives of the Past Ever Can," *Los Angeles Times*, June 13, 2021; Carolina A. Miranda, "Let's Dump TV Reboots That Jam Latinos into White Molds," *Los Angeles Times*, June 14, 2021.

10 María Elena Cepeda, "Beyond 'Filling in the Gap': The State and Status of Latina/o Feminist Media Studies," *Feminist Media Studies* 16, no. 2 (2016): 344–60, https://doi.org/10.1080/14680777.2015.1052005; Angharad N. Valdivia, "Latina Media Studies," *Feminist Media Histories* 4, no. 2 (2018): 101–6, https://doi.org/10.1525/fmh.2018.4.2.101; Angharad N. Valdivia, *The Gender of Latinidad: The Uses and Abuses of Hybridity* (Wiley-Blackwell, 2020).

11 Molina-Guzmán, *Latinas and Latinos on TV*, 120–21.

12 Cepeda, "Beyond 'Filling in the Gap'"; Valdivia, "Latina Media Studies"; Valdivia, *The Gender of Latinidad*.

13 Valdivia, *The Gender of Latinidad*.

14 Cepeda, "Beyond 'Filling in the Gap.'"

15 Cepeda, "Beyond 'Filling in the Gap'"; Frances Negrón-Muntaner, 'What to Do with All This Beauty?' The Political Economy of Latina Stardom in the Twenty-First Century," in *The Routledge Companion to Latina/o Media*, ed. María Elena Cepeda and Dolores Inés Casillas (Routledge, 2017), 287–305.

16 Rebecca Feasey, "The 'Charmed' Audience: Gender and the Politics of Contemporary Culture," *Spectator: The University of Southern California Journal of Film & Television* 25, no. 2 (2005): 39–48.

17 Mary Beltrán, "Image Analysis and Televisual Latinos," in *Race and Media: Critical Approaches*, ed. Lori Kido Lopez (New York University Press, 2020), 27–38; Rosa Linda Fregoso, *MeXicana Encounters: The Making of Social Identities on the Borderlands* (University of California Press, 2003); Myra Mendible, "Introduction: Embodying Latinidad: An Overview," in *From Bananas to Buttocks: The Latina Body in Popular Film and Culture*, ed. Myra Mendible (University of Texas Press, 2007), 1–28; Charles Ramírez-Berg, *Latino Images in Film: Stereotypes, Subversion, and Resistance* (University of Texas Press, 2002); Angharad N. Valdivia, *Latina/os and the Media* (Polity, 2010).

18 Molina-Guzmán, *Latinas and Latinos on TV*.

19 *Charmed*, season 1, episode 15, "Switches & Stones," written by George Northy, directed by Claudia Yarmy, aired March 17, 2019, on The CW.

20 Esteban del Río and Kristin C. Moran, "Remaking Television: *One Day at a Time*'s Digital Delivery and Latina/o Cultural Specificity," *Journal of Communication Inquiry* 44, no. 1 (January 2020): 5–25, https://doi.org/10.1177/0196859918825332; Valdivia, *The Gender of Latinidad*.

21 *Charmed*, season 1, episode 6, "Kappa Spirit," written by Emmylou Diaz, directed by Jeffrey W. Byrd, aired November 18, 2018, on The CW.

22 Ana Lopez, "Early Cinema and Modernity in Latin America," *Cinema Journal* 40, no. 1 (2000): 48–78; Molina-Guzmán, *Latinas and Latinos on TV*; Angharad N.

Valdivia, *A Latina in the Land of Hollywood and Other Essays on Media Culture* (University of Arizona Press, 2000).

23 *Charmed*, season 1, episode 4, "Dead Man Dating," written by Javier Grillo-Marxuach, directed by Richard Compton, aired October 28, 1998, on The WB.

24 *Charmed*, season 1, episode 2, "Let This Mother Out," written by Jessica O'Toole and Amy Rardin, directed by Vanessa Parise, aired October 21, 2018, on The CW.

25 *Charmed*, season 1, episode 3, "Sweet Tooth," written by Joey Falco, directed by Michael Allowitz, aired October 28, 2018, on The CW.

26 *Charmed*, season 1, episode 14, "Touched by a Demon," written by Joey Falco, directed by Stuart Gillard, aired March 20, 2019, on The CW.

27 Ramírez-Berg, *Latino Images in Film*.

28 Molina-Guzmán, *Latinas and Latinos on TV*, 89.

29 Bill Lawrence, dir., *Scrubs*, featuring Zach Braff, Donald Faison, Sarah Chalke, and Judy Reyes (2001–2009; Los Angeles: NBC/ABC, 2009–2011), television series.

30 Molina-Guzmán, *Latinas and Latinos on TV*, 37–38.

31 Ebony Elizabeth Thomas, *The Dark Fantastic: Race and the Imagination from "Harry Potter" to "The Hunger Games"* (New York University Press, 2020).

32 Matthew David Goodwin, *The Latinx Files: Race, Migration, and Space Aliens* (Rutgers University Press, 2021).

33 Molina-Guzmán, *Latinas and Latinos on TV*, 36.

34 Ellie D. Hernández, "The Future Perfect: Chicana Feminist Critical Analysis in the Twenty-First Century" *Chicana/Latina Studies: The Journal of MALCS* 5, no. 2 (2006): 60–91, www.jstor.org/stable/23014482; Aida Hurtado, *Intersectional Chicana Feminisms: Sitios y lenguas* (University of Arizona Press, 2020).

35 See Robert Gutierrez-Perez and Leandra Hinojosa Hernández, "Introduction: How to Read This Book: An Introduction for Everyone and No One," in *This Bridge We Call Communication: Anzaldúan Approaches to Theory, Method, and Praxis*, ed. Leandra Hinojosa Hernández and Robert Gutierrez-Perez (Lexington Books, 2019), xiii–xxv.

36 *Charmed*, season 1, episode 17, "Surrender," written by Sarah Goldfinger, directed by Megan Follows, aired March 31, 2019, on The CW.

37 Valdivia, *A Latina in the Land of Hollywood*; Valdivia, *The Gender of Latinidad*.

38 Santería is a syncretized religion that combines Catholicism, West African Yoruba, and sometimes spiritism. It is primarily practiced in the Spanish-speaking Caribbean.

39 *Charmed*, season 1, episode 13, "Manic Pixie Nightmare," written by Jessica O'Toole and Amy Rardin, directed by Melanie Mayron, aired March 3, 2019, on The CW.

40 Alanna Bennett, "Can the "Charmed" Reboot Overcome the Backlash Surrounding It?," *BuzzFeed News*, August 7, 2018, www.buzzfeednews.com.

41 Crystal Camargo, "Rebooting Whiteness, Complicating Latinidad: The Struggles of Latinx TV Remakes," *FLOW Journal*, June 8, 2021, www.flowjournal.org; Miranda, "Stuck in a Reboot Vacuum"; Miranda, "Let's Dump TV Reboots."

42 Patrick Cavanaugh, "Old School 'Charmed' Fans Are Trying to Stop the Reboot," *Comicbook.com*, February 14, 2018, https://comicbook.com.

43 Mary Beltrán, *Latina/o Stars in U.S. Eyes: The Making and Meaning of Film and TV Stardom* (University of Illinois Press, 2010).

44 Dave Zirin, "The Super Bowl's Woke Capitalism," *The Nation*, February 8, 2021, www.thenation.com.

8

Eventizing Premieres, Constructing Audiences, Performing Fandom

Remaking One Day at a Time *as a Cuban American Story*

KRISTIN C. MORAN AND ESTEBAN DEL RÍO

READING NOTE: Rebooted from a major television network to a streaming service and then to a niche television network, *One Day at a Time* demonstrates the precariousness of ethnic flips in the context of racial inequality. The reboot was produced by Norman Lear, the iconic creator of the 1970s original, but it shifted the characters and narratives from a women-led white family to a women-led Cuban American family. Although the reboot incorporated a Cuban American writer and co-producer and diverse writers' room, its format and structures remained defined by Lear's traditionally liberal sitcom narrative and aesthetic style, including a studio audience and a three-camera set. In this chapter, Kristin Moran and Esteban del Río examine the turbulence surrounding this ethnically flipped reboot through an analysis of the text, audience responses, and distribution. Specifically, they explore the complexities faced by ethnic writers and creators who desire to tell complex stories grounded in queer and Latina/x lived experiences in a capitalist industry still defined by gender, racial, and ethnic inequalities. Moran and del Río demonstrate the continuing limitations of flipped reboots and the structurally unequal conditions faced by women, LGBTQ, and ethnic and racial minority creators in contemporary capitalism.

Introduction

The remake of *One Day at a Time* (2017–2019, Netflix; 2020, Pop/CBS) premiered on Netflix in 2017, offering an updated version of Norman Lear's series of the same name that aired on CBS between 1975 and 1984. The legendary producer reinterpreted his 1970s women-centered, working-class, multi-camera sitcom for a new era, again filmed in front of a live studio audience. But this time, the characters and plot developments are centered on a Latina-led family wrestling with contemporary issues such as immigration debates, coming-out experiences, racial discrimination, combat veteran experiences, and workplace sexual harassment. The series producers felt an obligation to advocate for storytelling that hearkened back to Lear's progressive agenda of the 1970s by emphasizing social and political issues that felt more urgent during the first Trump administration. Lear became famous for his broadcast network programs in the 1970s and '80s that explored contemporary social issues of the time, such as *All in the Family* (1971–1979, CBS), *Sanford and Son* (1972–1977, NBC), *Maude* (1972–1978, CBS), and *The Jeffersons* (1975–1985, CBS). The original *One Day at a Time* (1975–1984, CBS) featured a white family in Indianapolis made up of a divorced mother and two teenage daughters. For this remake, Lear turned to executive producers and showrunners Gloria Calderón Kellett and Mike Royce to translate the original concept. It was Calderón Kellett's background as a Cuban American who grew up in Southern California that inspired the characters and storylines. The entirety of the show's run across Netflix and on CBS platforms saw public advocacy from Calderón Kellett, who hustled on social media to "eventize" each season's release. An industry term, eventizing describes the public relations campaign to build viewership, something especially important for streaming platforms.

In the remake, the 2017 series extended the narrative beyond gender-based politics and a progressive feminist agenda to one that embraces the intersectionality of its main characters. As political rhetoric became more toxic during the Trump era, the writers responded to specific instances with characters experiencing challenges that were relatable to the target audience. This chapter explores the promise of *One Day at a Time* (*ODAAT*) as a transformative text, engaging controversial social issues with Cuban American cultural specificity on the leading digital streaming platform at the time.

Netflix, along with other streaming services, represents a major disruption of the economic model, program delivery modes, and narratives of legacy broadcast and cable television. As Netflix came to dominate streaming platforms in the 2010s, one critic noted how narratives "have always been an outgrowth of the delivery mechanism."[1] As a remake, the show represents change not only in characters and storylines, but also in the purpose of television itself: to advocate for communities of color and provide information to engage in progressive cultural citizenship. In addition to Lear's imprimatur, the show features stage and screen legend and Latina icon Rita Moreno alongside a talented group of actors with a diverse writing room led by Gloria Calderón Kellett. But the translation from the white characters and topics of the original series to the remake's progressive Latinidad results from more than casting and staffing changes. The distribution on the digital streaming platform, producer agency and social media appeals, the economics of television, and the urgency of Latinx television representation during a time of racial reckoning all contributed to the poetics and politics of the reboot.

The show centers intergenerational Cuban American women, inviting audiences to identify with authentic, specific experiences that the characters use to navigate a range of controversial situations and topics from a progressive point of view. Many of the storylines, and much of the humor, feature intergenerational misunderstandings and tensions among the female characters, which adds complexity and historic context to the Cuban American experience. The three women illustrate the perspectives and issue cultures germane to Baby Boomers, Generation X, and Generation Z subjects, but also cast a generational arc of identity for a certain kind of Cuban American and Latina diasporic experience—one rooted in the histories of light-skinned Cubans who fled the revolution in the early 1960s.

The show was in production during the 2016 election campaign, and its persistent Latina-led advocacy for racial and social justice stood in direct opposition to the nativist racism of the Trump administration when it premiered in January 2017. The critical acclaim and enthusiastic fan base reaction that lauded the series for its progressive treatment of current events could not overcome the economic conditions of television, which rely on audience metrics to justify continued investment. While offering producers the space to create complex, progressive stories, Netflix dropped the show in 2019 after the third season. The cancellation was announced in a tweet, citing low viewership without providing specific audience data. On Twitter, Netflix announced, "We've made the very difficult decision not to renew One Day At A Time for a fourth season. The choice did not come easily—we spent several weeks trying to find a way to make another season work but in the end simply not enough people watched to justify another season."[2] After the Netflix cancellation, the show's fourth season was finally picked up by PopTV, which became part of ViacomCBS Entertainment and Youth Brands Group in late 2019. Season 4 was slated to have thirteen episodes, but only completed seven that made it to air and ultimately was a victim of the economic conditions of legacy television, not helped by COVID-19 cancellations.

As a contemporary sitcom, *ODAAT* was praised for its inclusive representations, and the hype surrounding each season premiere can be understood as "eventizing" with public relations efforts that made an event out of the premiere. The documented lack of Latinx representation across the media meant that this show had to be special. The labor of promotion rested on the showrunners and others involved in the production, including the social media feeds of the actors, since Netflix's promotional attention centered on programming that was assumed to be more lucrative. *ODAAT* needed critics and fans to demonstrate that Latinx stories could break through. What stands apart for this remake is the intentionality of the writers' room to invite writers of color and who identify as queer to foreground their experience. In an interview, Mike Royce explained how, as a cis white man, there were moments where he felt out of place, with the realization that it was because his experience was not the dominant narrative being told, and he understood that others had to take the lead.[3]

To make sense of the reboot, we see value in Cedric Robinson's notion of racial capitalism.[4] As discussed in the introduction, racial capitalism posits a necessary link between the economic dimensions of capitalism and the persistence of racial inequality. Within the context of commercial entertainment media, there is an undeniable emphasis on profitability and growth based on audience metrics, whether arriving from advertising or subscriptions. *ODAAT*'s remaking of a social issues–focused, female-led, multi-camera sitcom filmed in front of a live audience attempts to use commercial media platforms to progress through what Stuart Hall describes as the "struggle over the relations of representation to a politics of representation itself."[5] In other words, while the show is populated by Latina writers and actors with Calderón Kellett at the helm, it also articulates a culturally specific, intersectional Latinidad that defies essentialisms often assigned to Latinx characters and themes. This kind of nuanced, non-essentialist Latinidad has appeared on low-budget web series, but here *ODAAT* leverages Netflix, Sony, and CBS to work from a platform of high visibility and investment from global media corporations. But as other scholars argue,[6] for-profit corporations and even major non-profit institutions often appropriate diverse voices and equity agendas to serve their own profit-centered or reputational goals. The story of *ODAAT*'s four seasons tells of the remake of a beloved show, but also a reproduction of television economics in the digital age, with its attendant white heteronormative, patriarchal privilege, even in the guise of Latina voices.

The Production and Distribution Promise of Season 1

In a study of season 1[7] we argue that *One Day at a Time* represents the complexity and diversity of the Latinx experience in the United States by featuring characters and storylines that centralize the Cuban American perspective of the main characters, who live in Southern California. This runs counter to the prevailing pattern in television, where Latinas/os/xs are grossly underrepresented,[8] and those who appear typically speak from a pan-ethnic, non-specific, cultural location that obscures the regional, national, generational, religious, and linguistic differences one finds in Latina/o/x communities.[9] Television also holds a consistent record of neglecting Afro-Latina/o/x and indigenous perspectives, rendering these communities invisible in its stories.[10] Instead, *ODAAT*'s season 1 features Cuban American, Mexican American, Afro-Latina, Black, and queer Latinx characters whose perspectives run counter to the flattening of difference within Latinidad, identified by scholars of Latino-themed media.[11] The producers of the program told us that digital delivery allowed for the construction of Latinidad in *ODAAT* that defies the broad, benign cultural category favored by marketers, political analysts, and media producers and that has been common in much of Latino-themed media,[12] implying and hoping that this cultural specificity would entice Latinx viewers to tune in.

The characters' grappling with immigration debates, coming-out experiences, PTSD, and sexual harassment carries on the tradition of Norman Lear storytelling by tackling controversial, contemporary issues.[13] We posit that, free from the advertiser influence and production restrictions of commercial television, Netflix's platform empowered producers to pursue their own take on the "very special episode" tradition of engaging with social problems from a progressive Latina logic and centering Latinx themes. Our analysis looks favorably on the production context facilitated by both Netflix and Sony Television, as producer and showrunner Calderón Kellett told us in interviews that creatives were "supported to tell the stories we want to tell,"[14] and that there did not need to be a joke on every page of the script, which is often the case in legacy media. She reported that Netflix also provided flexibility in regard to episode length and allowed Calderón Kellett to "tell compelling stories that are much like a play" and, in her experience, atypical of a sitcom genre conventions.[15] According to Calderón Kellett, Lear chose to work with her because her experience growing up in a Cuban American family in Southern California and the richness of her background would inform the mother-daughter relationships at the center of the show. Both Netflix and Sony allowed for some autonomy and supported Calderón Kellett's storytelling in season 1, which was released in full on January 6, 2017. Two months later, in March, the show was renewed for a second season by Netflix amid enthusiastic reviews from television critics and a vocal fan base on social media. Here, Netflix, the dominant television streaming service, enabled creatives of color behind the camera and in the writers' room, to tell authentic stories tackling controversial social issues in a show produced by a major media conglomerate, Sony.

The production context of season 1 facilitated stories centering Cuban American perspectives that spoke from a myriad of identifiable racial, national, ethnic, gendered, and queer voices. We argue the more complex, culturally grounded, and diverse articulation of Latinidad moved away from the trap of understanding television stories about non-white characters as either positive/aspirational or negative/stereotypical.[16] Instead, the show invites audiences to identify with authentic, culturally specific perspectives of people of color and their relational interactions and negotiations with whiteness, masculinity, heteronormativity, and religion/spirituality. At the time, we predicted that, given the success of season 1, a narrative voice that centered culturally specific storytelling would portend continued audience engagement.

Constructing Audiences: Reflections, Reactions, and Critique

A central component of eventizing the premieres of each season has been the connection to fans and supporters of the show who were crucial to the public relations campaign that intended to bring audiences to the program. Resting on the producers' claim that digital delivery allowed for the cultural specificity of the Cuban American experience represented on the show, we aimed to collect impressions from the perceived target audience. Therefore, following from the textual and contextual analysis of season 1 of *One Day at a Time*, we conducted two focus groups with 80 percent of participants self-identifying as Latinx in April 2019.[17] The non-Latinx participants identified as Black. We intended to extend this audience research, but as required by pandemic conditions, we turned our attention to the narrative structure and distribution of text for this analysis. Nevertheless, the participants provide insight into the ways in which non-white audience members identified with the text. Each group was shown two clips from season 1: The first clip featured a family discussion about immigration status; the second was a climactic scene of Elena's "coming out." Most participants had not seen the show and were eager to share their impressions. Although we hesitate to make broad claims about the reception of the program, we can gain insight into how some audience members interpret the text.

As we reviewed the conversations with the participants, themes emerged that allowed us to understand how Latinidad was inscribed through the Cuban experience, but also the way in which being Mexican in California changed how the nuanced immigration story unfolded for these research participants. It was clear from their reactions that they found pleasure in the text and identified with the characters. They were, however, able to critique how *ODAAT* continued to privilege whiteness as a construct, even within a narrative that broadly claimed it intended to decenter whiteness in this updated remake.

Representation and Recognition

As expected, audiences were satisfied with the cultural references that felt familiar and they connected with the intergenerational family dynamics represented in the show. Isabel, one of the interviewees, stated, "I think I did see a lot of myself, and my family represented, just because I am also Latina, and there are those generational differences in mindsets of gender roles between my grandparents and my more open-minded parents." In the scene that was previewed, the matriarch, Lydia, played by Rita Moreno, shares that she benefited from the "Pedro Pan" initiative and came to the US legally.[18] There is support for this perspective in the dialogue from other characters and the counter-argument offered in the series by main character of Penelope that immigration has always been a contested condition embedded with the privilege of being able to "wait in line." The complexity of their positionality on immigration demonstrates how the representation can speak across generations. One participant, Paloma, explained,

> I also relate to the grandmother . . . she's like "Oh, I came here legally, why can't everybody else?" Very few people have the chance to come legally, and yet I also feel that it's . . . I mean, to what extent is it fair? My parents came here legally through employer sponsorship of my dad and we had to live here. My parents and my sister had to . . . take their citizenship test, pay a lot of money and so there has to be something in between, we need to give people the chance to come here and work legally. [To] be able to support their families, send money home and also if you want US citizenship to take the necessary steps.

The open narrative and cultural differences highlighted in season 1 allow for identification across characters and allow viewers to identify with the intergenerational nature of this comedy.

While participants applaud the ways in which the narrative modeled the ability to have civil discourse around controversial topics, in some ways the audience saw this as unrealistic, but nevertheless instructive. Through both topics, immigration and sexuality, there were moments of envy whereby the participants indicated they "wished" they could have those conversations. For example, participant Marisol noted in regard to immigration, "I personally have those conversations with my family and friends, and it just plays out way different and in a more complex way. . . . I mean, from my personal experiences it gets ugly." For her, the relatively civil discussion over dinner set up an ideal way of interacting rather than reflecting how discussion might play out within the early days of the Trump administration. Marcus, however, was more generous in his reflection on how the show represented the debate: "I liked how they showed a lot of different sides of immigration, which is such a huge topic right now. They showed people who were for it, people who were against it, people who have gone through it, and they didn't present it in an angry way. It was like everyone said what they wanted to say, and people were listening, which for a sitcom, that's huge." The participants that we talked to were not necessarily fans of the show, so the ongoing public enthusiasm evidenced from the fan community on social media was not always present in responses. In fact, the respondents' critiques offered about the shortcomings of the storytelling hints at broader audience dissatisfaction and disinterest in the show as evidenced by the diminishing audience share.

Centering Whiteness in Social Justice Situations

In the scene where characters commented on the difference between legal and illegal migration, participants were struck by the centering of the white Canadian who described himself as an "illegal alien" because he overstayed his student visa. The character solves his problem through family connections and financial status. The participants were critical of the emphasis:

MARISOL: When he used "Illegal Alien." I was just like "Ugh, here we go again." So, it felt personal just 'cause, like I said, I've gone . . . I've had to tell people that those are not the correct terms or that, that's not a right label to be giving these people . . . So then, that kind of creates a discomfort in me, like you said, then I'm not really allowed to laugh or I don't want to really laugh at some of the comedy. Then again some of the parts were funny.

MARCUS: I also kind of had an issue with Schneider in the first clip, because he was like "Let me tell you my story" but his story worked out so fine for him, and it was just like . . . I know it was supposed to be a joke, but also he has privilege that at least in that clip he did not acknowledge, and he seemed kind of oblivious or ignorant to, and I don't know, that kind of rubbed me the wrong way. He was just like "It was hard for me," it's like, well, you got a visa, you did this.

Luz: He could afford lawyers.
Marcus: Yeah, he could pay these fines. That's not everyone's experience.
Isabel: I think he does a good job of portraying the white liberal voice, where it's like "I'm an ally, but also I'm going to talk over your experience."
Marcus: Yes.
Isabel: And then he tends to get checked.
Luz: Yeah, "that reminds me of a time in my own experience where I suffered just like you guys."

In the back-and-forth dialogue between the participants, they unpack how the shifting discourse away from Cuban and Mexican immigration to Canada was a comedic device, but also centered whiteness in an attempt to flatten the differences in the immigrant experiences.

Focus group participants leveled the critique that the white characters were centered even in the discussion on immigration, which was expected to focus on Cuba and/or Mexico given the setting locale in Los Angeles. But the central discussion focuses on Canada and Schneider's student visa, rather than on Elena's friend and secondary character, Carmen, whose story about being undocumented remains in the background—quite literally when she explains that her parents have been deported to Mexico to justify why she has been hiding in Elena's bedroom. Given that the show is set in Los Angeles, it should be surprising that the Latina-driven stories are populated by white characters—from Schneider, whose self-adoption into the family is a repeated source of humor, to Penelope's co-workers and Lydia's love interest. Yet this should not be surprising, given that white characters and moments of white centrality operate from the racial capitalist logic of the industry's unequal economic underpinnings.

Interestingly, the intentionality of Latinidad as the central narrative device in this remake cannot guarantee the decentering of whiteness. In the same way as the original *One Day at a Time* functioned as a feminist text, with the single mother as the protagonist, it fell short as the series progressed in the broadcast lineup. Bonnie Dow[19] critiques the centrality of heteronormative romance as undermining the feminist political message in the same way that the tangential white characters get primacy in this Latinx remake.

In sum, respondents read the debates in *ODAAT* as idealized and instructional but critiqued the show for oversimplifying the current immigration crisis. While they identified with the family, they pointed out that the broader narrative structure centered whiteness—both with the white characters and in the absence of darker-skinned Latinas/os. In many ways, these audience responses show how a program based on storylines and characters from underrepresented groups cannot "do it all." Often, these narratives need to carry a large burden of representation. This burden is only intensified when the economics of television apply pressure for sustained, demographically profitable—or overall increases—in viewership. In the first season, producers expressed freedom to tell their stories, which garnered an affirming and quick renewal for a second season by Netflix in 2017. It appeared as though Latinx television representation had entered a new era, bolstered by streaming platforms whose flexibility and algorithms allowed for a different kind of storytelling. But these audience responses foreshadow problems that arise later for the show as it finds itself stretched out among competing goals: to tell stories from a Cuban American voice; to tackle controversial topics from a progressive, social justice point of view; to reach an audience that satisfies Netflix's bottom line; and to operate in a television universe that remains dominated by cisgender, straight, white, male executives.

Limits of Performing Fandom: The Cold Reality of Television Economics

Over the course of seasons 2 and 3 on Netflix, the program continued to garner critical praise and maintained a passionate, youthful fan base. The show and producers won a number of award nominations, including four Emmy nominations and GLAAD[20] recognition. Award wins included two Primetime Emmys for editing and Best Primetime Program Comedy from Imagen, an organization who recognizes positive portrayals of Latinos in the entertainment industry. Because Netflix did not share any audience metrics with producers, the feedback loop was limited to vocal fans on social media and critical reception. At the end of season 2, the extension of the program was unclear. As a result, producers' successive campaigns to build viewership on the streaming platform belied a different urgency: *renewal.* TV critic Maureen Ryan wrote in *Variety*, "Netflix is supposed to be different. It could prove it by renewing 'One Day at a Time.'"[21] And it did. The entirety of season 3 dropped on February 8, 2019, and took audiences into more complex storylines with Schneider's alcoholism, Penelope's jealousy as her ex-husband remarried, and the developing queer relationship between Syd and Elena. Netflix used the strategy of releasing a full season at once with *ODAAT*, which moved away from the appointment TV model of legacy television and did not use the weekly release now increasingly common with streaming video content.

Cedric Robinson writes that the development of capitalism in Europe followed the contours of racism, and that "it could be expected that racialism would inevitably permeate the social structures emergent from capitalism."[22] The history of television unfolds along the same axes of racial capitalism. The economics of television consistently operate from production, distribution, and reception logics that privilege "white supremacist, capitalist, patriarchy," to borrow a phrase from bell hooks. To the extent that television streaming platforms operate as disruptors of legacy media, Netflix could upend the economic model it inherited from the networks. Indeed, season 1 raised hopes that shows like *ODAAT* could get a green light and hold a sustained run on the platform, aided by sophisticated algorithms, contextualized by a plethora of new original shows, and propelled by the need for Latina-led stories and topics highly relevant to diverse Generation Z audiences. Instead, *ODAAT* was dragged back into the old ratings game, only this time without the ratings. But the push-pull of production costs, creative license, and audience metrics led not only to cancellation, but also to the deployment of producer agency and the recruitment of creatives into efforts to connect audiences with content. For example, in order to demonstrate to Netflix the power of the audience, on social media, Calderón Kellett and Royce encouraged fans to binge-watch the show, tweeting, "HUGE favor: If you want to support me & the show then PLEASE watch & tell friends & family to watch at least FOUR episodes in the next few days. Netflix decides what gets picked up based on views."[23] They shared with fans that this strategy was more important to streaming platforms than viewership over time, as binging indicates audience interest in the show.

Again, fans and critics continued to respond positively on social media even though Netflix hinted that the number of viewers was not suitable. Renewal became a more urgent matter for producers, as social media campaigns after season 3 intensified. We contend that as seasons progressed, the cultural specificity and intersectionality of the characters became less central, falling on genre conventions to hold more appeal as the economics of both streaming and legacy television bore down on the show's viability.

At the end of season 3, Netflix announced the show's cancellation, but a "#SaveODAAT" campaign flooded social media feeds and caught the attention of Sony. Nevertheless, Netflix's response to the decision to cancel was explained in a way that positioned the network as an unwilling participant, as much a victim as the show itself. The performative communication from Netflix on social media brings to mind concepts circulating widely in the current moment, such as "white fragility" and "gaslighting." Netflix blamed the conditions of distribution and the lack of audience instead of acknowledging its own agency and authority in the decision-making process. It became clear that while Latina cultural specificity and an engagement with serious topics excited fans and critics, it could not draw an audience that satisfied the streaming service's bottom line. Diversity in television has never been more important, but the whitewashing effect of television economics persists. The strategic communication around the canceling of the show rested on the neoliberal, capitalist logic that deflected attention away from the fact that this program, which was praised for its progressive Latinx characters, was another example of the limits of representation and a victim of the continued racial capitalism that buoys the inequality of the industry.

ODAAT's distribution drama points to the kind of narrative changes television programming could make if it were to become more antiracist, but also how television economics holds a gravitational pull toward whiteness and inequality in production and representation. This pull has been fueled by decades-long assumptions about what constitutes a lucrative audience and whose eyeballs are most valuable to sell to corporations. Early broadcast economics pushed narratives that appealed to the broadest mass audience relying on the lowest common denominator, which was translated to stories that appealed to the white audience experience—even when minority characters were the protagonists.[24]

Untethered to advertising revenue, streaming platforms offer the possibility of a radical shift away from patterns associated with legacy broadcasting. Both fans and critics were hungry for authentic television stories about people of color and took to social media to advocate for the show. Producers cultivated this energy with a media campaign aimed at finding a new platform. Pop answered the call.

When Pop picked up season 4 for distribution in 2020, the trajectory of the program had moved further toward edutainment, resembling the educational dimensions of programs like *East Los High*[25] and community advocacy not uncommon on Spanish-language news.[26] For example, the first episode, with guest star Ray Romano portraying a census collector, encourages the family "to be counted" to underscore the importance of participating in the US Census. In a 2020 interview with voting-rights advocate Stacy Abrams for the television festival Paleyfest, Calderón Kellett admitted the show aimed to "sneak in the broccoli" with storylines demonstrating how to vote and why voting is important. In this case, by season 4, decentering whiteness included edutainment and advocacy—and exploring Afro-Latina identity, mental illness, queer relationships, and citizenship. Although the program marketed itself as relevant for the Latinx audience highlighting the identities of main characters, the original appeal was that the cultural specificity could be identifiable to a wide range of audiences, even with more attention to instructive lessons that are more relevant to some audiences than others. The strategy was tested when *ODAAT* made its debut on PopTV.

The fourth season of *ODAAT* premiered on March 24, 2020, and was placed directly after Pop's hit show, *Schitt's Creek*. This intentional placement of a new series following an established "anchor" program represents a common practice in legacy television to maintain audience interest and introduce the audience to a new program. However, in this example the ratings for *ODAAT* dropped from its lead-in show by half, and the subsequent episodes fared little better as they aired during the next months. The first six episodes had been filmed prior to lockdowns and it is unclear how much COVID-19 impacted the viability of the series. April 28, 2020, was the final airing of the series that included filming in front of a live audience. Episode 7 is dubbed "The Politics Episode" and the educational element of the show was written prior to COVID-19. The political atmosphere ramping up to the 2020 presidential election was tense, with many people sharing the difficulty of having conversations with friends and family with opposing views. The intention of the episode was to model the process of preparing for these types of conversation so there was an urgency to ensuring that this show be available to audiences.

With the episode 7 script complete and no ability to film in the midst of the lockdown, Calderón Kellett shared during a panel for the ATX Television Festival in June 2020 that the producers hired an animation company, Smiley Guy Studios, and sent production teams to each actor's home to record the voice-overs. This COVID-era solution to limited production kept the series alive, but this episode turned into the unintentional finale. In fact, Sarene Leeds, writing for *Vulture*, states, "What makes the episode's shortcomings all the more dissatisfying is that this animated special is being promoted as a teachable moment." The article links to a tweet from Amnesty International thanking *ODAAT* for emphasizing "the importance of having tough conversations with your family." For a program that encountered difficulties finding a new distributor, "The Politics Episode," with its overt lessons on how to have civil discussions, perhaps sealed the fate of *ODAAT* as offering too much "broccoli" along with its laugh lines.

The 2020 production shutdowns caused by the COVID-19 public health emergency halted new pilots, live sports, and reality shows. This vacuum had CBS turning to its inventory of TV-ready programming. *ODAAT* had six episodes filmed in from its thirteen-episode contract when the pandemic hit, and an enthusiastic fan base. An encore of season 4 would air on CBS television in October 2020. Although the episodes had become decidedly narrower in their appeal, emphasizing an entertainment-education approach, the access that a broadcast channel offers gave *ODAAT* the single most viewers of an episode at one point in time. Over three consecutive weeks, the show aired two episodes during prime time on Monday night. Nevertheless, a condensed national prime-time broadcast run could not bring enough viewers to the set to warrant more. The CBS premiere achieved 1.6 million viewers, but the sixth and final episode that aired during prime time held only 1 million, as it lost viewers with each successive airing. The season's seventh installment, the animated episode that was the most aggressively educational, with its tackling of civil discourse in the context of the divisive 2020 election, never made it down the dial to CBS. Low broadcast ratings forecast the show's future and ultimate cancellation shortly thereafter.

Reconstituting Television Economics

The four-season run of *ODAAT* suggests that current television structure and economics, with all its technological innovation, audience fragmentation, and financial flexibility, continues to be driven by the same economic conditions that privilege narratives that center and appeal to the general public overshadowed by whiteness. We argue that the ethos of season 1 appealed across audience sectors and that assumption must have driven the decision to place the show into a prime-time, albeit cable-niched, location. Ironically, eventizing the hype and public discourse about the Latinx appeal contradicts the distribution strategy.

Norman Lear, as a celebrity producer, laid the groundwork for the publicity around the premiere of the remake of *One Day at a Time* and showrunners like Gloria Calderón Kellett. Eventizing the premieres of each season, a strategy that other programs now follow, points to the hustle that creators of color must engage in to be seen as viable. Calderón Kellett was able to promote the show with both Lear and Royce through a number of interviews picked up by industry trade publications as well as national public media reporting about Hollywood's lack of diversity. In the continued effort to promote her work and Latinx storytelling more broadly, Calderón Kellett was interviewed for NPR's *It's Been a Minute*, which aired on February 15, 2022, as her new show featuring Latinx characters, *With Love*, debuted. In spaces like these, Calderón Kellett can amplify the importance of the work of creators of color. In this episode, Calderón Kellett names many Latinx shows, including disclosing her experiences with *One Day at a Time*. The fact that *ODAAT* continues to be discussed and promoted highlights the desire for the diversification of content. In some ways, she has found herself positioned as a matriarch of the writers' room with a level of success that allows her to push boundaries and make room for others at the table. As a showrunner, executive producer, she is one creative among many who are making a difference. Calderón Kellett is an influencer, not just with the productions she is involved in but in her public media appearances calling out the need for diversity. The fact that more shows are being made is a testament to the work that is happening by Latinx writers, producers, and others behind the scenes in conjunction with the actors that we see who are making a change.

The work is not without cost. The extra labor required to prove that conditions warrant the creation of more texts outside of whiteness pressures the audiences, who are told that they "better show up" to support programming featuring non-white characters. Each show matters and the urgency to prove success reinforces the capitalist logic underpinning the actual work. The industry's record shows that executives exercise tolerance for mediocrity when there is a white cast aimed at white audiences, but the bar for shows that feature characters of color remains high with little room for error. *ODAAT* gained viewers over its three seasons on Netflix, growing from 720,000 viewers during its premiere weekend for season 1 to 840,000 for season 2, and the show reached 1.6 million viewers for the premiere weekend of season 3.[27] Yet this growth was not enough to satisfy Netflix's profit margin. In a recent example, ABC's *Promised Land*, a show "about two Latino families vying for wealth and power in California's Sonoma Valley," earned only three weeks on the broadcast channel before it was pushed to Hulu to ride out the season. In the February 15, 2022, interview, Calderón Kellett mentions *Promised Land* as the "only" Latinx show on prime-time television. By the time her interview aired nationally, the show had been pulled from ABC and moved to Hulu. In the week that followed, *Promised Land* creator Matt Lopez was left to clarify on social media that his show had not been canceled. Yet.

One Day at a Time was supposed to disrupt representation by showing complicated and intersectional characters that pushed the binary of positive and negative representations. The family is complicated. Their stories are complicated. It may be that the sitcom genre does not have the flexibility to account for this type of storytelling. Narratives that contain progressive, culturally specific content have a brief shelf life. Capsulated story arcs with clear intention and ending points seem to be the formula most appropriate for narratives that challenge dominant ideologies, and for now, decentering whiteness happens in short stints rather than open-ended serials banking on renewal. The entertainment industry continues to function in a way that replicates legacy television's economic assumptions privileging white audiences in the stories they continue to promote. Netflix hasn't disrupted the landscape enough to confidently release productions from the model that privileges white audiences and lowest-common-denominator strategies that flatten stories about people of color. In 2017, there seemed to be momentum and the anticipation of a sea change where more Latinx shows were going to be made, but the framework for judging success is stubborn. What we have witnessed is more green lights, but they don't stay green for long.

Nevertheless, the media landscape is vibrantly changing as of the writing of this chapter. While still woefully under-told, stories that feature Latinx themes and characters appear across television. Public discourse about media representation suggests that a dramatic shift might be happening. Labor unions and other advocacy groups are outing the industry for its lack of diversity, especially within positions of power that are behind the scenes. Calls to action are gaining momentum as the industry recovers from the impact of the pandemic. But without a reckoning with the economic model of television, which persists through disruptive technologies, we can expect that stories like those told on *One Day at a Time* will continue to drift toward the margins.

Discussion Questions

1. Both digital streaming and legacy commercial television canceled *One Day at a Time* due to insufficient audiences. How does this illustrate the notion of racial capitalism?
2. Given the systematic cancellation of Latinx programming in mainstream media, how can media outlets provide opportunities for Latinx stories to be shared? How might audiences advocate for more diversity in television to ensure that stories featuring characters of color are viable in entertainment media?

NOTES

1 James Poniewozik, "'One Day at a Time' and Why Netflix is Not Your Friend," *New York Times*, March 14, 2019.

2 Netflix (@netflix), "We've made the very difficult decision not to renew One Day At A Time for a fourth season. The choice did not come easily — we spent several weeks trying to find a way to make another season work but in the end simply not enough people watched to justify another season," Twitter, March 14, 2019, https://x.com/netflix/status/1106246147771764736.

3 Favianna Rodriguez, Gloria Calderón Kellett, and Mike Royce, "ONE DAY AT A TIME: Inside 'The Politics Episode' // ATX TV . . . from the Couch! Summer Event Series," *ATX TV*, June 16, 2020, video, 54:17, https://youtu.be/f8v9RrDm-hos.

4 Cedric Robinson, *Black Marxism: The Making of the Black Radical Tradition* (University of North Carolina Press, 1983).

5 Stuart Hall, "New Ethnicities," in *Stuart Hall: Critical Dialogues in Cultural Studies*, ed. David Morley and Kuan-Hsing Chen (Routledge, 1996), 441–49.

6 Sara Ahmed, *On Being Included: Racism and Diversity in Institutional Life* (Duke University Press, 2012); Jodi Melamed, *Represent and Destroy: Rationalizing Violence in the New Racial Capitalism* (University of Minnesota Press, 2011).

7 Esteban del Río and Kristin C. Moran, "Remaking Television: *One Day at a Time*'s Digital Delivery and Latina/o Cultural Specificity," *Journal of Communication Inquiry* 44, no. 1 (January 2020): 5–25, https://doi.org/10.1177/0196859918825332.

8 Dana Mastro and Alexander Sink, "Portrayals of Latinos in the Media and the Effects of Exposure on Latino and Non-Latino Audiences," in *Race and Gender in Electronic Media: Content, Context, Culture*, ed. Rebecca Ann Lind (Routledge, 2017), 144–60.

9 Esteban del Río, "The Latina/o Problematic: Categories and Questions in Media Communication Research," *Communication Yearbook 30* (2006): 387–429, https://doi.org/10.1080/23808985.2006.11679062; Isabel Molina-Guzmán, *Latinas and Latinos on TV: Colorblind Comedy in the Post-Racial Network Era* (University of Arizona Press, 2018).

10 Mari Castañeda, "Applying Latina/o Critical Communication Theory to Anti-Blackness," *Race and Media: Critical Approaches*, ed. Lori Kido Lopez (New York University Press, 2020), 101–15.

11 Angharad N. Valdivia, "Latinas on Television and Film: Exploring the Limits and Possibilities of Inclusion," *Routledge Companion to Media and Gender*, ed. Cynthia Carter, Linda Steiner, and Lisa McLaughlin (Routledge, 2013), 578–88.

12 Arlene Dávila, *Latinos, Inc.: The Marketing and Making of a People* (University of California Press, 2001); Christopher Chávez, *Reinventing the Latino Television Viewer: Language, Ideology, and Practice* (Lexington Books, 2015).

13 Sean Campbell, *The Sitcoms of Norman Lear* (McFarland & Company, 2007).

14 del Río and Moran, "Remaking Television," 12.

15 Personal communication with Calderón Kellett, May 2, 2017.

16 Kristen J. Warner, "In the Time of Plastic Representation," *Film Quarterly* 71, no. 2 (2017): 32–37, https://filmquarterly.org.

17 Focus groups were conducted at a medium-size private university in Southern California. Participants' ages ranged from 19 to 22 and each focus group had between 4 and 7 students. All names are pseudonyms.

18 A program that provided legal immigration waivers to thousands of Cuban children who arrived in the United States between 1960 and 1962.

19 Bonnie Dow, *Prime-Time Feminism: Television, Media Culture, and the Women's Movement Since 1970* (University of Pennsylvania Press, 1996).

20 GLAAD is a non-profit organization that aims to monitor LGBTQ storytelling and offers awards for programming that promotes inclusive representations.

21 Maureen Ryan, "Why Netflix Should Renew 'One Day at a Time,'" *Variety*, March 18, 2018, www.variety.com.

22 Robinson, *Black Marxism*, 2.

23 Gloria Calderón Kellett (@everythinggloria), "HUGE favor: If you want to support me & the show then PLEASE watch & tell friends & family to watch at least FOUR episodes in the next few days. Netflix decides what gets picked up based on views. I love this show & love writing this relatable family. PLEASE WATCH! Thank you," Twitter, February 13, 2018, https://twitter.com/everythingloria/status/963526244871499776.

24 Sut Jhally and Justin Lewis, *Enlightened Racism: "The Cosby Show," Audiences, and the Myth of the American Dream* (Westview Press, 1992).

25 Isabel Molina-Guzmán, "#Oscarssowhite: How Stuart Hall Explains Why Nothing Changes in Hollywood and Everything is Changing," *Critical Studies in Media Communication* 33, no. 5 (2016): 438–54, https://doi.org/10.1080/15295036.2016.1227864.

26 Kristin C. Moran, "Is Changing the Language Enough? The Spanish-Language 'Alternative' in the USA" *Journalism: Theory, Practice and Criticism* 7, no. 3 (2006): 389–405, https://doi.org/10.1177/1464884906065522.

27 Brett White, "Netflix Canceled 'One Day at a Time' at the Peak of Its Popularity, Nielsen Report Reveals," *Decider*, May 7, 2019, https://decider.com.

PART III

Challenging White Nostalgia in Contemporary Reboots

9

Producing Intersectionality

Decoding Black Women's Identity in HBO's Watchmen

MEGHAN S. SANDERS AND TINA M. HARRIS

READING NOTE: Focusing on HBO's televisual reboot of the cinematic adaptation of the critically acclaimed graphic novel *Watchmen* based on the DC comic book series, Meghan S. Sanders and Tina M. Harris engage critical race theory (CRT) to explore the intersectionality created through the dramatic visual representation of its protagonist as a strong, ethical, Black woman. Sanders and Harris interpret the television producers' decision to flip the racial casting as an opportunity to focus on complex social justice issues, such as transgenerational racial trauma and racial identity politics, that highlight continuing structures of racism in the United States.

Introduction

Films in popular culture serve many purposes, the most obvious being to entertain. Alan McKee and colleagues suggest that various forms of media are critical in articulating identities and cultural values as well as challenging them.[1] In this regard, entertainment media is arguably a strong force in the overall media landscape. In addition to giving audiences an avenue for pleasure, entertainment media is a source of robust discussion of society's ills, highlighting some of the toughest challenges faced by organizations, governments, and society. There are audiences who watch and producers who create films that tell stories of world history from this perspective. Some examples of visual texts used to tell painful aspects of US history include *Roots* (1977), *Rosewood* (1999), and *Amistad* (1997).[2] Film scholars Mollie Murphy and Tina M. Harris argue that films are critical "in shaping public narratives about historical and contemporary racial relations."[3] Such texts are successful in educating audiences about true historic events largely excluded from school textbooks and erased from cultural memory for being "too traumatic" for descendants of oppressors, thus reinforcing the framing of systemic racism as being a part of the past.

A more recent visual text addressing past and present societal ills is the HBO series *Watchmen* (2019), a partially flipped reboot of the film based on the critical acclaimed graphic novel based on the DC comic book series by the same name. In the movie and the graphic novel, the primary protagonist is an immortal white man. The HBO series revolves around a Black woman. Show creator Damon Lindelof intricately and pointedly weaves in historic events within the fictionalized narrative to educate audiences about whiteness, systemic oppression, and racial trauma. *Watchmen* audiences are continually taken on a narrative journey between the past and the present as new superhero archetypes fight the evil forces of structural and overt racism. The narrative unfolds over nine episodes, and, as our critique will demonstrate, the raced and gendered (i.e., intersectional) identities of the main character, Angela Abar/Sister Night, are central to Lindelof's goals of challenging audiences to engage critically with the series and a counterimage of Black womanhood.

In this chapter, we explore how the creative workers on the 2019 HBO *Watchmen* series used television to offer audiences counternarratives to contemporary notions of a post-racial ideology. As discussed in the introduction, post-racial ideology assumes that racial differences are no longer salient in contemporary US politics and society. To carry out the analysis, we performed a circuit of culture analysis, exploring aspects of the series' production, representation in the narrative, and audience responses.[4] We also address how Lindelof used his white privilege to decenter whiteness and the familiar white savior complex to focus on a powerful intersectional identity of a Black female superhero that celebrates and affirms Black identity during an especially volatile sociopolitical time in the US. We also present additional themes present in the narrative.

Critical Race Theory, Intersectionality, and *Watchmen*

Critical race theory (CRT) provides a fruitful lens through which to understand the contributions *Watchmen* makes to enlightening audiences about institutional racism and systemic oppression. CRT was born through Harvard law school students' objection to the lack of racial diversity in the school's faculty and its curriculum: "CRT is the heir to both CLS [Critical Legal Studies] and traditional civil rights scholarship."[5] CRT is committed to both "being 'critical'" and "a vision of liberation from racism through right reason."[6] An applied theory used across disciplines, it provides scholars with a productive framework to develop a voice and create "narratives that challenge racism and the structures of oppression."[7] The framework is built on six themes: (1) a recognition that racism is endemic to (North) American life; (2) an express skepticism of dominant legal claims of neutrality, objectivity, colorblindness, and meritocracy; (3) a challenge to ahistoricism in the law; (4) a recognition of the experiential knowledge of POC; (5) an interdisciplinary theory; and (6) the elimination of racial oppression.[8]

Visual images in mass media are a vehicle for potentially removing long-standing racial barriers.[9] Scholars argue that critiquing the media with CRT fosters critical race media literacy while deconstructing and contextualizing media images, power relations, and systems of oppression such as racism, sexism, and classism.[10] Thus, CRT simultaneously promotes critical media literacy and social justice, which can inform dialogue about race and racism among audience members, raise social consciousness regarding oppression, and mobilize people toward activism.[11] While CRT emphasizes race, its limitations lie in the exclusion of gender.

"Intersectionality" denotes "the various ways in which race and gender interact to shape the multiple dimensions of Black women's employment experiences."[12] The concept has been applied to the racism and classism existent in the mainstream/white feminist movement. Feminists collectively recognized patriarchal power yet often ignored or minimized other forms of oppression and discrimination experienced by Black women. Crenshaw's introduction of intersectionality captures the multilayered and complex realities of Black women and helps scholars explore these unique identities in valuable ways. This analysis of *Watchmen*, of its dominant themes, and social media reactions draws on the basic assumptions proposed by CRT and applies an intersectional lens, thus contributing further evidence to research that finds that that television shows and films are potentially effective and powerful tools for educating audiences about systemic oppression.

Socially Conscious Entertainment and the Social Justice Warriors

Entertainment psychology research discusses how entertainment can be used in multiple ways. Fictional stories explicitly focused on historical or contemporary social issues include them as subplots or include metaphorical references to social problems (e.g., *Avatar*) and may make abstract ideas more concrete and easier for audiences to understand, especially for those who feel they have little power or efficacy in addressing said problems.[13] Arguably, such media experiences can encourage reflection, contemplation, and action in ways that other media forms cannot. Such socially conscious entertainment, though not always created with persuasive intent in mind, can effect social change by increasing awareness about an issue, shift social norms, or even change behavior because they encourage connectedness with others, understanding, and cultural sensitivity.[14]

While television and film can illustrate negative aspects of interracial interactions and lack of fair representation, they can also illustrate the deconstruction of racial and social hierarchies.[15] The realm of comics is no different. Although heralded for their action, creativity, and fantastical elements, comic book narratives and their multimedia offshoots have historically and frequently provided commentary on race and politics.[16] For example, the anti-mutant prejudice seen in *X-Men* served as a metaphor for racism, antisemitism, and homophobia, and the Galactic Empire in the *Star Wars* series represented fascism. These depictions vary in how they address political messages and what social and political issues they address, yet they still center white heroes as winners and racial minorities as sidekicks and villains.[17] The picture is often bleaker for Black women. Black superheroines are often portrayed as bestial, hypersexual, and exotic in their connection to the African continent and mystic cultures (e.g., voodoo, animal totemism, nature, etc.), unlike their male and white female counterparts.[18] Additionally, many of these superheroines are members of superteams and rarely the focal point of the story (e.g., Storm, Pantha).

Rare exceptions to the lack of well-roundedness are characters such as Luke Cage and Black Panther (including T'Challa and his sister Shuri). In the contemporary comics, Cage is a husband, a father, *and* a superhero whom his community trusts to fight urban blight and the Avengers trust to lead them. More recent reboots of series featuring the characters Vixen and Black Panther (with Shuri taking the mantle) did so without excessive fetishization of cultures or bodies.[19] In these instances, these stories can improve the self-esteem and self-efficacy (i.e., belief in one's own abilities) of Black audience members.[20] Black children have historically used comic strips, cartoons, and comic books as a source for witnessing Black heroism and a means to become something bigger than themselves.[21] More broadly, "Superheroes reveal some of our most basic beliefs about morality and justice, our conceptions of gender and sexuality, and our attitudes towards ethnicity and nationality."[22] As the literature demonstrates, socially conscious entertainment media have great potential in shaping audience perceptions of others and/or themselves as racialized beings. This is particularly the case for graphic novels and their related stories.

The Original *Watchmen* Series

The original *Watchmen* story was released as a twelve-issue comic book by DC Comics. It was later released as a graphic novel and was named one of *Time* magazine's 100 best English-language novels of the last century. A film adaptation was released by Warner Brothers in 2009. The original story was written by Alan Moore in 1986 and takes place in an alternate 1985 where Richard Nixon is still president of the United States, and the white superheroes are outlawed public figures unless they work for the government. In this universe, the US won the Vietnam War, Watergate never happened, and the world is on the brink of World War III. The story is told primarily from the perspective of five mostly retired US superheroes investigating the death of one of their own; however, the core of the story is a commentary on what was happening in the US at the time it was written.

The original graphic novel and 2009 film boldly addressed political messages while following the characters from the 1940s through the 1980s. The story features "regular" people without superpowers and technology who have taken it upon themselves to decide what is best for humanity. These themes are simultaneously a critique of whom societies trust to guard the fate of humanity and of Reaganism. Readers and viewers are ultimately forced to question how one addresses social and moral concerns and explores the motives for one's actions. But the story also features a wealth of messages about government skepticism, power politics, distrust of authority, and a conservative moral code exemplified in many ways in the character Rorschach.[23] The 2009 film was more of a retelling or adaptation of the graphic novel, staying fairly true to its stories. While it featured social commentary, it was more political in nature, with subthemes related to energy resources. It did not feature themes related to racism, nor did it prominently feature the women characters. The main characters were also predominantly white men, and characters of color were referenced only as historical figures who were no longer alive during the story's current events.

In the *Watchmen* universe, only three of the main characters in the novel and film were prominently featured. The main woman character in the earlier stories was not a superhero and served as more of a secondary character. The HBO series focused on a new main character, a Black woman, presenting a race and gender flip for the story's protagonist. Like Moore, Lindelof wanted to tell a story through *Watchmen* the series that reflected cultural anxieties and shone a critical lens on what was currently happening in the US. In rebooting the series, he wanted to tell a contemporary story in the same universe as the original, focusing on the 2019 equivalent of a nuclear standoff: racism and policing.[24]

HBO's *Watchmen*

The HBO series *Watchmen* premiered in October 2019. Between live viewing, replays, and streaming views, the show became the network's most-watched series premiere since *Westworld* in 2012.[25] The series follows the tradition of recent superhero films and television series (e.g., *Black Panther* [2018], *Luke Cage* [2016–2018], and *Black Lightning* [2017–2021]) by centering an African or African American superhero valiantly fighting for social justice in a dystopian society.[26] The series picks up in 2019 in the same timeline as the original novel. Robert Redford has been president for decades, a version of reparations has been paid to a subgroup of Black people, and guns are strictly controlled. At the center of this story is Angela Abar/Sister Night (played by Academy Award winner Regina King), a Black police detective-turned-vigilante in Tulsa, Oklahoma, who investigates the murder of a friend and fellow officer. For years, police have worn masks as a form of privacy and protection, starting when a white supremacist group (the Seventh Kavalry) slaughtered a large group of police officers, forcing many surviving officers to leave the force. Angela is married to a man named Cal, who is a stay-at-home father. Audiences later learn that Cal is really Dr. Manhattan, a former physicist who obtained near-omnipotent powers after a laboratory accident. After years of living with these powers, he had developed distance from personal relationships and humankind but found a reconnection with Angela, whom he decided to give up his powers for. It is these powers that story's primary antagonists and white supremacists wish to wield to gain absolute power.

According to *TV Guide*'s Keith Phipps, Abar is "a woman determined to work for justice who has to continually re-evaluate what that means."[27] Much like the graphic novel's authors, Lindelof wanted the story to have a beginning, middle, and end (a classic narrative arc) that took to task ideas about and behaviors associated with racial dynamics in the US in a non-condescending way.[28] While there are significant white characters and homages to the original storyline, the series deviates from its predecessors by decentering whiteness. In doing so, it also brings to the forefront (and back to life) a secondary Black character from the original graphic novel and film: Hooded Justice. The limited series immediately forces its audience to contemplate the connections between race and power, and what happens when the powerful place themselves above the law. The series sets this tone by beginning with the true story of the 1921 Tulsa Massacre.

The Tulsa Massacre of 1921

In the early 1900s, 1910s, and 1920s, a number of racially motivated massacres took place around the US, including in Washington, DC, Atlanta, Chicago, Knoxville, New York, and East St. Louis. These attacks resulted in beatings, deaths, and destruction of primarily Black-owned properties and/or those frequented by Black individuals. To connect with this history, *Watchmen* begins with a domestic attack that many audience members and even the show's creator and writers reported having little knowledge of prior to their involvement with the series.

In 1921 in Tulsa, Oklahoma, one of the worst race-based attacks in US history occurred. More than 2,000 Black residents populated the area known as the Greenwood District. This district spanned thirty-five to forty blocks of business and residential properties, and had its own school system and more than 600 businesses, including grocery stores, restaurants, movie theaters, and hospitals. It was considered one of the wealthiest, if not the wealthiest, Black communities in the US. Several residents were multimillionaires, earning the area the nickname "Black Wall Street." Much of the community's prosperity was attributed to the drive, motivation, and entrepreneurial spirit of soldiers returning from World War I and feeling a need and ability to open businesses serving the Black community. However, the thriving area was resented by many Whites, who felt that this accomplishment of the "American Dream" gave the Black residents too much value, esteem, and worth within the community.

Tensions came to a head when a White woman alleged a Black teenager attacked her in an elevator. A lynch mob formed, and the town became a powder keg of violence. Greenwood residents were killed in drive-by shootings, by decapitation, and by air bombings. Homes and businesses were looted and burned, leveling Black Tulsa and leaving an estimated $1.5 million in damages (around $20 million by today's standards). Martial law was declared, the National Guard was activated, and survivors were placed in prison camps for as long as eight days. They were forced to clean up the ravaged area and forbidden from talking about what happened, or they would be run out of town. Official documents state that over 300 Black individuals were killed and buried in unmarked mass graves, though many believe the real number to be much higher, as many public records were burned after the Massacre. Black and White descendants alike have family stories of bodies being dumped in the Arkansas River. More mass graves have been discovered as recently as late 2019, which attests to the pervasiveness of the Massacre.

The 2019 *Watchmen* series picks up thirty years after the end of the graphic novel as a continuation of that story *and* of the story of Tulsa with an alternate present day, as though the Tulsa Massacre was a well-known and ingrained part of US history and within the *Watchmen* story universe. In line with CRT, the narrative illustrates how racism is endemic to everyday life. This is markedly different from other race films that often "romanticize racism, recuperate stereotypes, and promote the ideology of a postracial 'colorblind' society."[29]

Watchmen possesses transformative power through the many texts and subtexts presented through Angela's story. We use thematic analysis to make sense of the rich data in the nine hour-long episodes of the series. Thematic analysis is used for "identifying, analyzing, organizing, describing, and reporting themes found within a data set."[30] Scholars are able to produce "a rich and detailed, yet complex account of data"[31] while also providing a structured approach to managing and interpreting the data. Space limitations prohibit us from presenting all of the themes we identified; therefore, we provide a few exemplars demonstrating how Angela's intersectionality is used to dismantle racism in practical and powerful ways.

Emerging Themes from *Watchmen*

Intersectional superhero is the first dominant theme observed throughout the series. Angela is never explicitly described in this way, but her on-screen presence throughout the series frames her as intersectional. In episode 1 ("It's Summer and We're Running Out of Ice"), viewers are introduced to Angela and her family. She is a counterimage because she is relatable and does not perpetuate stereotyped images often associated with Black women. The intersectional superhero theme captures the complexities of Angela's raced and gendered identities that are critical to how she identifies. She is immediately forced to navigate these multiple identities while also fulfilling her duties as a superhero/police officer fighting the white supremacist militia, the Seventh Kavalry. Her role of mother to white children is a race flip of the mammy trope in that she is their adoptive and actual mother, rather than a domestic caretaker. Instead, we learn she assumes motherhood because her partner and his wife were murdered, which left the children orphaned. Angela and her husband, Cal, raise them as their own. Throughout the series, we also see that she has a healthy, loving relationship with Cal that defies the jezebel stereotype, thus presenting a Black woman as a multidimensional, beautifully complex being.

The first episode sets the stage for understanding the breadth and depth of Angela's wholeness. She is viewed and treated as the strength of the entire community, as illustrated by her interactions with the different characters, and she is incredibly intelligent, as evidenced by her ability to unravel the conspiracy taking place throughout the series. So, like the archetypal hero, she exhibits strength, cunning, and leadership. But she also has a tortured past, witnessing the violent deaths of her parents and surviving an attack in her own home. This episode begins with Angela doing a science demonstration for children at her son's elementary school. She appears to have a "normal" life, as she answers the children's difficult questions about her life as an officer, which many believe to be in the past. The scene eventually shifts to Angela assuming her role as mother upon returning home with her son, greeting her daughter and husband on the lawn, but then dashing off to assume her superhero duties. She seamlessly retreats to her basement where she "suits up" to become Sister Night and join the other police officers at an emergency meeting about the Kavalry. When she and the other officers learn of the Kavalry's uprising, Angela takes charge and strategizes with her colleagues about how to ambush them and thwart any attacks being planned. She is a very vocal authority figure amongst them. At the meeting's conclusion, we see her shift back into the roles of mother, wife, and family friend as she and her family share a joyous dinner with her boss, and friend, Judd Crawford. They all appear to be enjoying their time together, which illustrates her ability to transition between her roles and recognize their value in defining her as a woman and in relation to others. She is a superhero, yet she is able to balance all of the roles and fight evil in the process. Angela reflects intersectionality through membership in two historically marginalized groups (womanhood and Black racial identity) and actively fighting the systems that define who she is perceived and understood to be.

Interracial accomplices is also a very prominent theme. Throughout the series Angela has close personal and/or professional relationships with non-Black characters. Some of them, as is the case with Judd and Looking Glass, end in betrayal, while others (like her relationship with Lady Trieu) are relationships of convenience. The one we will focus on most for this theme is Angela's relationship with FBI Agent Laurie Blake. Early on, viewers witness an antagonistic relationship between Angela and Agent Blake (introduced in episode 3), who is investigating the murder of Judd Crawford. Laurie is determined to identify the assailant. She believes Angela is the culprit and begins to aggressively pursue and interrogate her. Laurie's suspicions seem somewhat valid because of Angela and Judd's friendship. The assumption is bolstered upon learning Angela snuck into Judd's home and secretly discovered a Klan robe, creating questions about Judd himself and his relationship to the Kavalry.

These two characters are juxtaposed with one another. Similar to the original story, Blake is the daughter of two of the original Minutemen and she has a romantic history with Dr. Manhattan (who is currently living as Cal, Angela's husband). Unlike Angela, she is very aware of her past and lineage. But it is Angela who has the most stable personal relationship. Dr. Manhattan gave up his seeming omnipotence out of love for Angela, choosing to live as a Black man—something he would not do for Laurie. While both are strong women in the upper ranks of law enforcement, that is where their allyship ends for most of the series. A grudging respect but high suspicion and lack of trust is reminiscent of the tension between white feminists and womanists. For example, in episodes 3–5, audiences witness Angela and Laurie's deepening commitment to moral righteousness despite the obstacles faced. They continue working independently and sometimes antagonistically toward that end. As their paths continue to cross and the women remain suspicious of each other's motives, they engage in a power struggle as they fight for the same things: truth and justice. After Angela is betrayed by fellow police officer Looking Glass, who tells Laurie that Angela is responsible for Judd's death, Angela believes she is in the fight alone. Laurie joins forces with Angela after learning the real killer's identity and that Judd's widow Jane was also a racist, thus shifting them from enemies to accomplices (episode 7). They do not explicitly articulate an allegiance to each other; rather, the audience is primed by the story arc to believe there is an unspoken mutual agreement that they are in this fight together for justice, racial and otherwise. Laurie is the accomplice (not ally) because she and Angela have gender in common, but her white privilege makes her unable to completely empathize with racism and the Black experience. Through a critical lens, one can reasonably conclude that decentering Laurie, though she is a main character in the original *Watchmen* story, is Lindelof's liberatory move to illustrate real-world tensions in the feminist movement and directly acknowledge how it ignores racism. Similarly, it may be concluded that centering Angela in the narrative allows Lindelof to spotlight two forms of systemic oppression through intersectionality, thereby helping audiences understand and visualize how multiple oppressions shape reality and worldviews for Black individuals, women, and Black women. It must be noted that audiences are compelled to view Angela as a groundbreaking character reminiscent of *Scandal*'s Olivia Pope. Both women are revolutionary in reflecting the multidimensionality of Blackness and womanness while centering Black feminism, social justice, and power—both political/societal and physical—in ways mainstream media does not often do.[32]

Transgenerational trauma manifests when Angela meets her grandfather William (also known as Hooded Justice), who has been subjected to decades of vile racism in Tulsa. Racial trauma as the psychological injury overwhelms a person's capacity to cope. It is caused by experiencing firsthand or vicariously witnessing a racially motivated incident.[33] In Black families, this racial trauma can become transgenerational as stories and struggles are passed down from generation to generation. Angela literally lives her grandfather's experience in episode 6 when she overdoses on "nostalgia pills" made for William. The pills were originally developed to help individuals with memory-related diseases retain their memories, personalities, and identities. Unlike the ways in which nostalgia has been discussed in other chapters in this volume, the nostalgia pills allow for someone to relive their own memories rather than solely experiencing a great affection for and reflection on a broad, abstract time period. In taking the pills made for someone else, Angela is allowed to live her grandfather's memories and abuses (beginning with the Tulsa Massacre) from his perspective. The audience joins her on this first-person perspective journey. The unfolding scenes include flashbacks to William's traumatic childhood and adulthood experiences of fighting racism and white supremacy in the community as well as within the police force. William's subjection to multiple forms of racial abuse (i.e., lynching, beating, police brutality) is physically, psychologically, and emotionally damaging and results in "cumulative racism" (i.e., accumulation of experiences with racism over time) that fuels his rage against the perpetrators and society.[34] Cumulative racism is symbolized by the nostalgia pills, and Angela swallowing them is the transference of generational trauma. Through the pills, William also passes on his superhero status to Angela because of their lineage and shared Blackness, which consumes Angela and cements her commitment to confronting racism and white supremacy. Culture writer Jen Chaney also argues that the pills illustrate "the ways in which history regularly gets whitewashed and sanitized in American culture, and how nostalgia—the sense that things were better back in the day, which is usually only true if you happen to be a straight, white, Christian man—makes it that much harder for social progress to happen."[35]

Transgenerational trauma is evident in Angela's interactions with William during her "nostalgia" pill overdose. Angela is fighting racism as an officer and superhero by actively working against the Kavalry. Her trauma is rooted in the murder-bombing of her parents in Vietnam and her grandmother's death, which leaves her an orphan (episode 7). But it is also rooted in her grandfather's experiences. Audiences get glimpses into her lifelong racial trauma and struggles through her intersectional experiences in a racist patriarchal country. Viewers are also privy to differences in William's and Angela's lived experiences in facing white supremacy as a Black man and a Black woman with an intersecting identity.

Thematic Analysis of Audience Tweets

To explore audience responses to the narrative's themes and subtexts regarding race, we analyzed audience tweets posted the week of the series premiere (October 20–26, 2019). The series premiere was chosen because it included the largest volume of social media engagement regarding the series. Posts about the series decreased substantially with each subsequent episode. Tweets posted by news organizations, nonprofits, and foundations, as well as messages that simply shared links to information or news stories without providing a statement or opinion, were not included. This yielded a total of 473 tweets for analysis, all of which were analyzed. We gathered texts because they provided real-time and live responses.

Only one post during the series' premiere week referenced Angela's intersecting identities, and only to mention that the character had an intersectional identity as a Black woman. The majority of the messages focused on overall storyline, primarily around the Tulsa Massacre. By opening the series with the Tulsa Massacre, *Watchmen* challenges ahistoricism in the law as articulated by CRT. Audience response not only reflects the creator's, writers', and actors' intentions to create genuine interest in learning more about the Massacre, but also alludes to questions of how history is recorded, whom it serves, and the need to remember even the most heinous of human atrocities so as not to repeat them. This connection was apparent during the time of data collection, where "Black Wall Street" rather than the name of series was trending. Many tweets expressed audience surprise at not having previously been aware of the Massacre, and gratitude toward the series for enlightening them.

Some responses reflected a sense of frustration for not having learned about these events in school, while in others there was a lack of surprise and a resigned acceptance. Although the reenactment was not what audiences were expecting, there was an appreciation for the needed history lesson and for providing a framework from which to honestly discuss racism in the US, both historical and current. Users also created a sort of historical society around the Massacre, often sharing links to news articles and websites with more information about the historical event, and other largely unknown events in Black and US history. This observation mimics the purpose of the nostalgia pills, which Lady Trieu says she really created "so people could learn from the past, to evolve and transform and better themselves."[36] This education was not without pain, as a number of posts suggest the presence of transgenerational trauma in real life. Some viewers said that watching the recreation of the Tulsa Massacre elicited a similar sadness and pain of watching videos of police killings of Blacks that are still occurring generations later. Tweets also included references to the series educating white people whether they wanted or not, and humor in the backlash of some whites, particularly *Watchmen* "fanboys," against the inclusion of race as such an integral element of the series.

Although the majority of audience responses on websites such as Metacritic and Rotten Tomatoes were either critical or lukewarm, in the case of active Twitter engagement, only a minority (23 of 473) were negative. Many of these posts were in response to others' messages, as opposed to originating with the user. Most of the negativity was in regard to the series' emphasis on race relations and racism. Some felt the inclusion of the storyline was a gimmick to pander to liberal ideologies and/serve as liberal propaganda, and encouraging further racial division and a "race war" in the US. Others argued that the storyline was not representative of and even tarnished the *Watchmen* canon, focusing too much of the series on politics.

Conclusion

Like other texts discussed in the introduction as the impetus for this volume, the HBO iteration of *Watchmen* was helmed by white men creators and producers. But in departure from them, discussions of racism are front and center in all other aspects. The limited series goes beyond a flipped reboot and serves as a case study of how entertainment texts can effectively counter racial nostalgia that flipped reboots discussed throughout this volume seemed to elicit from audiences. Based on the data shared here, the series was generally received positively by new audiences who shared appreciation for the series discussing racism head-on, even with the dissatisfaction of longtime core audience. Despite the reboot using properties with an established base, the approach and focus of the storytelling as well as the casting was a risk to HBO given the political climate in the US and increasing anti-Black sentiment globally.

Specifically, *Watchmen* is a powerful visual text because it offers audiences an alternative conceptualization of Black womanhood through the character of Angela Abar/Sister Night. Though our critique here only scratches the surface, it reveals the series' potential as a visual text to highlight systemic oppression through the lens of an intersectional character. She is unlike other superheroes because she does not have supernatural or extraordinary strengths. Instead, her strengths lie in the fact that she is the human embodiment of the exceptional intellectual, and possess moral, and emotional strength necessary for dismantling systemic oppression. Angela and other superheroes share a strong moral code that drives their commitment to fighting for the powerless and against the evil powers dedicated to the demise of humanity. Angela differs from white superheroes through her explicit engagement in orchestrated efforts to fight institutional racism and nonconformity to the mythical caricature of "superheroness." She is fighting against evil; however, it is her life's mission to do so from an intersectional positionality that is new for some audiences. Her on-screen presence is powerful because her femaleness and Blackness are strategically and effectively used by Lindelof and the show writers to completely decenter whiteness. Lindelof offers audiences a counterimage of both superheroes and Black women. Angela resists conforming to the familiar tropes of the mammy, Jezebel, or Sapphire and introduces audiences to a character who defies the negative connotations associated with her intersectionality. Moreover, she possesses relatable, human qualities that serve to represent, affirm, and empower historically marginalized groups.

Brett Stoudt argues that privilege must be further scrutinized in order to deconstruct institutional racism.[37] He further noted that "the absence of this critical gaze helps to normalize the structures that reproduce asymmetrical advantages and protect its benefactors from a sense of culpability or urgency towards their contributions to injustice."[38] Failure to illuminate how privilege is challenged perpetuates the existing racial hierarchy, thereby limiting the potential for CRT and other theoretical frameworks to level the playing field. In interviews, Lindelof expressed anxiety about being the voice of intersectionality as a White male.[39] Nevertheless, he boldly used his White male privilege to center a platform for a marginalized reality, which was achieved by having a sixteen-person writing team that was 75 percent women and writers of color.[40]

In keeping with CRT, Lindelof purposely presented a narrative from the viewpoint of an intersectional woman to address serious issues he felt were missing from public discourse about race and television in general.[41] He used the tragedy of the 1921 Tulsa Massacre to push the proverbial envelope and challenge the audience to deal with real-world issues. As noted by the analysis of the tweets and show reviews, some "mainstream" (read "white") audiences were resistant to the narrative because they believed it to be too political, though it must also be noted that fans of the original story did not take issue with the political and social commentary present there. The double standard highlights and normalizes the belief that films where whiteness and maleness are framed are set up as the ideal. It is our contention that Lindelof aimed to disrupt this approach to entertainment and successfully introduced a powerful superhero character who disrupts audience sensibilities regarding otherness. Moreover, this new narrative deals with the hard truths that audiences, the film industry, and many others are unwilling to face. The retelling of the 1921 Tulsa Massacre in *Watchmen* is a powerful narrative used to demonstrate that there are events in US history typically omitted from textbooks and cultural memory. The retelling of the Tulsa Massacre resonated particularly with the majority of the audience, as evidenced by the social media analysis. Many posts included statements and questions regarding one of the most heinous crimes in US history, an event we still do not know the full effects of to this day and perhaps never will, as much information was erased from official documents. The fictional account included in the series illustrates entertainment can not only provide a sense of enlightenment and education, but it also serves to prompt audiences to question the status quo when it comes to who is in charge of and allowed to tell history, and the need for honest reckoning with a violent, racist past and present. The centering of a Black female superhero amplifies the salience of this message in ways that the usual formula (white male savior) does not. In essence, Lindelof engages "the characters to represent and problematize the barriers that have and continue to divide people of color and whites, making the invisible visible."[42]

Lindelof and King, through her portrayal of Angela, challenge audiences to perceive Black women as powerful beings who defy preexisting notions of what it means to be Black and female. More importantly, the series functions as a narrative critical "in shaping public narratives about historical and contemporary racial relations."[43] *Watchmen* pointedly addresses systemic oppression and white supremacy during a time in US history where race relations are volatile, and BIPOC and some well-meaning whites are working together to dismantle various societal structures. We specifically identified the dominant themes of intersectional superhero, interracial accomplices, transgenerational trauma, and identity politics that collectively speak to the reality of racism through visual text. By using Angela in the superhero genre, *Watchmen* is evidence of the power of mass media to challenge perceptions of otherness while decentering whiteness in mainstream entertainment.

Discussion Questions

1. Identify three elements of the racially and gendered flipped reboot of *Watchmen* that decenter whiteness and challenge dominant Hollywood representations of superheroes.
2. Discuss how Lindelof's production decisions and the storytelling in the flipped *Watchmen* reboot challenge the contemporary racial nostalgia.

NOTES

1 Alan McKee et al., "Defining Entertainment: An Approach," *Creative Industries Journal* 7, no. 2 (2014): 108, http://doi.org/10.1080/17510694.2014.962932.

2 Jeremy Stoddard, Alan Marcus, and David Hicks, "The Burden of Historical Representation: The Case of/for Indigenous Film," *History Teacher* 48, no. 1 (2014): 15, www.jstor.org/stable/43264376.

3 Mollie K. Murphy and Tina M. Harris, "White Innocence and Black Subservience: The Rhetoric of White Heroism in *The Help*," *Howard Journal of Communication* 29, no. 1 (2017): 1–14, https://doi.org/10.1080/10646175.2017.1327378.

4 Paul du Gay et al., *Doing Cultural Studies: The Story of the Sony Walkman*, 2nd ed. (Sage, 2013).

5 Angela P. Harris, "Foreword: The Jurisprudence of Reconstruction," *California Law Review* 82, no. 4 (1994): 743, https://doi.org/10.2307/3480931.

6 Harris, "Foreword," 743.

7 Christopher B. Knaus, "Shut Up and Listen: Applied Critical Race Theory in the Classroom," *Race Ethnicity and Education* 12, no. 2 (2009): 142, https://doi.org/10.1080/13613320902995426.

8 Adrienne D. Dixson and Celia K. Rousseau, "And We Still Are Not Saved: Critical Race Theory in Education 10 Years Later," *Race Ethnicity and Education* 8 (2005): 70, https://doi.org/10.1080/1361332052000340971.

9 Tina M. Harris and Kirsten Weber, "Reversal of Privilege: Deconstructing Imperialism, Racism, and Power in the Film *White Man's Burden*," *Communication Law Review* 10, no. 1 (2010): 55.

10 Tara J. Yosso, "Critical Race Media: Challenging Deficit Discourse About Chicanas/os," *Journal of Popular Film and Television* 30, no. 1 (2002): 59.

11 See Harris and Weber, "Reversal of Privilege"; Sonia Saraiya, "HBO's *Watchmen* Ambitiously Reimagines a Classic," *Vanity Fair*, October 17, 2019, www.vanityfair.com.

12 Kimberle Crenshaw, "Demarginalizing the Intersection of Race and Sex: A Black Feminist Critique of Antidiscrimination Doctrine, Feminist Theory and Antiracist Politics," *University of Chicago Legal Forum* (1989): 139.

13 Albert Bandura, "Social Cognitive Theory of Mass Communication." In *Media Effects: Advances in Theory and Research*, 3rd ed., ed. Jennings Bryant and Mary Beth Oliver (Routledge, 2009), 94–124.

14 Meghan S. Sanders et al., "Entertainment Media and Social Consciousness," in *The Oxford Handbook of Entertainment Theory*, ed. Peter Vorderer and Cristoph Klimmt (Oxford University Press, 2021), 781–98.

15 Susan E. Kirley, *Typical Girls: The Rhetoric of Womanhood in Comic Strips* (Ohio University Press, 2021), 134.

16 Dani Di Placido, "Who Is HBO's 'Watchmen' for, Exactly?," *Forbes*, December 3, 2019, www.forbes.com.

17 Sheena C. Howard and Ronald L. Jackson II, "Introduction," in *Black Comics: Politics of Race and Representation*, ed. Sheena C. Howard and Ronald L. Jackson II (Bloomsbury Press, 2013), 1–8.

18 Jeffrey A. Brown, "Panthers and Vixens: Black Superheroines, Sexuality, and Stereotypes in Contemporary Comic Books," in *Black Comics: Politics of Race and Representation*, 134.

19 Brown, "Panthers and Vixens."

20 See Albert Bandura, "Self-Efficacy Mechanism in Human Agency," *American Psychology* 37, no. 2 (1982): 122–47; Carolyn A. Stroman, "Television Viewing and Self-Concept Among Black Children," *Journal of Broadcasting & Electronic Media* 30, no. 1 (1986): 87–93, https://doi.org/10.1080/08838158609386610.

21 Howard and Jackson, "Introduction."

22 Brown, "Panthers and Vixens," 133.

23 Marc DiPaolo, *War, Politics and Superheroes: Ethics and Propaganda in Comics and Film* (McFarland & Company, 2011).

24 Emily St. James, "HBO's *Watchmen* Tells Stories About America's Racist Past in America's Racist Present," *Vox*, October 20, 2019, www.vox.com.

25 Alex Welch, "Sunday Cable Ratings: 'Watchmen' Debuts, 'The Walking Dead' Dips Again," *TV by the Numbers*, October 22, 2019, https://tvbythenumbers.zap2it.com.

26 Dino-Ray Ramos, "'Watchmen' Premiere Draws 1.5 Million Viewers, Delivering HBO's Strongest Digital Debut Since 'Westworld,'" *Deadline*, October 21, 2019, https://deadline.com.

27 Keith Phipps, "Watchmen Review: Damon Lindelof's Take is Custom-Fitted for Our Effed-Up World," *TV Guide*, October 15, 2019, www.tvguide.com.

28 St. James, "HBO's *Watchmen* Tells Stories About America's Racist Past in America's Racist Present."

29 Murphy and Harris, "White Innocence and Black Subservience."

30 Lorelli S. Nowell et al., "Thematic Analysis: Striving to Meet the Trustworthiness Criteria," *International Journal of Qualitative Methods* 16, no. 1 (2017): 1–13, https://doi.org/10.1177/1609406917733847.

31 Nowell et al., "Thematic Analysis," 2.

32 See Kristina Brüning, "Olivia Pope: A Black Post-Feminist Subject? Analyzing *Scandal*'s Intersecting Post-Feminist and Colorblind Discourses," *Feminist Media Studies* 19, no. 4 (2019): 463–78, https://doi.org/10.1080/14680777.2018.1508049; Tina M. Harris et al., "'It's Handled!': The Complex Intersection of Race and Gender in Scandal's Olivia Pope," in *Gladiators in Suits: Race, Gender, and the Politics of Representation in "Scandal,"* ed. Kimberly R. Moffitt et al. (Syracuse University Press, 2019), 304.
33 Thema Bryant-Davis, "Healing Requires Recognition: The Case for Race-Based Traumatic Stress," *Counseling Psychologist* 35, no. 1 (2007): 138.
34 Tina M. Harris and Kyle Stanley, "Identity Politics of Blackness in the (Mass) Communication Classroom and Beyond," in *The Routledge Handbook of Ethnicity and Race in Communication*, ed. Bernadette Marie Calafell and Shinsuke Eguchi (Routledge, 2024).
35 Jen Chaney, "*Watchmen* Beautifully Wrestles with Toxic Nostalgia," *Vulture*, November 24, 2019, www.vulture.com.
36 *Watchmen*, season 1, episode 5, "Little Fear of Lightning," written by Damon Lindelof and Carly Wray, directed by Steph Green, aired November 17, 2019, on HBO.
37 Brett G. Stoudt, "The Role of Language & Discourse in the Investigation of Privilege: Using Participatory Action Research to Discuss Theory, Develop Methodology, & Interrupt Power," *Urban Review* 41, no. 1 (2009): 8.
38 Stoudt, "The Role of Language & Discourse," 8.
39 Braxton, Greg, "*Watchmen*'s Provocative Portrait of Race in America has its Own Creator Worried," *Los Angeles Times*, October 20, 2019, www.latimes.com.
40 St. James, "HBO's *Watchmen* Tells Stories."
41 Yosso, "Critical Race Media," 53
42 Harris and Weber, "Reversal of Privilege," 7.
43 Murphy and Harris, "White Innocence and Black Subservience," 49.

10

Contesting the Flipped Rebooting of *Charmed*

ISABEL MOLINA-GUZMÁN

READING NOTE: Flipping the ethnic, gender, racial, or sexual identities of original programs comes with rewards and risks. Rebooted programs with such flips hold the opportunity to bring back audiences of the original while targeting a new, more diverse generation of viewers. With a focus on racial nostalgia during a moment of increasing white nationalism, Isabel Molina-Guzmán focuses on the reboots' online anti-fandom and opposition by the original actors. In doing so, she highlights how disruptions to Hollywood's reproduction of racial and gender inequality in flipped reboots are challenged by actors who financially benefit and audiences who are comforted by television's normative whiteness.

Introduction

Twenty years after the premier of The WB's *Charmed* (1998–2006), its fans received notice of The CW's "fierce, funny, feminist" Latina/x reboot (2018–2022). News of the reboot was met with wicked resistance by fans of the original show (OG *Charmed*), who circulated an online petition, and by original cast member Holly Marie Combs, who launched a Twitter campaign against the reboot. At the same time, some Latina/x audiences and critics also challenged the casting and marketing of the reboot because it only featured one Latina-identified actress.[1] The debate between audiences speaks to the complex nature of racial, ethnic, and gender inequality in contemporary Hollywood rebooted television. The premier of the rebooted *Charmed*, like many flipped reboots, became caught in the conflict between the reproduction of white privilege in the television industry, global nationalist politics grounded in Euro-centered racial nostalgia, and the increasing expectations of ethnic and racial minority audiences who desire increased visibility and media representations.

Combs, who played middle sister Piper, and fans of the OG *Charmed* accused the rebooted *Charmed* of erasing the feel-good, middle-class, white-women-centered narratives of the original's Millennial vibe. As an example of the reproduction of white privilege in television reboots, Combs and OG fans publicly communicated their unhappiness with the reboot's failure to include the original white cast and producers, none of whom were invited to be involved in the reboot production. In other words, instead of a flipped reboot, Combs and OG fans expected a revival of the original show featuring its white women cast, characters, and original producers. On the other side of the debate, some Latina and queer Latinx critics and audiences took umbrage with CW executives' marketing of the show as a Latina *Charmed*.[2] For these audiences and reviewers, the lack of authentic or "real" Latina actors drew into question whether the reboot was indeed a Latina/x show. Instead, the marketing of the show as a Latina *Charmed* was perceived as a gratuitous attempt to lure Latina/x audiences while hiring Afro-Caribbean and mixed-race Canadian actresses to play US Latina characters. Only one of the main actors identified as Puerto Rican.

In this chapter, I situate the production and narrative structures of the OG *Charmed* within its postfeminist ethos to analyze a representative set of Twitter and Choice.org posts by OG cast members and reboot anti-fans. Specifically, I focus on tweets and comments that favored the white cast, storylines, and postfeminist values of the original or decried the reboot as too "politically correct," "too woke," too feminist, too brown, and too entrenched in politicizing Trump's nationalist agenda.[3] I conclude with a reflection on *Charmed*'s anti-fandom relationship to the ethnic, racial, and gender inequalities that shape US mainstream television and movie productions.

Charmed's 1990s Postfeminist (White) Girl Power

Popular postfeminist film and television representations flourished throughout the 1990s and early 2000s at a time when women's labor force participation was at a peak. According to the US Federal Reserve and the Bureau of Labor Statistics, by the year 2000 women in the workplace and families with dual income households had reached an all-time high of 60 percent. Changes in social demographics during the 1990s were also marked by a steady decline in marriage rates and an increased percentage of women who were not married. During the turn of the millennium, the United States also entered a period of rapid ethnic and racial demographic change. For example, by 2010 Los Angeles and New York became majority-minority cities with large Latino populations. In 2024, the racially, ethnically, regionally diverse Latino community remained the largest ethnoracial minority demographic in the United States.[4]

From 1990 to 2010 popular depictions of postfeminist characters lacking in any substantive feminist politics seemed to be everywhere.[5] Postfeminist television of this era depicted women characters as overwhelmingly white and beautiful, socially in control of their lives and sexuality, and economically powerful in terms of their professions and conspicuous consumption of luxury products, services, and practices. Finally, the narrative world of these postfeminist characters was a world free from sexism, racism, and poverty, often standing in contrast to the anti-women, anti-Black, and anti-Latino realities for these communities in the United States.[6] As such, postfeminist television programs naturalized the dominant cultural belief that gender equality had been achieved and white women in particular were responsible for achieving it.

Charmed, like programs of that era, represented the postfeminist sensibilities of middle-class wealth, heterosexual love, and socially acceptable white femininity, and recirculated the popular media representations that white women in Western society were now equal to white men. By highlighting the lived-world context against which postfeminist characters and stories are told in this section, I'm not suggesting that these programs have a responsibility to represent reality. Rather, I am suggesting the postfeminist world constructed by media producers is an idealized version of white upper-middle class heterosexual womanhood, a version of the world that has not really existed especially for majorities of women-identified people throughout the world.[7] It is this fictional world the actors and fans of the original wanted to nostalgically relive during Trump's first administration and a historical moment of increased gender, racial, and ethnic conflict throughout the world.

The Postfeminist World of OG *Charmed*

Constance Burge originally created *Charmed*, which premiered in 1998 as part of a wave of postfeminist television programs celebrating the power of white girls and women. Burge was a writer for another 1990s postfeminist program, *Ally McBeal* (1997–2002, Fox). *Charmed* was produced for Aaron Spelling and Spelling Productions, the company responsible for *Beverly Hills, 90210* (1990–2000, Fox) and *Melrose Place* (1992–1999, Fox). The OG *Charmed* was picked up by the nascent The WB Network, which built its success in part through its original postfeminist programming, such as *Buffy the Vampire Slayer* (1997–2003), *Gilmore Girls* (2000–2007), and *Dawson's Creek* (1998–2003). In 2006 CBS Corporation shut down UPN and Warner Brothers Entertainment closed The WB, and they merged their respective original programming into one network, now known as The CW. The rebooted *Charmed* produced by CBS Television Studies premiered on The CW in 2018 as part of a new lineup of original Sunday night programming.[8]

Building on The WB's audience- and cult-favorite *Buffy the Vampire Slayer*, which itself was a reboot of the cult movie by the same name, WB executives bought the rights to the more socially conservative, less violent, and less edgy *Charmed* (1998–2006). Recalling that Hollywood is characterized by a social network that reproduces itself through gender and racial inequality and remembering that little if anything on television is truly new, the show featured already popular white actresses from previous Aaron Spelling shows, Alyssa Milano (*Who's the Boss*, *Melrose Place*) and Shannen Doherty (*Little House on the Prairie*, *Beverly Hills, 90210*), alongside the lesser-known Holly Marie Combs (*Picket Fences*). It quickly captured audiences' attention and premiered to record-setting ratings, a record broken only by the debut of *Desperate Housewives* six years later (2004–2012, ABC). Before *Desperate Housewives*' television run, *Charmed* was the longest-running show to feature a group of women lead actors. In 2024 the OG *Charmed* is streamed and syndicated in the United States as well as more than twenty countries throughout Asia, Europe, and Latin America. The original's consistently strong ratings helped to anchor the nascent WB network's lineup of postfeminist girl power.

Like *Buffy*, the show featured strong white women leads, but it differed in its focus. *Buffy* focused on often gory fight scenes and the sexual tension between the lead vampire slayer character, played by Sarah Michelle Gellar, and reformed vampire Angel, played by David Boreanaz. Discussing his vision for Buffy in a *Time* article headlined "Proof That Joss Whedon Was Ahead of the Pop-Culture Feminism Curve," Whedon, who also wrote the movie and was a writer on the original *Roseanne* (1988–1997, ABC), said, "If I can make teenage boys comfortable with a girl who takes charge of a situation without their knowing that's what's happening, it's better than sitting them down and selling them on feminism."[9] Buffy represented a sexier, happier, easier-to-sell superficial form of feminism for audiences. This popular representation of feminism was at the core of The WB's shows and success, including *Charmed*.[10] Because US network television is a capitalist form of cultural production, the economic objective for network executives is to maximize profits by maximizing audience ratings. As discussed in the introduction to this collection, one method for maximizing profits is to copy the formulas of already successful shows. It is not accidental that WB executives, who already owned the broadcasting rights to *Buffy*, would also bet on Spelling Productions and Burge's take on Whedon's profitable formula.

Burge focused *Charmed*'s postfeminist narrative on the sisterly relationships and collective magical power, a very second-wave feminist sentiment. Second-wave feminism values women's collectivity as a symbol of domestic strength. In *Charmed* the characters' development centered on the domestic relationship between three sisters who lived in the same household, and their gentler use of matriarchal magical power to symbolize their feminine strength. Together the casting, plot, and narrative of the original show, as star Alyssa Milano puts it, made it "a perfect postfeminist girl-power show. Even independent of their special powers, these women are financially independent, hyper-feminine, and culturally acceptable to mainstream audiences."[11] Although there are action and fight scenes galore in both *Charmed* series, the villain plot is secondary to the character development surrounding the sisters' relationships with each other, the peripheral men in their lives, and their communal sisterly magical strength. OG *Charmed* is an exemplar of what Rosalind

Gill defines as a postfeminist cultural artifact—a pure celebration of predominantly white girl power devoid of political references and defined by "female autonomy, agency, choice."[12]

Anti-Fandom and Postfeminist Desires

The observation made by television scholar Douglas Kellner more than thirty years ago continues to be true today: "television is often out of sync with social experience, and there may be dissonance between the Today of its news and the Yesterday of its entertainment programs."[13] For the anti-fans and the actors of the OG *Charmed*, their dislike of the reboot stemmed from a shared desire for a revival of yesterday's apolitical postfeminist entertainment and against a reboot informed by the politics of today's news coverage of nationalist political resentment against global equity movements and immigration, specifically Asian and Latina/o American immigrants. In sum, anti-fans wanted to revive a show grounded in a nostalgic return to whiteness, women's heteronormative identities, and middle-class economic power.

On the one hand, fandom is driven by audiences' sense of empathy and their ability to identify with or aspire to be like the characters, actors, celebrities, musicians, or even sports teams.[14] On the other hand, anti-fandom is caused by a disconnect between the rebooted text and audiences' definition of themselves as different from and superior to. With regards to *Charmed*, anti-fan responses position the original show as the ideal against which to read the reboot. Specifically, the reboot's claim to feminism in the pilot's marketing line, "fierce, funny, feminist," challenged OG audiences who viewed the original with nostalgia and perceived the original and themselves as feminist. In situating the reboot as authentically feminist, CW executives poked the smoldering fires of the contemporary politics of resentment, as evidenced in anti-fandom towards the flipped reboot. Racially, ethnically, and gender-flipped rebooted shows such as *Charmed* and *Doctor Who* (see chapter 11 on *Doctor Who* anti-fandom) bring in new audiences as much as they motivate domestic and global fans of the original to engage in anti-fandom.

As an example of the nostalgic drive of anti-fandom, a report by Caroline Westbrook on the reboot controversy focused on the concerns of anti-fans and the original cast. Westbrook focuses on a social media

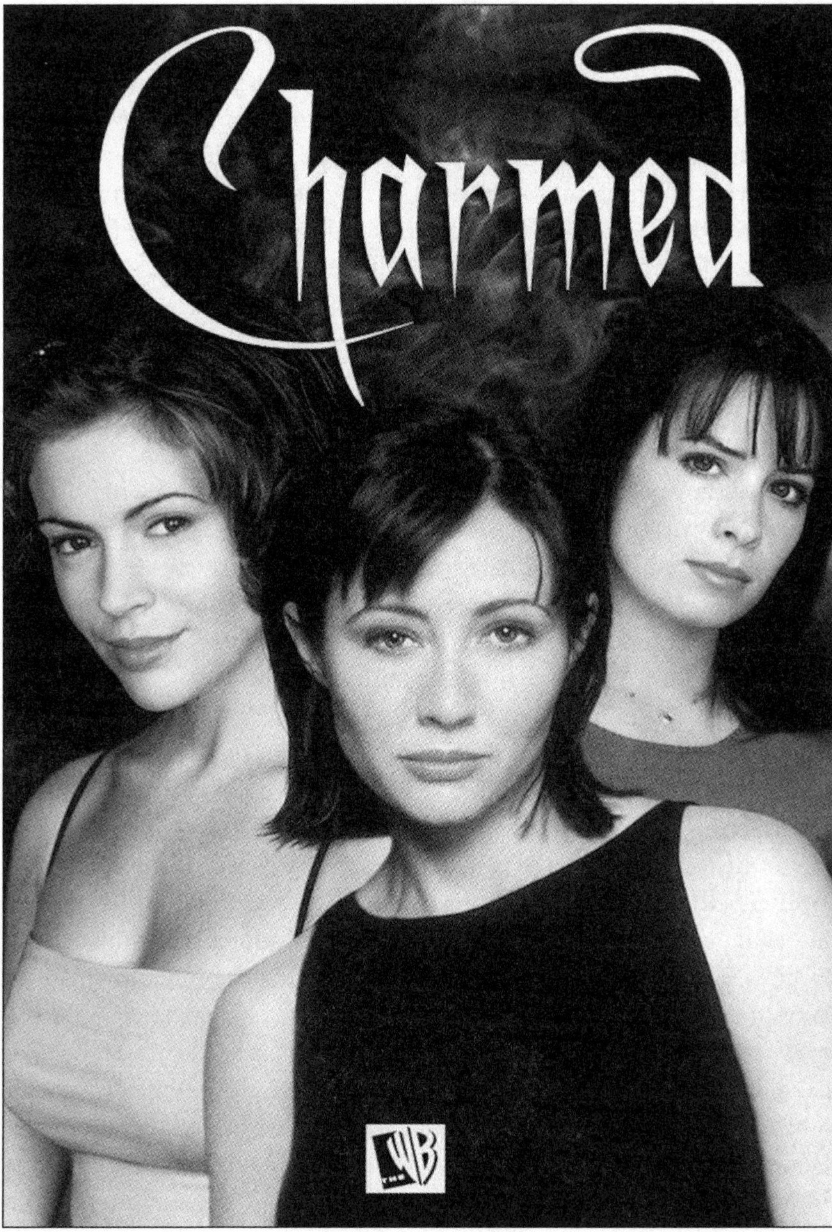

Figure 10.1. An official WB poster of the original cast: Alyssa Milano, Shannen Doherty, and Holly Marie Combs. *Source*: The WB.

exchange directed at the reboot's tagline: "Charmed was created by a woman. About women. For women (& gay boys like me). It was the longest running show with a female cast. It's stars campaign for equality to this day. Rebooting it with a 'feminist twist' is insulting."[15] The original's feminism is situated within the gender of the short-lived showrunner, the actors, and the feminist politics of Alyssa Milano, who became a vocal #MeToo activist—all of which the anti-fan clarified in a follow-up response: "The phrase 'feminist twist' felt like a slap in the face to me, the women in my life & the women involved in the show. It turns feminism into a marketing ploy, cashing in on the very real stories driving #metoo or #RoseArmy, both of which have heavy ties to the cast of Charmed."[16] For this fan the apolitical postfeminist values of the original, a show they identify with, are threatened by the reboot tagline that calls their feminist identity into question. The fan's tweet went viral when it was retweeted by original lead Holly Marie Combs and subsequently picked up by news and entertainment outlets. Combs actively campaigned against the reboot in part because of the sidelining of the original producers and actors, the reboot's marketing as feminist, and the lack of recognition of the OG *Charmed* as a feminist show.

In later tweets on the platform now known as X, Combs, who, along with Alyssa Milano became an executive producer on the OG *Charmed*, clarified that her resistance to the reboot revolved around not being included in the production of the reboot. In doing so, Combs draws attention to the role of revivals in resuscitating the careers of white actors and producers that maintain Hollywood's institutionalization of inequality. Interestingly, few of the OG fans or actors mentioned that showrunner Burge was quickly replaced by Brad Kern during the first season—the same Brad Kern who was fired from *NCIS: New Orleans* in 2018 for his toxic behavior in the wake of the #MeToo movement. Kern is accused of sexual harassment and creating a hostile work environment dating back to his days as the showrunner for *Charmed*.[17] When asked about the accusations, Milano said she never witnessed any wrongdoing by Kern: "In our working environment, the first, second and third names on the call sheet were all women. We ran a very fair set environment, and it breaks my heart that anything that was happening over in that writer's room was not [respectful], especially on a show about female empowerment."[18] That the writers' room of a supposedly feminist show would be run by a toxic cis-male producer is not surprising given Hollywood's power structure and the dominance of white male heterosexual producers in the television industry.

OG anti-fans nostalgically remembered the celebration of sisterhood and depiction of powerful white women as symbols of a new "feminist" ethos. Responding to news of the reboot on *Entertainment Weekly*, an anti-fan defended the postfeminist values of the original: "I'm pretty turned off by the redundant need to mention a 'feminist' storyline. Charmed represented feminism by nature. Why try to sell some commercialized faux narrative when sisterhood and womanhood is genuinely what the Charmed legacy is all about?"[19] Feminism by nature for this anti-fan is a reference to the biological sex of the OG actors. Biological female birth naturally equates to feminism for them. In response to the same *Entertainment Weekly* story about the reboot's feminist storylines, Combs tweeted, "Guess we forgot to do that [feminism] the first go around. Hmph."[20] In another media interview, Combs uses a critique of ageism in Hollywood to again call out the tagline as well as the exclusion of the original actors:

> "Let me say first that I appreciate the jobs and opportunities the *Charmed* reboot has created," Combs said. "But I will never understand what is fierce, funny, or feminist in creating a show that basically says the original actresses are too old to do a job they did 12 years ago. I hope the new show is far better than the marketing, so the true legacy does remain."[21]

Despite the original's sexualized depictions of the sisters, which Alyssa Milano described as typical of television productions of the time, the white heteronormative femininity of the lead characters, the politically safe narrative of second-wave feminist sisterhood, and the show's creation by a woman showrunner, a rarity in television production, decidedly marked the original as a postfeminist show. Anti-fans of the reboot identify with that safer older depiction of commercialized feminism. During the show's run, Milano and other *Charmed* stars became, as they remain, vocal activists for (white) women's equality in Hollywood. Much of the resistance to the reboot ironically focused on the producers' and network executives' claim to the reboot as "feminist" with contemporary "feminist storylines" that by implication denigrated anti-fans' postfeminist values.

To characterize the reboot as feminist, and by implication the original as not feminist, calls into question the nostalgic values anti-fans associate with the original. Feminist media studies scholars suggest that postfeminism is not actually a form of feminism or part of the genealogy of feminist movements. Instead, postfeminist media is defined as a popular depoliticized depiction of feminism that, as Whedon pointed out, is easier to market to global audiences—men, women, and queer folks. However, to anti-fans the original is the true feminist text. For instance, this tweet exemplifies the tension for anti-fans between a depoliticized postfeminist representation and the more explicitly political feminist claims of the reboot: "#STOPCHARMEDREBOOT @TheCW You claim that your reboot is 'feminist' Please explain how replacing grown women with teenage girls is feminist."[22] Given that none of the reboot actors are actually teenagers, the reference to age in this post perhaps more accurately signals a discomfort with other changes to the cast in terms of the ethnicity, race, and sexuality of the characters that rupture anti-fans' nostalgia for the original.

Similar sentiments circulated in the Choice.Org petition against the reboot, such as this comment:

> There is a great number of universal human values carefully cherished in the original "Charmed" series that should not simply be abandoned and spoiled by fake "feminism". If a woman is only equal to a man when she has special magical powers, it is no feminism—it is discrimination. Not to mention the LGBTQ twist to this farsa. Gay people need no magic to be just as human as anyone. Please put a hold on this discriminating, greedy reboot, it is an insult to anyone that has ever seen a single episode of the original show.[23]

The anti-fan's logic questions a depiction of feminism dependent solely on casting women as having special powers, and says that doing so is discriminatory presumably because it affords women equality only when they are playing witches. It is not clear who is being discriminated against in the petition comment—men, gay men, women, women not cast as magical? And the anti-fan overlooks that as Combs and other anti-fans suggest, such as in the previously mentioned tweets, the original was feminist precisely because it featured women leads. That said, the anti-fan comment reinforces the underlying desire by original fans for a de-political postfeminist revival starring the original actors, who are now more than twenty years older than when they played the *Charmed* witches. Anti-fans' desire for a revival located in the turn of the millennium and reject the reboot's explicitly political storylines and the ethnic, racial, and sexual identity flip of the actors and characters. Objections by anti-fans as indicated in the above tweets and comments illustrate a resistance to the reboot producers' rejection of the more conservative, feminine, entertaining, and less political representation of white women empowerment emblematic of postfeminist TV programs.

Charmed's Anti-fandom

Underlying the anti-fan discourse analyzed in the previous section is the expectation mainstream television should situate whiteness and heteronormativity as the norm. Indeed, it was a common practice of many of the #stopcharmedreboot posters to include edited images and memes of the original white actresses as if to draw a contrast with the reboot's ethnic and mixed-race actors. Alongside the images of the original actors, ran comments such as "we want the original cast"[24] and "No thanks. We need the original cast BACK!"[25] In these examples anti-fans centered the whiteness of the original cast, idolized the original's actors, and the postfeminist narrative of white women's hyperfeminine empowerment that fueled their hatred of the reboot.

By flipping the ethnic, racial, and sexual identity of the characters in the reboot, media executives, the first-season showrunners, and their predominantly women and queer writers' room intentionally challenge Hollywood's capitalist structure of inequality and explicitly situate the reboot within the contemporary racial and gender politics of the Trump era. Challenging the racist and sexist structures of Hollywood media that predominantly benefit white men, three of the *Charmed* reboot's original executive producers were women who were executive producers on The CW multiethnic telenovela remake hit *Jane the Virgin* (2014–2019): Jessica O'Toole, Amy Rardin, and Jennie Snyder Urman. The fourth executive producer, Carter Covington, who identifies as a gay man, received executive production credit for *Faking It* (2014–2016, MTV), a romantic comedy featuring an intersex character. Producers of successful television programs often get hiring preference to develop other shows. Given that most television executives and showrunners are white men, television and films have mostly remained in the creative control of white men, such as the production of OG *Charmed*. Because Urman and her writing partners previously launched other shows that successfully brought in diverse audiences, they were able to disrupt the structurally unequal hiring practices and develop The CW's *Charmed* flipped reboot and as a result enable a more diverse creative pipeline.

After declining Urman's initial pilot script based on a prequel set in 1970s New England and featuring the white women characters "Tina, Paige, Annie," CW network executives announced the flipped reboot and its more political and neoliberal multicultural reimagining of the show. The network greenlighted a reboot featuring three women-of-color actors as the sisters and consciously set the pilot within Trump's presidency and the #MeToo movement. Using a blind casting process, the producers selected three women of color to play the roles of the sisters Macy, Maggie, and Mel. Nuyorican actress Melonie Diaz previously starred in *Fruitvale Station*. Mixed-race Canadian actress Sarah Jeffery played the role of Jennifer Lopez's daughter in *Shades of Blue*. And Madeleine Mantock, a British-Caribbean actress, was best known for her roles in BBC dramas such as *Casualty* and cult-favorite USA Network's *Into the Badlands*.

A significant and at times inflammatory focus of the anti-fan discourse centers on disdain for the sexual, ethnic and racial (ethnoracial) flip of the actors from white women to women of color and from exclusively heterosexual witches to the inclusion of specifically queer storylines surrounding the character Mel Vera, played by Melonie Diaz. Melonie's character attends graduate school in women's studies, and all of Mel's romantic and sexual interests are women. A running theme through the series is Mel's opposition to hiding that she is a witch, perhaps a symbolic parallel to hiding one's queer sexuality. And as previously discussed (see chapter 7), Mel represents the voice of feminism on the reboot through her explicit feminist dialogue in storylines dealing with issues of sexual consent, sexual assault, and sexual harassment.

These plotlines, along with the reboot's explicit depiction of Mel as a feminist, who is often disdainful of the men characters of the show, makes her a primary target of anti-fans. In echoes of the *Doctor Who*

Figure 10.2. Official CW poster for the *Charmed* reboot featuring Sarah Jeffery, Madeleine Mantock, and Melonie Diaz further highlights the racial differences of the reboot cast and characters. *Source*: The CW.

anti-fandom discussed in chapter 11, a fan tweeted: "Enjoying the #charmedreboot more these days but still doesn't match the original and they still really hate men. I dislike Mel no matter how much I try not to." Fans of the original were particularly offended by the explicitly feminist language of the show, the casting of lesbian characters, and the use of non-white actresses, as summarized by this Choice.Org petitioner,[26] "I am so over the feminist crap being shoved down our throats. The original version was perfect the way it was if you wanted to pick up using the original sisters' kids and make one of them a Physicist, a Lesbians, and a college student then so be it. But this is a disgrace." Posters and bloggers across the gender and sexual spectrum, at least according to their profile pictures and other posts, engaged in anti-feminist rhetoric by stereotyping Mel as angry, assertive, aggressive, and castrating, common negative stereotypes of feminists. For example, in a blog of the pilot that featured an image of the reboot actors superimposed with "I hate them so much!" and the original cast with "I miss them so much!," this anti-fan observed, "Mel is so angry over her mom's death and so feminist that when a guy disagrees with her opinion and makes a snide comment about her mom, she punches him."[27] The review concludes like other anti-fans by arguing the feminist politics of reboot are forced, depicts men as toxic demons, and Mel as an unrelatable man-hater. The hyper-feminine and sexualized representation of the youngest sister, Maggie, and the romantic heterosexual coupling of Macy insulated these characters against negative feminist stereotypes.

Whether the anti-fans or the reboot fans are engaged in racism is impossible to filter out. Yet anti-fans desire for a *Charmed* revival is an implied and explicit rejection of the multiracial women-of-color starring as the Charmed ones (the fictional father of characters Maggie and half-sister Macy is a Black man). Dislike for the mixed-race and Latina/x characters are grounded in anti-fan expectations for the gendered and racialized nostalgic drive of watching television. As Lynn Spigel documents, television audiences derive pleasure from the medium's ability to function as a mirror reflective of their gender and racial ideals, dreams, and fears.[28] Anti-fans privilege whiteness, normative femininity, and heterosexuality, idealizing and craving a revival of *Charmed* and its idealized past over the socially complicated present of the reboot. Specifically, the desire by anti-fans is for a revival starring the original actors, continuing original storylines grounded in a postfeminist past, and avoiding the discomfort with contemporary racial, gender, and sexual culture and politics. The racialized rejection of the reboot is grounded in a collective nostalgic drive for heteronormative, white, middle-class girl power.

Television's Collective Racial Nostalgia

Scholars define collective nostalgia "as a sentimental longing for, or wistful feelings associated with, a past period of time for one's group."[29] In the context of the US under the Trump era, collective nostalgia signals the romanticization of a historical period perceived as privileging the status of white, middle class, and heterosexual men. The collective nostalgia of anti-fans for a revival speaks to their sentimental longing for a reaffirmation of their own social status, racial, sexual, and gender identity and politics. The original characters and storylines reinforce anti-fans' idealization of gender, racial, and sexual norms characterized by white privilege, normative femininity and masculinity, and heteronormative sexuality.

The OG *Charmed* taps into characters and storylines dependent on traditional and conservative representations of race, ethnicity, gender, sexuality, and feminism; with one exception, media representations of witches, even the hypernormative witches of the OG *Charmed*, have long been associated with social outsiders who challenge the sexual and gender norms of Western society. It is perhaps this subtle nod to the closeting of the characters' outsider status as witches that makes OG *Charmed* a compelling text for gay and lesbian anti-fans even as the original reinforces the nostalgic norms of heteronormative sexuality. Superficially postfeminist television programs such as the OG *Charmed* appear to flip the script on normative representations of womanhood. However, postfeminist mainstream media depictions of women and feminism continue Hollywood's traditional storylines that depict white men through their public lives as heroes, villains, historical figures, et cetera, and white women through their private lives as wives, sisters, mothers, and heterosexual lovers. At its best, anti-fan resistance to *Charmed*'s political flipped reboot speaks to the collective yearning for a return to a simpler past perceived as a socially and politically less complicated era, a time that privileged white middle-class heterosexual femininity. At its worst, it foregrounds television's structural racism and the social resentment of ethnic, racial, and sexual difference.

To understand OG fans' dislike of the racially and sexually flipped *Charmed*, I contextualize the reboot's production and reception within the collective racial nostalgia that fuels Trumpist nationalist discourses and policies grounded in racism, xenophobia, sexism, and resentment. It is a political discourse that positions gender and ethnoracial inequality and disenfranchisement as the norm, a norm central to racial capitalism as discussed in the introduction to this collection. Trump's 2016, 2020, and 2024 presidential campaigns tapped into a public and global resurgence of nationalistic politics grounded in a collective racial nostalgia and white resentment.

As a form of collective nostalgia, racial nostalgia is dependent on the perception that white cultural, social, political, and economic dominance is in decline.[30] From slavery to segregation and contemporary immigrant concentration camps, racial nostalgia in the United States is intrinsic to the nation's capitalist formation, culture, and governance. Beginning with the nation's colonial settler beginnings, US identity as an imagined collective identity depends on the historical and political erasure of enslaved Africans, indigenous genocide, and segregation based on ethnicity, race, and indigeneity. Trump's "Make America Great Again" platform elevates the politics of racial nostalgia and racial resentment to its most dehumanizing, anti-immigrant, anti-Black, and anti-women form.[31] The rhetoric of Trumpism taps into the gender and racial anxiety of working- and middle-class citizens, mostly but not exclusively white men, who believe the "American Dream" ideology of heterosexual domesticity and economic security is no longer within their reach. Some cultural critics call this population of mostly men "the left behinds." Those populations who perceive themselves as left behind by the politics of social justice and racial equity and who blame immigration and the gains of the Women's, LGBTQ, and Civil Rights movements for their disenfranchisement. Racial nostalgia therefore is closely linked with racial capitalism and the nationalistic politics of white resentment in the United States.

Flipped reboots such as *Charmed* tap into some audiences' affective responses of racial nostalgia and resentment. The domestic and global rise of white nationalism and its dependence on racial nostalgia increasingly shapes audiences' pleasure in contemporary popular culture. With regard to the reboot, Urman and CW executives position the show's narrative and character development explicitly in response to Trump's nationalistic and toxic rhetoric. In an interview with *The New York Times*, Urman said of the reboot, "In the development process, we imagined the show as a prequel set during the rise of the women's movement . . . Then the election happened. There was the shock of the morning after, and the anger at being shocked. It felt like we should be examining this present moment instead."[32] CW executives greenlighted Urman's creative decision to pivot away from a prequel based on the original characters to its more political and racially and ethnically flipped reboot. The reboot's diverse writers' room kicked off the pilot with a focus on sexual harassment and the #MeToo movement. Interviewed for the same article, Melonie Diaz, who is of Puerto Rican descent and was the first actor cast in the show, echoed the cast's commitment to the political reframing of the reboot: "I'm never going to get over the 2016 election. I'm angry on a visceral level. The way I feel is, 'How can we not be talking about this? The world is a dumpster fire!'" The sentiments expressed by

Urman and Diaz were also echoed by CW executives, who supported the strategic decision by the producers to pivot the show's creative plan to address the contemporary political landscape, and the reboot's writers' room.[33] Reboots sometimes challenge Hollywood's power structures and the gender and racial nostalgic drive of television. It is difficult to ignore *Charmed*'s anti-fans' desire for the nostalgic return for a revival of postfeminist white girl power.

Anti-Fandom and Racial Nostalgia

Where some fans see themselves reflected in the content, anti-fandoms emerge from audiences not seeing themselves in the characters or storylines. Such was the case for some of *Charmed*'s anti-fans, who could not or did not want to see themselves reflected in the reboot's politically progressive, mixed-race, Latina, and queer characters. For example, a repeated racialized and gendered insult leveled at the reboot was that the Latina and mixed-race women are ugly compared to the beautiful white actors of the original, for example:

> We want a warm, magical, entertaining show like the original one, where the sisters are nice and lovely, not to mention beautiful. We don't want some three third-rate "actresses" with wooden emotions, playing the ape all the time and being rude and unpleasant in general. If you want to run another corrupting show for spoiled teenagers about the ones alike, you mustn't name it after a good show that has nothing to do with this bullshit.[34]

Referring to the women as "playing the ape" is a racially loaded phrase used by people to derogatively describe and stereotype Black people as less than human. Indeed, it was the insult that Roseanne Barr leveled at President Obama's Chief of Staff Valery Jarret, an insult that resulted in the cancellation of her revival (see chapter 2). To the anti-fan above, the white OG actors are beautiful, and the women of color of the reboot are less-than-human apes. Unlike Combs and McGowan's more implicit racists insults, the racist insult is explicit for this anti-fan. These responses reinforce the connection between white postfeminist nostalgia and its racist, sexist, and homophobic assumptions, as is often the case with anti-fans of the flipped reboots.[35]

One smaller thread in the anti-fan responses to the reboot centered on the explicitly queer, feminist, and anti-Trump themes of show. After watching the premier of the reboot, an OG anti-fan tweeted: "The original #Charmed was not even half this political. Way over the top. This is a definite no for me."[36] Another poster who identified as a heterosexual cis-man anti-fan tweeted this more explicit response: "Grab your girlfriends? Because guys can't watch it?! THIS is why people dont want this reboot. You are making it for all the wrong reasons. #Charmed #CharmedReboot #StopCharmedReboot."[37] For this poster, his position as a heterosexual male viewer was clearly challenged by the queer and feminist themes of the reboot. Signers of the petition equally shared their virulent response to the flipped and political reboot, such as "this pc crap is bs."[38] Similar to the racist signaling of the word of "ape," the term *political correctness* ("PC") is often invoked by conservatives who engage in race baiting to denigrate cultures and cultural texts or languages that do not cohere to Eurocentric perspectives.

After two years of criticism of the reboot, a 2020 example further highlights the racial stakes and tensions. In 2020, Combs and Rose McGowan became embroiled in a controversy that the writers and some fans of the original and the reboot characterized as racist and anti-women. In response to a video posting by Combs and McGowan that criticized Netflix for removing the original and keeping the reboot, of which they jokingly said "it sucks," a fan of the original tweeted an edit of the video and commented "It really doesn't sit right with me that white women from the OG Charmed consistently put down a new #Charmed with a POC cast . . . you hate to see it . . ."[39] Reboot actor Jeffery picked up on the video and the tweet with a response of her own: "I truly hope they find happiness elsewhere, and not in the form of putting down other WOC. I would be embarrassed to behave this way. Peace and love to y'all."[40] Further highlighting the racial subtext of Combs's resistance to the reboot is this Reddit post:

> They seem to think it somehow takes something away from the original. instead of celebrating that they helped pave the way for more shows led by women, by women of colour, by people of different sexual identities, they're choosing to be petty. I think in part it's that they weren't consulted or something but then I don't see why they woulld/should be (they

> weren't producers until much later in the series and chances are those were vanity titles tbh) the OG show is lauded as this great feminist show (its far less feminist than people like to remember) yet the actresses cannot find it in them to be supportive of and lift up other women.[41]

Anti-fans' calls for a revival and the responses of the original *Charmed* actors to the flipped reboot further exemplify the consequences of collective racial nostalgia and its nationalist implications. For example, an anti-fan tweeted,

> These women taught me at a really young age that I could do whatever I wanted and no man could stop me if I really tried. They even if they didn't know it felt like sisters to me as well as mother figures. *Charmed* was something I used to wake up early to watch with my father. This is my childhood, and I don't think that the "Reboot" can even be called a Charmed Reboot, because that is not what it is.[42]

Another twitter anti-fan who supported the petition against the reboot tweeted, "It's not Charmed. Nothing will ever come close to the acting, the writing, story lines and on-screen chemistry."[43] Or, as another anti-fan wrote less eloquently, "I'm signing because I feel they are shitting on my childhood."[44] The anti-fan responses to the flipped reboot speak to collective racial nostalgia of Hollywood television, a nostalgia for the normative dominance of whiteness, white middle-class femininity, and the characters' presumably white fictional families. OG fans' desire for a revival and nostalgic representations of whiteness and white femininity relies on entertainment media's reproduction of inequality that ultimately devalues feminism, Latinidad, and Blackness.

Finally, the disdain of some anti-fans focused on the diverse cast as an economic ploy, another way to race-bait without being explicitly racists. For example, these tweets illustrate the racial dog-whistle of diversity: "I wish they would just #StopCharmedReboot but they don't pay attention to fans and they are just doing this for money targeting other new audience. Shame" and "This rebellion against the reboot has never been about race. CW could've hired white people and I still wouldn't want the reboot. As someone with Latino/Caribbean blood please tell me again how I'm mad there's Latino Representation 👏🥀."[45] The second tweet is by a Puerto Rican anti-fan, illustrating the cultural dominance of white normative femininity on television for some Black and Latina/o fans of the original, particularly around Black representations of Latinidad. Anti-Black Latina/o responses are the norm rather than the exception, as Tanya Kateri Hernandez documents in *Racial Innocence: Unmasking Latino Anti-Black Bias and the Struggle for Equality*.[46] The responses by fans of color are not monolithic, however, as some OG audiences found the diversity of reboot a positive representational take: "Im about to finish first season of charmed and already want the second season to start! I love the diverse cast!! #charmedreboot #charmed2019 #madeleinemantock #sarahjeffery #meloniediaz #afrolatino #latinx."[47] The racial differences between the reboot and the original became more apparent with the addition of the character of Jordan Chase, played by Jordan Donica, who joined the show in the second season as a Black Whiteligher (a protector of witches).

Throughout the reboot's run, the conflict between the OG and reboot writers over the casting and the storylines was picked up by entertainment news such as *People* and *Entertainment Weekly*. For example, the OG writers engaged in a similar racially coded back-and-forth, such as this tweet by OG writer Curtis Kheel, "As an original #Charmed writer, I can tell u what happened next: Piper, Phoebe & Paige vanquished the 3 imposters right after they invaded Halliwell Manor. Then @H_Combs blew up the portal to that other universe & quipped: 'We wish them well.' #seriesfinale #CharmedReunionMovie." The reboot writers responded through their official Twitter account, presumably in reference to the lack of diversity and toxic environment of the OG show, "Unlike with the OG version of the franchise, we had a strict 'no assholes' hiring policy in the writer's room. We feel mostly sorry for these people, because unlike them we actually like each other and had the BEST time."[48] Indeed, the reboot producers gave a credit to Constance Burge, the original creator of the OG *Charmed*, but left out Brad Kern, who executively produced the majority of the OG episodes.

A Nostalgic Conclusion

Charmed's anti-fandom focused on the wish for a revival of the original white actors and producers and their collective racial nostalgia for

Figure 10.3. Another official CW poster featuring Jordan Donica, Melonie Diaz, and Sarah Jeffery. The image further highlights the racialization of the reboot cast and characters. Unlike the first season promotional image, Jeffery is wearing her hair naturally curly instead of straightened. *Source*: The CW.

and celebration of idealized white womanhood. Anti-fan posts illustrate Kathleen Loock's argument that television revivals that recast the original members of the programs and continue the original plot line "embrace the more conventional and conservative reactivation of family-friendly" characteristics.[49] Revivals, such as the one desired by OG fans, are a form of uncomplicated and less-challenging television that celebrates nostalgia for a simpler racial time. In turn, the decision by the producers and network executives to situate the reboot within contemporary ethnic, racial, gender, and sexual politics disrupt this nostalgic desire to memorialize a less complicated moment in the lives of the audience.

For Combs the desire for a revival is also grounded in a nostalgic return or recognition of her stardom and eventual role as a producer of the original *Charmed*. Her critique reinforces white privilege and the hard-fought battles for women creatives in Hollywood productions. Television revivals provide an opportunity for the original actors, who are usually white, and the producers, who are usually white and male, to return to positions of visibility and power. As part of her initial response to the news, Combs tweeted:

> Here's the thing. Until you ask us to rewrite it like Brad Kern did weekly don't even think of capitalizing on our hard work. Charmed belongs to the 4 of us, our vast amount of writers, crews and predominantly the fans. FYI you will not fool them by owning a title/stamp. So bye.[50]

In the original, Combs and Milano received writing and production credit for their creative work on the set in the final year of the series. Both women were also reported to be in support of a revival that incorporated their off- and on-screen talent, but not a stand-alone reboot that, in the words of Milano, felt "really disrespectful" in the lack of their involvement.[51] By taking to task the exclusion of the original, all-white, cast and crew, Combs explicitly stakes claim to her power in an industry that continues to discriminate against older women, women of color, and women in general. And at the same time, although not consciously, she reinforces the white heteronormative privilege of Hollywood. In doing so, Combs's response maintains the racial capitalist structures of televisual production that in all its forms remains embedded in racial, sexual, and gender inequality.[52]

Ultimately, the responses by these fans and the original cast are indicative of the ways in which the representational is, as Stuart Hall argues, always informed by the "coupling of difference and power."[53] Representations of difference, of othering, are intimately interconnected with white hetero-patriarchal structures of power critical to racial capitalism. Television revivals are located within that place of power. In the case of the *Charmed* reboot that so openly rejects postfeminist ideology and white femininity in favor of a more political yet still neoliberal multicultural present, both the original cast and its fans grieve the loss of that power and privilege that fuels a sense of representational and structural loss.

Although the use of colorblind casting did not result in an all-Latina cast, it did result in a women-of-color ensemble performing mixed-race Latina/x characters. The backlash against this type of "diversity programming in television" exists alongside the right-wing, nationalist backlash to President Obama's post-racial era. Responses by OG fans to the reboot illustrate how television has not moved beyond racial difference but instead remained constrained by the nostalgic and nationalist politics of gender, sexuality, and race that continue to limit more progressive politics and initiatives.[54] Anti-fan reactions to comments by network executives, the showrunners, and actors opposed the reboot's narrative unabashedly located within this generation's US Black and Latina/o/x movements, and the feminist activisms of the Trump era. Both the casting and writing of the reboot explicitly questioned the privileging of gender and racial values of the OG fans. In conclusion, by challenging the postfeminist values and whiteness of the original, the reboot functions as a departure from mainstream TV's conservative ethos and the gendered and racialized nostalgic tendencies of reboots and revivals.

Discussion Questions

1. Discuss how the rebooted *Charmed* challenges postfeminist television and its values around gender and racial norms.
2. Define the concept of collective racial nostalgia and discuss the role of nationalism in anti-fan responses to flipped TV and films such as *Charmed* or other examples.

NOTES

1 I use the term *Latina* to discuss cisgender actors and characters. The term *Latinx* is used for nonbinary or queer-identified actors or characters. For a discussion of the terms and the critique of *Latinx* see Richard T. Rodríguez, "X Marks the Spot," *Cultural Dynamics* 29, no. 3 (2017), 202–13, https://doi.org/10.1177/0921374017727880.

2 See chapter 7 in this collection for an in-depth discussion of the inclusion of Latinidad in the reboot.

3 Methodological note: I collected and analyze Combs's original tweets against the reboot and responses to the tweet as well as Twitter users' comments on @CharmedReboot, #stopcharmedreboot and change.org petition "Say No to the 'Charmed' Reboot." Additionally, I collected bloggers and media critics responses to the multicultural US, British, Canadian casting of the reboot.

4 Caroline Short, "Households That Reported Being English or German Topped List of Owner-Occupied U.S. Households," prepared by the Demographic Division of the US Census Bureau (Washington, D.C., 2024), www.census.gov/.

5 Angela McRobbie, *The Aftermath of Feminism: Gender, Culture and Social Change* (Sage, 2008).

6 McRobbie, *The Aftermath of Feminism.*

7 Amy Shields Dobson and Akane Kanai, "From 'Can-Do' Girls to Insecure and Angry: Affective Dissonances in Young Women's Post-Recessional Media," *Feminist Media Studies* 19, no. 6 (2019): 771–86, https://doi.org/10.1080/14680777.2018.1546206.

8 "Charmed," program notes (The CW, 2018), https://tinyurl.com/bdh6ppcj.

9 Lily Rothman, "Proof That Joss Whedon Was Ahead of the Pop-Culture Feminism Curve," *Time*, March 2015, https://time.com.

10 Sarah Banet-Weiser et al., "Postfeminism, Popular Feminism and Neoliberal Feminism? Sarah Banet-Weiser, Rosalind Gill and Catherine Rottenberg in Conversation," *Feminist Theory* 21, no. 1 (2019), 3–24, https://doi.org/10.1177/1464700119842555.

11 Bruce Fretts, "The Women of The WB Wow Audiences," *Entertainment Weekly*, December 25, 1998, https://ew.com. Burge, *Charmed*'s creator, left after the second season due to rumored conflicts with showrunner Brad Kern. In the wake of the #MeToo movement, Kern came under investigation by CBS in 2018 because of accusations of gender and racial harassment and its creation of a toxic production environment. See Tierney Bricker, "The Wicked Behind-the-Scenes Drama of the Original Charmed: Feuds, Firings and Feminist Fury," *E! News*, October 12, 2018, www.eonline.com.

12 Rosalind Gill, *Gender and the Media* (Polity, 2007), 3.

13 Douglas Kellner, *Media Culture: Cultural Studies, Identity and Politics Between the Modern and the Postmodern* (Routledge, 1995), 43.

14 For an in-depth study of anti-fandom and social media, see Mel Stanfill, *Fandom Is Ugly: Networked Harassment in Participatory Culture* (New York University Press, 2024).

15 Phillip Lee Curtis (@PoshLopez), "Charmed was created by a woman. About women. For women (& gay boys like me). It was the longest running show with a female cast. It's stars campaign for equality to this day. Rebooting it with a 'feminist twist' is insulting," Twitter, January 26, 2018, https://twitter.com/PoshLopez/status/956785920241410048.

16 These were responses to the aforementioned tweet by Phillip Lee Curtis (@PoshLopez).

17 Maureen Ryan, "Brad Kern and the House That Moonves Built at CBS," *Vulture*, August 3, 2018, www.vulture.com.

18 Maureen Ryan, "Alyssa Milano on 'Charmed,' Brad Kern Allegations and the Path to Reform," *Variety*, December 14, 2017, https://variety.com.

19 Chris McPherson (@ChrisMcPhersn), "I'm pretty turned off by the redundant need to mention a 'feminist' storyline. Charmed represented feminism by nature. Why try to sell some commercialized faux narrative when sisterhood and womanhood is genuinely what the Charmed legacy is all about?," Twitter, January 26, 2018, https://twitter.com/ChrisMcPhersn/status/956797680042291200.

20 Holly Marie Combs (@H_Combs), "Guess we forgot to do that the first go around. Hmph," Twitter, January 28, 2018, https://twitter.com/H_Combs/status/956918071515475969. For *Entertainment Weekly* coverage of audience response to news of the reboot, see James Hibberd, "Charmed Reboot Gets CW Pilot Order, Adds 'Feminist' Story Line," *Entertainment Weekly*, January 25, 2018, https://ew.com/.

21 Nicole Drum, "Fans React to 'Charmed' Reboot Premiere," *Comic Book TV*, October 17, 2018, https://comicbook.com.

22 The Fountain of Truth (@thegreattrevi), "#STOPCHARMEDREBOOT @TheCW You claim that your reboot is 'feminist'. Please explain how replacing grown women with teenage girls is feminist," Twitter, February 14, 2018, https://twitter.com/TheGreatTrevi/status/963719851385806850.

23 Comment from Nikola Djuric on September 14, 2008 on Choice.org petition: AJ Jacoby, "Stop the *Charmed* Reboot," petition, Change.org, March 29, 2018, www.change.org/p/cw-network-stop-the-charmed-reboot.

24 Holly Fans (@HollyFansSpain), "We want the original cast!!!! #STOPCHARMEDREBOOT," Twitter, May 9, 2018, https://x.com/HollyFansSpain/status/994302923940220928.

25 Alonso Solis (@AlonsoFSolis), replying to @cw_charmed, "No thanks. We need the original cast BACK!" Twitter, https://x.com/AlonsoFSolis/status/997157967907536898.

26 Comment from Julie Miles on June 19, 2019, on Choice.org petition: Jacoby, "Stop the *Charmed* Reboot."

27 S. F. Gebel, "Charmed Reboot Review: Worse Than Even the Trailer Foreshadowed," *Reading with Highlighters*, October 17, 2018, https://readingwithhighlighters.wordpress.com.

28 Lynn Spigel, *Welcome to the Dream House: Popular Media and Postwar Suburbs* (Duke, 2001).

29 Christine Reyna et al., "The Good Ol' Days: White Identity, Racial Nostalgia, and the Perpetuation of Racial Extremism," *Group Processes & Intergroup Relations* 25, no. 3 (2022), https://doi.org/10.1177/13684302211057454.

30 Reyna et al., "The Good Ol' Days."

31 Reyna et al., "The Good Ol' Days."

32 Megan Angelo, "The Witches of 'Charmed' Are Out to Slay Demons. And the Patriarchy," *New York Times*, October 5, 2018.

33 Cidney Contreras, "Feud Erupts Between Writers of the Original Charmed and Reboot," *Entertainment Weekly*, June 13, 2022, www.eonline.com.

34 Comment from Erik Gordon October 18, 2018 on Choice.org petition: Jacoby, "Stop the *Charmed* Reboot."

35 For research on ethnicity and race in anti-fandom, see Melissa Click, ed., *Anti-Fandom: Dislike and Hate in the Digital Age* (New York University Press, 2019); Michelle Rivera, "Hate It or Love It: Global Crossover of Reggaeton Music in the Digital Age" (PhD diss., University of Illinois, 2014); and Mel Stanfill, *Exploiting Fandom: How the Media Industry Seeks to Manipulate Fans* (University of Iowa Press, 2019).

36 Victorious (@BrokenPalabras), "The original #Charmed was not even half this political. Way over the top. This is a definite no for me," Twitter, October 15, 2018, https://twitter.com/BrokenPalabras/status/1051643115747053568.

37 Thomas (@Thomstarr), "Grab your girlfriends? Because guys can't watch it?! THIS is why people dont want this reboot. You are making it for all the wrong

reasons. #Charmed #CharmedReboot #StopCharmedReboot," Twitter, September 18, 2018, https://twitter.com.

38 Comment from Robert Talmadge on Choice.org petition: Jacoby, "Stop the *Charmed* Reboot."

39 Onté Grey (@ontegrey), "It really doesn't sit right with me that white women from the OG Charmed consistently put down a new #Charmed with a POC cast . . . you hate to see it . . . ," Twitter, October 12, 2020, https://x.com/OnteGrey/status/1315746397250113537.

40 Sarah Jeffery (@sarahjeffery), "I truly hope they find happiness elsewhere, and not in the form of putting down other WOC. I would be embarrassed to behave this way. Peace and love to y'all," Twitter, October 12, 2020, https://x.com/sarahjeffery/status/13158169139229777922.

41 Comment from @CaseyRC: r/CharmedCW, "Does anyone know why the original charmed ones actresses are such nightmares about the reboot?," Reddit, 2021, www.reddit.com.

42 Comment from Yasmin Gidney on Choice.org petition: Jacoby, "Stop the *Charmed* Reboot."

43 Karen @stormy_weather8, "It's not Charmed. Nothing will ever come close to the acting, the writing, story lines and on-screen chemistry," Twitter, February 8, 2018, https://x.com/stormy_weather8/status/961744319295221760.

44 Comment from Dustin Turner on Choice.org petition: Jacoby, "Stop the *Charmed* Reboot."

45 Charmed Daily (@charmeddaily), "I wish they would just #StopCharmedReboot but they don't pay attenton to fans and they are just doing this for money targeting other new audience. Shame.," Twitter, March 16, 2018, https://x.com/CharmedDaily/status/974730090767581184; Charmed Fan (@buddhistmermaid), "This rebellion against the reboot has never been about race. CW could've hired white people and I still wouldn't want the reboot. As someone with Latino/Caribbean blood please tell me again how I'm mad there's Latino Representation #StopCharmedReboot," Twitter, https://x.com/BuddhistMermaid/status/973596852716175360.

46 Tanya Katerí Hernández, *Racial Innocence: Unmasking Latino Anti-Black Bias and the Struggle for Equality* (Beacon Press, 2022).

47 wolf eating up shadows (@lainbeom), "Im about to finish first season of charmed and already want the second season to start! I love the diverse cast!! #charmedreboot #charmed2019 #madeleinemantock #sarahjeffery #meloniediaz #afrolatino #latinx," Twitter, June 10, 2019, https://x.com/Lainbeom/status/1138053168875679744.

48 Maureen Lee Lenker, "*Charmed* May Be Over, But the Feud Between the Original and the Reboot Is Not," *Entertainment Weekly*, June 13, 2002, www.ew.com.

49 Kathleen Loock, "American TV Series Revivals: Introduction," *Television & New Media* 19, no. 4 (2018): 299–309, https://doi.org/10.1177/1527476417742971.

50 Holly Marie Combs (@H_Combs), "Here's the thing. Until you ask us to rewrite it like Brad Kern did weekly don't even think of capitalizing on our hard work. Charmed belongs to the 4 of us, our vast amount of writers, crews and predominantly the fans. FYI you will not fool them by owning a title/stamp. So bye," Twitter, January 26, 2018, https://x.com/H_Combs/status/956781792517701633.

51 See Alexandra D'Aluisio, "Alyssa Milano Slams 'Disrespectful' Reboot of 'Charmed' (Exclusive)," *Us Weekly*, May 21, 2019, www.usmagazine.com.

52 USC Annenberg's Inclusion Initiative and UCLA's Hollywood Diversity Report both cite inequities in television production.

53 Stuart Hall, "Race, Culture, and Communications: Looking Backward and Forward at Cultural Studies," *Rethinking Marxism* 5, no. 1 (1992): 10–18, https://doi.org/10.1080/08935699208657998.

54 Peter Kuryla, "Barack Obama and the American Island of the Colour Blind," *Patterns of Prejudice* 45, no. 1–2 (2011): 119–32, https://doi.org/10.1080/0031322X.2011.563150.

11

Shock! Horror! The 13th Doctor Will Be a Woman

Reading Online Misogynist Response as Transphobic Gender Confusion

JOKE HERMES AND SOPHIE EEKEN

READING NOTE: Returning to the relationship between nostalgia and dominant gender norms in television as a culture industry, the analysis by Hermes and Eeken focuses on the anti-women discourse by some *Doctor Who* anti-fans. Specifically, the authors compare anti-fan and fan responses to the Doctor Who Gender Reveal when, for the first time in the decades-long history of this perpetual sci-fi reboot, the main protagonist was cast as a white woman. Through their analysis the authors move beyond the knee-jerk e-bile comments that by now almost customarily come the way of women actors and producers and toward an understanding of how these comments facilitate a conversation, however uncouth and uneasy, that speaks to inequality and cultural citizenship, that is inflected with notions of audiences' nostalgic belonging, and that informs us about the needs and wants of different publics in society, and media texts' contribution to all of to it.

Introduction

Like other "legacy" figures in popular media culture, Doctor Who, a shape-shifting humanoid alien who travels through time and space, after twelve installments as a guy, got a rebooted facelift with a gender flip to a woman. As one of the oldest still-running perpetually revived TV series, *Doctor Who* is a phenomenon with a huge worldwide fan base. For most of the Doctors' existence, they have been "he." After the upheaval over "13," the Doctor has reincarnated again as a man, although notably now a man of color, played by actor Ncuti Gadwa, whose breakout role was as a gay teenager in the series *Sex Education* (2019–2023, Netflix). Yet it was the BBC online Reveal video in 2017 that garnered a veritable storm of reactions, many of them deeply upset and hostile toward the idea of a woman playing the Doctor. Such reactions to women taking on established male roles are not uncommon. Similar to negative responses to ethnic and racial flips in rebooted shows such as *Charmed* (chapter 10) and *Party of Five* (chapter 5) discussed in this collection, the anti-fandom surrounding the gender recasting of Doctor Who may be read as a symptom of the continuing underlying sexism and patriarchal structures in the cultural practices of societies.

The Gender Reveal

In hindsight and with actor Jodie Whittaker having come to the end of her stint as the thirteenth Doctor, it feels almost ridiculous to go back to the avalanche of heated reactions to the BBC's Reveal of the new Doctor in 2017. Looking back, it seems little more than a flash in a pan, your everyday outbreak of misogyny, painful to behold but soon over. But was it a mere moment of disgust at men losing their representational privilege to women? Or was it something more culturally and socially significant?

It all started on July 16, 2017, with a video: "Shock, horror: the next actor to play the eponymous protagonist in *Doctor Who*, the BBC's long-running science fiction television series, turned out to be a woman."[1] Despite twelve actors having played the Doctor, none of the Doctor's embodiments had until then been female. In previous work in 2019, we inquired how the Reveal video was interpreted and made meaningful in comments posted on YouTube by a variety of fans and viewers, ranging from negative to neutral to positive.[2] Here, we would like to continue discussion of how legacy figures have the power to activate broadly shared gender anxieties bound in heteronormative and cisgender nostalgia.

In the first part of this chapter, we focus on the reactions to the Reveal, collected in 2017 and 2018 from YouTube.[3] The comments show a gamut of emotions and a surprising amount of anger and disgust. We then move to online discussions of Jodie Whittaker's seasons as the Doctor. We conclude by asking ourselves what exactly the core issues were in anti-fan discussion of a female Doctor. Beyond discourses of male disenfranchisement hover discourses grounded in transphobia and a deep cultural distrust of the BBC. Thus, an analysis of the response to Whittaker's casting provides an opportunity to reconsider how audiences understand gender in media representation and its relationship to issues of institutional governance. If gendered representation and governance are intertwined, discourses of legacy figures in media entertainment need to be less about role models and more about how they are informed by our notions of social justice.

For those unfamiliar with the series (and with apologies to its fans), *Doctor Who* feels nostalgic and old-fashioned. For audiences of a certain age, it is reminiscent of the children's television of the late 1960s and '70s, the period in which the first seasons were made. Although the Doctor's look and dress code have clearly changed, the Doctors all use a "sonic" screwdriver as their main weapon and generally do not physically fight or use what Yvonne Tasker somewhat jokingly called "masculinity."[4] The Doctor is a rebellious Time Lord who flees Gallifrey, their species' home planet, in the TARDIS space and time machine. Curious by nature, the Doctor ends up in the midst of adventure after adventure. These usually begin with the investigation of some intriguing event or phenomenon that turns into the Doctor having to protect innocent beings from evil forces. In doing so, the Doctor relies largely on ingenuity and wit. Throughout his incarnations, he has mostly been aided by female companions. For those who want to read more about the Doctor and the Doctor's fans, suggestions are included in the notes section at the end of this chapter.[5]

2017: The Reveal

The Reveal was posted on YouTube and Facebook as well as on the BBC site. In the first year, the Reveal was viewed 3,214,641 times on the BBC's web site and prompted 31,691 written comments. The video was also posted on Facebook, where it was viewed over eleven million times and garnered 44,900 comments. As the BBC moderates its own website, we chose to focus on videos posted by fans on YouTube in which they commented on the casting decision. In Spring 2018 there were over fifty thousand videos tagged "Thirteenth Doctor" on YouTube and over four million comments tagged "Female Doctor Who."[6]

Such a large volume of spontaneously offered material was irresistible and much easier to retrieve than Facebook posts dispersed over groups and pages. The downside in using YouTube is that commenters remain anonymous through the use of screen names. YouTube's user comments, in addition, have a bad reputation. Indeed, *The New York Times* typifies them as "juvenile," "aggressive," "misspelled," and "sexist."[7] There was a risk, then, that our analysis would fall victim to a built-in bias toward the most sexist and negative comments. A random check of open-group Facebook comments, however, suggested that this was not the case. On the open Facebook Doctor Who page, comments and their tone corresponded to those we found on YouTube.[8] Also, while generally, both on YouTube and Facebook, the comments posted beneath the Reveal video and reaction videos were negative in tone, there were also those who defended the choice of a woman as the new Doctor.[9] Plus, as you will see from their screen names, which we have include with the quotes, whatever their views, many commenters have a real sense of humor that is difficult not to like.

The 2017 Comments

In the comments to the Reveal reaction videos, a clear majority disapproved of the casting and perceived it as a means of aggressively pushing a progressive political agenda. Mostly these comments bespeak antifeminist ideology. "This feminist takeover is a joke, everything they touch, they kill," Mark Evans, one of the many commenters, wrote.[10] The anger against feminism expressed here is akin to the anti-fandom found in other reboots where the gender and racial identity of the characters are flipped, such as Isabel Molina discusses in this collection with regards to the postfeminist anti-fandom of the *Charmed* reboot.

> The change wasnt made for diversity sake, it was mad to replace yet another 'white male character' with a 'minority' (which to feminism, women are classified as minorities . . . somehow). This whole thing is to take men and specifically white men, and replace them as much as they can. Which is the main reason I hate the decision. (Shiirow)

> Yup. The first commandment of Feminism is 'Vagina gud, penis bahahahaaad.' If wonder woman ever did anything that made men not look like inferior subhumans, Feminists would go amok. (My Ingroup Idol Did Nothing Wrong)

These anti-fans agree that feminism is the problem. They see the flipped gender casting of Doctor Who as an extremist threat: "Those followers of feminism that act to suppress and silence those of the male gender, classic fascist tactics, are perfectly reasonably compared to Nazis, hence the portmanteau feminazi."[11] The logic underlying these comments is that the BBC has been taken over by a left-wing elite minority, and that this minority, despite its progressive posturing, is actually of an extreme, right-wing variety.

Another line of thought that runs throughout these comments blames the former showrunner Steven Moffat (2010–2017) ("Moffat killed the show," according to Thewolv0667). The last couple of seasons were "proof" of bad writing, driven by "SJW motives." *SJW* stands for "social justice warrior" and is used by online communities as a derogatory term for anyone who supports diversity initiatives, including ethnic, racial, and gender equity movements. The casting of a female Doctor by a new showrunner is seen as a final blow to the show's earlier entertainment value. The casting of Jodie Whittaker thus came to stand for feminism, and the perceived ways in which it disturbs what Sara Ahmed calls "the promise of happiness, or the social pressure to maintain signs of getting along." In this context, women generally—and feminists specifically—are typecast and represented as "killjoys."[12]

There is also a small number of commenters (most of them responding to Tessa Netting's positive reaction video discussed below) that were optimistic about the gender change. Their posts characterized the move as bringing something "fresh" to the series. A female Doctor, some suggested, signaled possibilities for new storylines in an exceptionally long-running series: "Honestly I am so excited to see all the areas of the show it can open up. It gives them so much they can explore" (Heavenly Imaginings).

Gender Anxiety

Crucial to understanding reactions to the Reveal video is that the themes of patience and emancipation accounted for only a tiny portion of the comments compared to those that we grouped under grief, trauma, conspiracy, hostility, and treason. The preponderance of negative comments about the gender of the Doctor speak to how deeply this change in representation (de)stabilized the commenters' sense of identity and community, similar to the anti-fandom analysis of *Charmed*. From the beginning of the series in 1963 and up until the twelfth Doctor, the producers maintained a stable narrative structure and the promise of continuity guaranteed by the gender of the Doctor. Roger Silverstone has termed this the "ontological security" that television can offer.[13] For a considerable number of viewers and fans, changing the Doctor's gender exposed the fragility of the dominant social order. It was not the specific actor playing the Doctor that mattered so much as the instability of gender as a category and the perceived power of the BBC over nostalgic imaginings of the world, our future, and the powerlessness individuals may feel in fast-changing societies.[14]

A deep nostalgia for traditional gender norms where men, specifically white men, are the source of power and control colors feelings of grief and loss for the series fans, as illustrated below:

> There is no bright side to this situation for many of the Doctor's longtime classic and nuwho fans. We see this as a time of mourning, as indeed, #TheDoctorIsDead. (Krychick SPP)
>
> Rip . . . and i thought that he would just regenerate. (RedCowCat)

Commenters grieving the loss of their narratively dead and beloved Doctor were aware of other audiences more positive and emancipatory arguments about the arguments:

> The doctor was a non-stereotypical role model for boys. Not a fighter, but an intellectual. Yet someone who could still be "cool". Taking this away we're left with a load of GI Joe's unless the trend keeps shifting and we get male heroes who aren't sleeping with every second girl and picking up mass murder with weapons within 5 minutes. (James Grieves)

It seems to be the case that *why* the Doctor's gender matters to fans is important: Is it the character's *becoming* a woman or *being* a woman that is so problematic?

In the most negative comments, cis-male gender is endowed with a mythic status and idealized masculinity serves as a guarantee against the status of men in society declining, as FallenSnowWolf argues:

> This was my problem with Ghostbusters [another recent popular film to cast women in men's roles] but people need to understand that you can just take a character and change its sex and say it works but they do not realize that men and women have very different characteristics and writers dont realize this that women dont like seeing their female characters act like men. The only people that are happy are a small group that is really loud or bata males for a lack of a better word. Women want men to be manly and women to be feminine. The average woman hates SFC and love their men like men. (FallenSnowWolf)

The fact that *Doctor Who* was rebooted in 2005 after cancellation in 1989 adds to commenters' worries. A similar demise is cynically predicted:

> [B]e prepared for a 10 year cancellation folks, with a bit of luck in 2027 we'll have the same effect the 2005 reboot had, great stories, great actors and actresses but above all the Doctor being who he always was and always should be, a Man. (Sewell_27)

The idea that the Doctor's regeneration as a woman is a social conspiracy by feminists appears to provide users with a target for their grief and trauma. Comments adhering to this view describe feminism as a radical anti-male movement.

In television and film programs, the fan theory goes, (white) males are targeted for elimination. Feminism becomes a fight not for "actual" diversity, but rather for female domination.

> This was blatant misandry and pandering to feminists in the name of "diversity". The more male characters they can remove from lead roles, the happier they seem to get (Axess2084)

Commenters found it astounding that the BBC would adhere to what was perceived as new diversity norms in the media: "It is certainly concerning, BBC is drinking the Social Justice kool aid" (Scott Schinke). For these commenters the world has gone off-kilter. Balance and reason have been lost. There is no respect for historically established "dynamics":

> The doctor we know was always a man, he always had female companions, and its a theme that the show is known for, it is the dynamic of the

> show, a man taking a woman around the universe and back again. For me this is breaking the concept of the show, it is now not a lonely man showing ladies round the universe, but a Feminist . . . . . . (Gary Moore)

There is also a smaller number of reactions that offer blatant misogyny, transphobia, and homophobia, sometimes couched in jokes and off-color humor: "Nurse who?" (Mank Deme). Other comments illustrate disgust, misogynism, and transphobia:

> Basically, in brief terms- Now that Dr Who is morphed into TRANNY gay married Charles Manson SUPERGAY child Abductor & possible molester, the morons at BBC cant understand why this kids show is failing. . . . . . . The show is dead. (Friedrich Schultz)

> Is he now trans? Conveniently right at the height of all this far left, ultra feminist transgender crap? It was a calculated decision, and Chriss Chibnall [the new showrunner in 2017] knew exactly what he was doing. (Jay Pond)

This type of statement represents the most outspoken criticisms of the new Doctor. They read like "geek fragility."[15] Geek fragility is reminiscent of "white fragility," that is, the hostility expressed by white subjects in the face of racial stress:

> a state in which even a minimum amount of racial stress becomes intolerable, triggering a range of defensive moves. These moves include the outward display of emotions such as anger, fear, and guilt, and behaviors such as argumentation, silence, and leaving the stress-inducing situation. These behaviors, in turn, function to reinstate white racial equilibrium.[16]

Likewise, geek fragility "is a constructed fantasy, a world in which young white men outside the traditional definitions of masculinity are victims turned heroes, entitled to their rewards."[17] Cult texts such as *Ghostbusters* in Blodgett and Salter's research, or *Doctor Who*, are particular properties for geek subcultures, where the original film and television series can become something as sacred as the Judeo-Christian Bible.[18] The previously mentioned comments, despite being in the minority, evoke the "geek" culture of *Doctor Who* fandom by deploying discourses of betrayal in the face of their key text being rebooted to be more representationally inclusive. Their geek sense of treason, however, is also echoed in the multitude of milder comments that combined gender conservatism, fear of change, and populist distrust of elite institutions, such as the BBC.

Counternarratives to Doctor Who's Anti-Fandom

Patience!

How then did other recurring themes by fans counter the ideology of gender anxiety and distrust outlined above? Some simply tried to bypass the whole issue of gender. "Withholding judgment" or neutral comments sought to solicit fans' patience by appealing to their "loyalty and trust" in the series' legacy. These neutral commenters are built on fan nostalgia and respect for previous iterations of the show.

> So, there's some reasons, but time will tell. With reservations, will give it a chance, hoping it will prove us wrong. I've contemplated, same as you, but I think we owe that to The Doctor ;) (CS)

> Why wouldn't you [watch the new season]? Because it's a woman? You have no idea how she's going to be as the Doctor and the fact that you don't even want to give her a chance because of her gender means you're not a real fan of the series anyways. (LonerStoner)

These comments suggest that gender or the identity of the Doctor should never be an issue for true fans of the series: "It shouldn't matter whether the Doctor is a man, women, black, white, ginger, or blonde" (Ashnuim Games). Others express amazement over how important biological gender is for others: "If gender doesn't matter to people then why are they making such a fuss over it? Give her a chance she may be fantastic!" (Paul Richards).

Advocating patience conveyed both hope and worry. The new female Doctor was not immediately assumed to be a failure. Success, however, would depend on the production team's ability to develop a female lead character in line with previous iterations of the Doctor: "As for the Doctor being female, I'm OK with the idea. However, it will depend on the way the story is told" (Stewart Nicolson). Implied in fan reservations is the assumption that a female lead is a more difficult and risky choice than the "usual" male casting. While denying that gender is important, there is a sense of solidity in tradition and that tradition happens to be that the Doctors are always men.

Emancipation

Gender anxiety and denial of the importance of gender difference is complemented by a particular type of positive gender ideology. Casting a woman as the Doctor thus becomes part of a wider move toward inclusive media representation: "it's a small step that feels more like a giant leap for equality and inclusion on television" (Doc Trower). *Doctor Who* became a symbol of social progress:

> I feel like it's really important to introduce, like a different gender. I think that BBC introduced a female doctor to make a change. An actual change. (Retroforbes)

Dreamfaller63 was moved to tears and felt that now s/he was allowed to assume "her place. I don't have to be the companion anymore, the sidekick. I can be the smart sexy space lady. All I've ever wanted. Thank you Doctor Who for taking this long overdue step." Others too see the re-gendered Doctor as proof that women can now imagine themselves to be anything in any role:

> I love that the doctor is a female because now I feel like I can actually be the doctor not just pretend to be her. (Eleanor Richardson)

> I'm anxious for her season to begin! Yay!! Finally a woman! (Marta Peterson Womack)

> I cant wait for the female doctor!!!! How can we effect change in the world when only half of it is invited or feel welcome to participate in the conversation. (EmmaTEr_123)

> SOOOO happy the new doctor is Female! Have been waiting for a role model like that in this show for ever, and I expect great things from her :D (Piano Kallan)

Given #MeToo activism and the increasing attention to the male domination of media industries during the gender recasting of this role, it was not particularly radical to applaud the casting of a woman as the Doctor. Nonetheless, it is a distinct and happy moment for those fans who read it as a symbol of emancipation and equality. As Dreamfaller63 put it, "Boys had 54 years of the doctor. . . . It's time the other half of the population gets their share." This type of political reasoning can be traced back through both socialist and liberal feminism to first-wave Suffragette activism.[19] We note, however, that emancipatory politics such as these can also easily fall prey to either essentialism, which equates bodies with an innate gender, or to forms of reasoning that discount intersectional logic in the functioning of social power relations at the expense of people of color.[20] Emancipatory gender ideology may be less far removed from gender anxiety than you would expect.

Rearguard Battles

Overall, the comments read as a battle over what might be called "cultural citizenship." Commenters exercise the right and take on the responsibility to engage with others in conversation about their worries, hopes, and dreams, and what might be the best world for most of us.[21] Together the comments speak to a diverse fan community that uses the series to yearn for a more normative past or hopeful present and future, to reflect upon social and political conflicts while always revering the Doctor. In all but the most extreme comments, commenters do not appear to relegate women to defined cultural spaces or representational roles. The problem for some fans becomes the act of *changing* the Doctor's long-standing gender more than the character's performance of femininity or the writers' development of the character. Gender clearly mattered, but it mattered to viewers and fans in different ways. We cannot say whether it is the fans' and viewers' sense of common ownership over the series that started the debate, or whether the Reveal video simply served as an opportunity for venting existing gender anxiety, or, most likely, both.

Whichever the case, the Reveal video functioned as the kind of "incitement to discourse" through which gender and race emerge as contested social categories in the present moment.[22] Audiences' feelings of happiness and contentment become tied to the historical privileges accorded to some and their resulting oppression of others. Given that transgenderism and gender-neutral toilets in workplaces and public buildings are likewise engendering enormous discussion, it seems that the Reveal video was explicitly used, at least in part, to tap into these pre-existing anxieties and as a symbol of the loss of a normative and recognizable social world in which men are men, and men and women are never the same. In this world, women are never able to achieve the status of the Doctor. For the vocal majority of the fanbase, the instability of the Doctor's gender became supremely upsetting. Their emotional response became intertwined with feelings of injustice, powerlessness, and dependence of what are perceived as unaccountable cultural and social institutions.

Five years after the recasting of *Doctor Who*, the ferocious energy of the reactions to the Reveal has all but dissipated. Checking YouTube again for reaction videos of the seasons that featured Jodie Whittaker (or "13" as she is referred to), we do not find much discussion of the gender flip. There are fans who declare their love for the new Doctor and quote from the series or who leave comments underneath Jodie Whittaker making fun of all the negative reactions that have come her way.

There are some commenters who continue to return to negative sentiments about the showrunner not doing a good job, such as "did her dirty" (Hannah Barch). Negative commenters reiterate that the show "has failed" (i.e., its ratings were not very good) and there are some who reiterate attacks on the idea of a female Doctor. In these comments, we reencounter the themes of grief and betrayal. Betrayal quotes still invoke words like *lesbian* and *trans*, *woke* and *social justice warrior* as insults, and the feeling of having been betrayed by the BBC remains as strong as ever. Within the negative comments there is a group to whom Whittaker has proven herself as an actress, notwithstanding the "bad writing." As septile vg says: "Jodie is so great here im sorry for her for bad writing two seasons :(." Corbin Vickers adds, "It's a shame that the first female doctor had to be ruined by the writing of this series."

In general, it seems to us that there is less e-bile.[23] Negative videos and comments are clearly a minority. When you have clicked on one negative video, the YouTube algorithm generally offers you the next, but it did not manage to come up with much. Had such videos been available, they would have been suggested to us. We could not find traces of the previous strong links between negative comments and gender and diversity either. Anti-fans of the recast Doctor Who seemed to have decamped to another bit of the internet and were not bothering to engage through YouTube.

The Jodie Whittaker Fanbase

The sheer size of the Reveal material may have hidden that Jodie Whittaker has a strong fan base. (Or her personal fans simply waited for the storm to blow over.) Five years after the Reveal, comments such as below are easy to find. Monsore long, for example, writes: "She was wasted imo. She's a great actress and had hardly any good episodes." Violet Herald replies to a remark by Night Bot,

> She can act. The problem is, due to the writing, her character feels a bit off and forced. Same thing happened to prequel Anakin Skywalker. George Lucas wasn't very good at making dialogue. In this example though, Chibnall's just not cut right.

Kate Hall concurs:

> Completely agree. We've seen that she can do the crazy/witty side of the Doctor and we've seen glimpses of her being able to do the serious aspects but I feel she needs more grand scenes to really show us she's the Doctor, scenes like Capaldi's War Speech or Smith's stonehenge speech.

Five years past the Reveal video there are also far more conversations between commenters who are not critical of the gender flip on cultural grounds. Kota Hope's reply to Mysterygamer MGClues shows that there is fan discussion that has no truck with either gender anxiety or essentialism:

> @Mysterygamer MG:Clues: You're right, and I can see that happening. Though this type of situation happens so much in fandoms that one can only flip a coin at this point for how the fans will turn. Which is too bad, as I love this Doctor. I don't have a problem much with this doctor as I have a writer's brain, as my mom calls it, and understand what the show was going for. I don't focus too much on the commentary of the story for real-world things, as I do for the story itself in the show. That's why I love doctor who. And so many people write for doctor who, in books and audios, and create a story within the universe that it is amazing. I just hope that the fandom doesn't give up on this show, just because of this doctor. (Kota Hope)
>
> @Kota Hope: yeah. though with some those youtubers spreading negativity it may be hard (Mysterygamer MCClues).
>
> @Mysterygamer MGClues: Yep . . . (Kota Hope)

Weaponized Sarcasm

One of the YouTubers still spreading negativity against the recast is The Critical Drinker. In 2020 The Critical Drinker posted a slightly less than five-minute video "'Fugitive of the Judoon'—Doctor Who's most stunning and brave episode ever" that sarcastically comments on the show's attempt to be inclusive.[24] It underlines the bad ratings and serves up misogyny as humor. Also engaging in sarcasm, other commenters bond with the Drinker. D.P. Robertz remarks, "Now we know why the Doctor has never settled down with anyone. He's a strong, independent black woman who don't need no man."

This inspires Guy Incognito and a number of other commenters:

> She left Gallifrey for cigarettes 60 years ago and never looked back. (Guy Incognito)
>
> AND she's "body-positive" (Freewheeler !)

> D. P. Robertz This is the best comment, sistah!! (Sigma Cronos)
>
> You meant transgender (Rusty Padlock)
>
> Uhhh huuuuh honey. (Click my fingers in a sideways motion) (Cheekvegg)
>
> Witch Doctor are we talking about? Get it? Witch Doctor!!! (WideAwake)
>
> I'm so proud of Chibnall, he's so brave and revolutionary! For so long i've wanted an overweight, butch, middle aged black lesbian doctor, and they've finally delivered on that dream. I think this is what we all wanted, deep in our hearts. Such a brave. (DarthWall275)

Replacing the shock horror of the early reactions, sarcasm has become the weapon of those who feel betrayed by television producers and the erosion of a social era where these fans felt powerful.

In addition to comments that simply repeat "the show ended" (Adam J. Cuthbert, Paul W.) or "died" (Dark Highwayman) with earlier show-runners, other commenters turn to sarcasm to suggest that the "death" of Doctor Who is part of the entire collapse of culture as they knew it: "What a decade it has been for cinema. SW, GoT, Dr Who, Ghostbusters, MIB, Terminator, ... What's next? Indiana Jones? Oh yeah, 007 too" (kohisaaa kohisaaa). All of the films are ones that have been rebooted through gender- or racially flipped casting.

Sarcasm, generally understood to be a form of irony, is also related to anxieties over social power or inequality. A cross-cultural study concluded that "the most common reasons for using sarcasm were 'to be funny' and 'have fun with friends.'"[25] However, the authors note that men are more likely to use sarcasm than women and that women tend to be the target of sarcasm. Surveying sarcasm literature, Drucker and coauthors note that "during the 1970s and 1980s, several studies found evidence showing an anti-female bias in the appreciation of humor. Humor deriding women was considered funnier than humor deriding men, among both female and male participants."[26] While generally sarcasm may be more widely used by women and against men in the recent comments (to keep to an overgeneralized and flat gender distinction for now), it seems safe to say that sarcasm is weaponized in these discussions for bonding among the gender-conservative commenters who identify as men.

"Filking" the Doctor

Fortunately, and as in 2017, there is more than gender-conservative disenchantment. There are those who simply disregard the bemoaning of the soon-to-be-expected or actual death of the Doctor to claim her (rather than him or them) for themselves.

> 13 is great, love almost every episode of hers "Are you two seeing each other?" "I don't think so. Are we?" Doctor being a lesbian (and me here loving it) (Femme Funtime)

> "13 being 13 for 13 minutes straight" there is absolutely nothing "straight" about Thirteen (The Reyyan is hiding in the Chernobyl Fleshlight)

> I just realized the 13 doctor is me if I was the doctor (Pink-A-Palouza)

These comments illustrate how here too filking and romantic fantasies are part of fan culture. They were a welcome sight among the sarcasm and negative feedback we also found. Filking is a fan-fiction creation where songs, singing, or musical videos are used to express their enjoyment of the texts. It's a misspelling of the word "folk," a sing-along activity common in fan conventions. The examples above are comments presented in filk form.

Conclusion

The initial wave of public feeling over the new gender of the Doctor after the Reveal showed how a woman cast as the Doctor became what Ahmed calls a "blockage point." She "disturb[ed] the promise of happiness," which Ahmed suggests she would "redescribe as the social pressure to maintain signs of getting along."[27] As in the earlier study, we find that an argument can be made for how the fight over ownership over the Doctor and over the gender identity of the Doctor can be understood as the performance of cultural citizenship, which shows itself as fierce discussion.[28] In the comments, the Reveal became a political platform, a space in which users could discuss their hopes and dreams for society in ways that link affect, emotion, and discursive practice.[29]

Grasping this entanglement of affect and discourse poses a significant methodological challenge.[30] As Ahmed puts it,

> emotions do things, and they align individuals with communities—or bodily space with social space—through the very intensity of their attachments. Rather than seeing emotions as psychological dispositions, we need to consider how they work, in concrete and particular ways, to mediate the relationship between the psychic and the social, and between the individual and the collective.[31]

Our only access to all these connections and mediations is through language, and language that is regularly doubly or triply coded through humor, sarcasm, and implicit references that we will not have picked up on. Ideally, a discourse-analytical approach such as this is followed by "live" contact with Doctor Who viewers and fans. We would love to talk with them about nostalgia and the world they see going asunder. We are also curious about the "stickiness" of binary gender definitions in both the gender-conservative comments and the women's emancipation comments. Only for those who declare their lesbian romantic interest in the Doctor, we expect the insult "tranny" would be something of a joke, but that too needs checking.

Taking a bird's eye view across the years, three positions now suggest themselves in the discussion of the Doctor. Most prominent is the one that objects to women being cast for legacy male roles; far less prominent is the position that such "recasting" does not undermine the social order. The third position implicitly takes faith in the social order further and undoes the heteronormative contract by turning the Doctor into a lesbian love object. It seems, then, that the minor shift in the cultural power that is associated with being represented as a legacy figure has a seismic effect. At issue in discussion of a female Doctor is more than male disenfranchisement or even transphobia. The deep distrust of the BBC and of the showrunners is surely also a sign of how the formal mission of public institutions has been regarded as mere camouflage. To see such institutions become accountable to new gender politics can only be a shock if they were felt to be embedded in older systems of social relations that provided well-defined and safe spaces for classes, religions, genders, and cultures.

Gender seems to be a remarkably strong activator of anxiety and nostalgia. When the BBC announced *Sex Education*'s Ncuti Gadwa (who played Eric, an attractive and outspoken gay character) as the new Doctor, none of the early commenters let rip the way they did when Whittaker was announced. If Black men who happily embrace a gay identity on screen are so much less a problem than white women, it is the gender of legacy figures in media entertainment that matters. As gendered role models they have, in a way, imprisoned our notions of social change and justice. Notably, the first commenters on YouTube reacting to a fan compilation of earlier Doctors introducing Gadwa mostly worry about the writing and, of course, about the BBC.

> Looks interesting, the actor seems to have charisma, no I just hope the writing doesn't let him down. (christian emden)

> Great trailer! Concerning though that fans on YouTube are putting more effort into advertising the new doctor than the BBC! (Alex Webb)

The moment of the 2017 Reveal and the massive (and predominantly negative) response seem to indicate a moment of deep gender confusion. As soon as the actual season featuring Jodie Whittaker as the thirteenth Doctor started, the attacks on the BBC as "social justice warriors" and "feminist traitors" died down. We noted clear signs in the online responses to the Reveal that much more is going on than simple hatred and disgust at a world that is taking away male privilege and thereby "destroying tradition." What can we learn from the 2017 flash-in-the-pan outbreak when we compare them to the conversations within isolated camps five years later? The amount of sarcasm has notably lessened. It seems to be related to the shock suffered by fans and the strength of their feelings.

It is important, we think, to query more closely how sarcasm can be responded to in a cultural citizenship discussion. Demanding respect for a diversity of gender, race, and sexual identifications to us seems crucial. To be a "killjoy" and not appreciate how sarcasm is also a gateway for satire would, however, hurt such a project. We can only hope that fierce discussion such as of Doctor number 13 has made clear that nostalgic investment needs to be made space for and that discourses of legacy figures in media entertainment need to be less about role models and more about how they are informed by our notions of social justice.

Discussion Questions

1. What do the anti-fan responses to the flipped gender casting of *Doctor Who* tell us about the UK's contemporary social order? Within the social order, who is privileged and who is perceived as threatening?
2. What do anti-fan responses tell us about the normative expectations of gender and racial nostalgia in reboots, remakes, and revivals?

NOTES

1 Author's own quote.

2 Sophie Eeken and Joke Hermes, "*Doctor Who*, Ma'am: YouTube Reactions to the 2017 Reveal of the New Doctor," *Television & New Media* 22, no. 5 (2021): 447–64, https://doi.org/10.1177/1527476419893040.

3 An example of negative response: Internalized Misogyny posted "The Female Doctor: Why People are ACTUALLY Pissed," July 22, 2017, www.youtube.com/watch?v=zhev3GI6oug; an example of a positive response: Tessa Netting posted "THE 13TH DOCTOR REACTION!! A Female Doctor Who," July 29, 2017, www.youtube.com/watch?v=ezMzya21XuE; an example of a neutral response: Mundanematt posted "A female Doctor Who . . . a pandering risk or righteous move?," July 16, 2017, 11:22, www.youtube.com/watch?v=TNLpDI_7wA4. Since making this video, Mundanematt has changed his screen name to Matt Jarbo; the other two videos are no longer available on YouTube.

4 Yvonne Tasker, *Spectacular Bodies: Gender, Genre and the Action Cinema* (Routledge, 2012).

5 A rich literature discusses the Doctor and their fans. Here are some references: Piers Britton, *TARDISbound: Navigating the Universes of Doctor Who* (I.B. Tauris, 2011); David Butler, ed., *Time and Relative Dissertations in Space: Critical Perspectives on 'Doctor Who'* (Manchester University Press, 2007); James Chapman, *Inside the Tardis: The Worlds of Doctor Who* (I.B. Tauris, 2013); John Cordone and Michelle Cordone, "Who Is the Doctor? The Meta-Narrative of Doctor Who," in *Ruminations, Peregrinations, and Regenerations: A Critical Approach to Doctor Who*, ed. Christopher J. Hansen (Cambridge Scholars Publishing, 2010),

8–21; Matt Hills, "Mainstream Cult," in *The Cult TV Book: From Star Trek to Dexter, New Approaches to TV Outside the Box*, ed. Stacey Abbott (I.B. Tauris, 2010), 67–73; Mat Hills, *Triumph of a Time Lord: Regenerating Doctor Who in the Twenty-First Century* (I.B. Tauris, 2010); Matt Hills, "Rebranding *Doctor Who* and Reimagining *Sherlock*: 'Quality' Television as 'Makeover TV Drama,'" *International Journal of Cultural Studies* 18, no. 3 (2015): 317–31, https://doi.org/10.1177/1367877913513692; Danny Nicol, *Doctor Who: A British Alien* (Palgrave Macmillan, 2018). A specifically feminist perspective can be found in these publications: Jared Aronoff, "Deconstructing Clara Who. A Female Doctor Made Possible by an Impossible Girl," *International Journal of TV Serial Narratives* 3, no. 2 (2017): 17–30, https://doi.org/10.6092/issn.2421-454X/7627; Brigid Cherry, "Extermi . . . Knit! Female Fans and Feminine Handicrafting," in *Fan Phenomena: Doctor Who*, ed. Paul Booth (Intellect, 2013), 106–15; Lorna Jowett, "The Girls Who Waited? Female Companions and Gender in *Doctor Who*," *Critical Studies in Television* 9, no. 1 (2014): 77–94, https://doi.org/10.7227/CST.9.1.6; Lorna Jowett, *Dancing with the Doctor: Dimensions of Gender in the Doctor Who Universe* (I.B. Tauris, 2017); Lorna Jowett, "'Is the Future Going to Be All Girl?' Doctor Who and the Frustrations of a Feminist," *CSTonline* (March 23, 2018), http://cstonline.net; Patricia Melzer, *Alien Constructions: Science Fiction and Feminist Thought* (University of Texas Press, 2010); Richard Wallace, "But Doctor?—A Feminist Perspective of Doctor Who," in *Ruminations, Peregrinations, and Regenerations: A Critical Approach to Doctor Who*, ed. Christopher J. Hansen (Cambridge Scholars Publishing, 2010), 102–16; Rebecca Williams, "Desiring the Doctor: Identity, Gender and Genre in Online Science-Fiction Fandom," in *British Science Fiction in Film and Television*, ed. Tobias Hochscherf and James Leggott (McFarland, 2011): 167–77.

6 We focused on comments of the first videos posted in three categories (critical/negative, positive, neutral). These three fan videos each had high viewing rates (over 30,000 views), generating around a thousand or more reactions per video. Our grounded theory analysis was based on the 4,230 responses to the three YouTube videos as well as the 31,691 responses to the official BBC Reveal video. Our focus on YouTube entails that we have no feedback from those who did not post comments or who do not use social media. Nor could we check commenters' gender as, unlike Facebook, YouTube uses screen names. Comments are the main way in which videos are discussed and an essential part of YouTube as a cultural form. Mike Thelwall's article is helpful in arguing why this is a valid method: Mike Thelwall, "Social Media Analytics for YouTube Comments: Potential and Limitations," *International Journal of Social Research Methodology* 21, no. 3 (2018): 303–16, https://doi.org/10.1080/13645579.2017.1381821. Others have also discussed YouTube as a specific cultural form. We used two sources: Peter Schultes et al., "Leave a Comment! An In-Depth Analysis of User Comments on YouTube," *Wirtschaftsinformatik Proceedings* 42 (2013): 659–73, http://aisel.aisnet.org/wi2013/42; Pelle Snickars and Patrick Vonderau, *The YouTube Reader* (Kungliga

Biblioteket, 2009). Grounded Theory as a method of research is described accessibly in Juliet M. Corbin and Anselm Strauss, "Grounded Theory Research: Procedures, Canons, and Evaluative Criteria," *Qualitative Sociology* 13, no. 1 (1990): 3–21, https://doi.org/10.1007/BF00988593. The foundational text is Barney Glaser and Anselm Strauss, *The Discovery of Grounded Theory* (Aldine, 1967).

7 Schultes et al., "Leave a Comment!," 660.

8 *Doctor Who* (official page), Facebook, www.facebook.com/DoctorWho/.

9 Our grounded analysis resulted in three clusters: *patience*, *emancipation*, and *gender anxiety*. They are based on the themes of praise, patience, love, conspiracy, hostility, treason, and trauma. We theorized these clusters as speaking to three affective practices in which television drama comes to intersect with feminist ideology, women's emancipation, and the loss of status, importance, and funding for public service. In two of these three clusters (*emancipation* and *gender anxiety*), gender is defined in binary categories and linked to gender nostalgia versus gender progress. *Patience* is built around the suggestion that gender may not be as important as it is made out to be by the other discussants. A definition of "affective practice" can be found in Margaret Wetherell, *Affect and Emotion* (Sage, 2012).

10 Mark Evans comment on Tessa Netting, "THE 13TH DOCTOR REACTION!! A Female Doctor Who." All quotes are verbatim. We have neither corrected language nor added anything to the cited quotes. We have used (long) excerpts. Where sentences have been left out of a running quote, this is indicated by an ellipsis (. . .). We choose not to mark passages with "sic," for misspelling is the norm rather than the exception in the YouTube comments we studied.

11 Ryan Gunn commented on "Thirteenth Doctor Reveal—Doctor Who," *Doctor Who*, July 16, 2017, video, 1:00, www.youtube.com/watch?v=_-_bSdWEYK8.

12 Sara Ahmed, "Killing Joy: Feminism and the History of Happiness," *Signs* 35, no. 3 (2010): 584, https://doi.org/10.1086/648513.

13 Roger Silverstone, *Television and Everyday Life* (Routledge, 1994): 5–8. Silverstone is quoting Anthony Giddens here.

14 Judith Butler, "Violence, Mourning, Politics" (Lecture, Feminist Theory Address, University College London, London, March 8, 2002).

15 Bridget Blodgett and Anastasia Salter, "*Ghostbusters* Is for Boys: Understanding Geek Masculinity's Role in the Alt-Right," *Communication Culture & Critique* 11, no.1 (2018), 149, https://doi.org/10.1093/ccc/tcx003.

16 Robin DiAngelo, "White Fragility," *International Journal of Critical Pedagogy* 3, no. 3 (2011), 57.

17 Blodgett and Salter, "*Ghostbusters* Is for Boys," 195.

18 Leora Hadas, "Resisting the Romance: 'Shipping' and the Discourse of Genre Uniqueness in *Doctor Who* Fandom," *European Journal of Cultural Studies* 16, no. 3 (2013): 330, https://doi.org/10.1177/1367549413476011.

19 Liesbet van Zoonen, *Feminist Media Studies* (Sage, 1994).

20 Judith Butler, *Bodies That Matter: On the Discursive Limits of Sex* (Routledge, 2011); Gloria Wekker, *White Innocence* (Duke University Press, 2016).
21 Joke Hermes, *Rereading Popular Culture* (Blackwell, 2005).
22 Michel Foucault, *The History of Sexuality: Volume 1: An Introduction*, trans. Robert Hurley (Random House, 1976), 17–18.
23 Emma Jane, "'Your a Ugly, Whorish, Slut': Understanding E-bile," *Feminist Media Studies*, 14, no. 4 (2014): 531–46, https://doi.org/10.1080/14680777.2012.741073.
24 The Critical Drinker, "'Fugitive of the Judoon'—Doctor Who's Most Stunning and Brave Episode Ever," *The Critical Drinker*, January 29, 2020, video, 4:47, https://youtu.be /watch?v=l_-hqqcS_xg.
25 Dawn Blasko, Victoria Kazmerski, and Shariffah Sheik Dawood, "Saying What You Don't Mean: A Cross-Cultural Study of Perceptions of Sarcasm," *Canadian Journal of Experimental Psychology/Revue Canadienne de Psychologie Expérimentale* 75, no. 2 (2021): 118, http://dx.doi.org/10.1037/cep0000258.
26 Ari Drucker et al., "On Sarcasm, Social Awareness, and Gender," *Humor* 27, no. 4 (2014): 552, https://doi.org/10.1515/humor-2014-0092.
27 Ahmed, "Killing Joy," 584.
28 Floris Müller and Joke Hermes, "The Performance of Cultural Citizenship: Audiences and the Politics of Multicultural Television Drama," *Critical Studies in Media Communication*, 27, no. 2 (2010): 193–208, https://doi.org/10.1080/1529503 0903550993.
29 Hermes, *Rereading Popular Culture*.
30 Annette Hill, *Media Experiences* (Routledge, 2019), 61.
31 Sara Ahmed, "Affective Economies," *Social Text* 22, no. 2 (Summer 2004): 119, https://doi.org/10.1215/01642472-22-2_79-117.

12

"It Was All a Dream"

Black Social Mobility and Recycling 1990s Black Situation Comedy

PATRICK JOHNSON

READING NOTE: If racial nostalgia in the rebooted *Charmed* signals the nationalistic values of white resentment, then this chapter turns to the continued recirculation of 1990s Black sitcoms to examine the potential of Black nostalgia by young television audiences. By talking with young Black Millennial college audiences, Patrick Johnson documents the role nostalgia plays in reinforcing heteronormativity and middle-class respectability. His analysis illustrates how the recirculation of Black middle-class characters creates a sense of "cruel optimism" that finds pleasure in the banality of everyday life that pushes the structural racism and inequality faced by first-generation students of color to the temporary background.

Introduction

Pointing to the proliferation of film adaptations of classic television series, commemorative box sets, reunion tours, and retrospective television programming, Simon Reynolds argues that we are in the age of retro, which he describes as "a self-conscious fetish for period stylization (in music, clothes, design) expressed creatively through pastiche and citation."[1] For some Black Millennials, the widespread availability of cultural artifacts from the past can result in a "strange kind of nostalgia," marked by "a yearning for a golden age that one never personally experienced."[2] As Nikki Ndukwe contends,

> Nostalgia for the '90s entails remembering a time that seemed simpler: no social media, cool style, awesome music and amazing television that

made us laugh. Nowadays, it's hard to walk down the street without seeing a hip millennial dressed in styles from their local vintage shop that mimic that of a 1995 sitcom character.[3]

The continuing syndicated, streamed, and digital cycling of Black situation comedies from the 1990s, such as *Martin* (1992–1997, Fox), *A Different World* (1987–1993, NBC), *The Cosby Show* (1984–1992, NBC), *Moesha* (1996–2001, UPN), and *The Fresh Prince of Bel-Air* (1990–1996, NBC), are among the media texts that contribute to Black Millennials' reverence for an era that preceded them.

The situation comedy's "feel good" ethos makes it a particularly rich site for thinking through what Badia Ahad-Legardy describes as "afro-nostalgia." Rejecting the notion that Black people's relationship with the past is exclusively traumatic, Ahad-Legardy offers afro-nostalgia as a means for not only thinking about the pleasure that Black people derive from returning to the past but also how such engagement allows Black people to reimagine possibilities within a given present. Ultimately, Ahad-Legardy implores us to take seriously the ways "the black historical past" inspires "'good feelings' in the present."[4]

Drawing on individual and focus group interviews with twenty-six Black college students, this chapter explores 1990 Black situation comedies' relationship to Black Millennial audiences' ideas about social mobility by providing a cultural lens through which they can imagine future versions of themselves. The data for this chapter was collected between March 2015 and November 2016 at West Coast University, an elite public research university in the Western region of the United States. Audiences were between eighteen and twenty-three years old at the time of the study. Audiences have been given pseudonyms to maintain their anonymity. Situating television consumption as an everyday learning practice, JoEllen Fisherkeller argues that the medium provides young people with materials for imagining "their particular version of the American Dream, in which they will be successful professionals, and live 'better', either economically or politically."[5] Such strategies are imaginative because "they are symbolic links connecting who the students are, their possible selves, and the circumstances of the particular adult worlds into which they want to move."[6] Much like a hip-hop music producer digging in crates of old vinyl, Black Millennial audiences return to the Black televisual past to sample strategies for their dreams and aspirations. Through the continual syndication of shows such as *The Fresh Prince of Bel-Air*, *Martin*, *Moesha*, and *Living Single*, audiences acquire "the ability to maintain hopes and dreams for the future, even in the face of real and perceived barriers," immersing themselves in "a culture of possibility" that allows them to envision their lives in the future.[7]

In this chapter, I first explore the myth of the American Dream as a dominant theme in 1990s Black situation comedies and how audiences relate to this theme in the programs. The American Dream is understood as a narrative that binds those in the United States through specific themes and assumptions, chief among which is the promise that anyone can succeed. Second, I examine Black Millennial audiences' own educational, professional, and social aspirations in relation to shows. Finally, recognizing that audiences occupy what Jacqueline Bobo and Stuart Hall describe as the negotiated reading positions of Black audiences, neither fully accepting nor rejecting the dominant themes encoded in media texts, I examine how audiences trouble critics' reading of the shows as only advancing narratives of unobstructed ascent.[8]

The Black Situation Comedy and the American Dream

Replete with imagery of Black educational and professional ascent, much of 1990s Black television constructs a United States where the American Dream is accessible to all its citizens. The America of the 1990s situation comedy was one where religious faith, hard work, and ingenuity all but guaranteed that one could improve one's lot in life regardless of racial and gender identity. This ideology undergirded *The Cosby Show*, which, Leslie Innis and Joe Feagin assert, left viewers with the impression that the Huxtable family would continue their upward mobility, and by extension Black people as a whole could also achieve upward mobility.[9] *The Cosby Show*'s popularity can be attributed to the producers' and writers' ideological commitment to presenting a world where race is not an impediment to social mobility.

The Cosby Show serves as the progenitor for many of the most popular 1990s Black situation comedies, comedies that represented the intersection of race and class in idealistic ways. And like *The Cosby Show*, *The Fresh Prince of Bel-Air*, *Living Single*, and *Moesha* presented "an ostensibly egalitarian, post-civil rights, 'post-racial' world" that simultaneously assuaged white concerns about race and class while offering Black viewers a tutorial on how they, like the faces they saw on-screen, could acquire a piece of the American Dream.[10] The programs' ability to appeal to a broad range of audiences ensured that they reached the requisite number of episodes to live on in syndication and thus be available for sampling by subsequent generations of viewers. As Bambi Haggins argues, it is through reruns that the American Dream "is refurbished for the contemporary spectator" and is codified through repetition.[11]

Black Millennials' Rebooting of the American Dream

Through their consumption of 1990s Black situation comedies, audiences learned that the American Dream was achievable, an idea that was reinforced through several elements of the shows. Todd, a twenty-one-year-old sociology major, recognizes that 1990s Black situation comedies' representations of universal situations, themes, and concerns resonate with audiences across racial lines. This is evident in the following interview excerpt:

> TODD: You still had the themes of family values, the themes of respect, parenting, education, sacrifice. It was a lot of common themes, looking back now you can kind of relate to those themes. Going to college. Striving to be successful. Independence. You see those back then.
>
> PJ: Do you think those themes are important?
>
> TODD: It helps people relate to them. A lot of those shows were highly popular, not just among Black America but among America in general . . . I can resonate with wanting to go to college. I can resonate with parents sacrificing to raise their children and to send them off to college and get them to be independent.

Todd's observations reflect an understanding of how 1990s Black situation comedies often subscribed to what Herman Gray describes as "separate but equal discourses."[12] In such shows, Black characters reside in predominantly Black worlds but live lives that mirror characters in white-casted situation comedies. In doing so, the programs "maintain a commitment to the universal acceptance into the transparent 'normative' middle class," while also challenging the chains of equivalence that equate Blackness with poverty.[13] In the process, the programs reinforce the impression that Black people in the 1990s had access to educational, professional, and social opportunities that previously eluded them during the Jim Crow era.

Pointing to the representation of social mobility in *Moesha*, Taj, a twenty-year-old junior majoring in African American studies, acknowledges the purchase of linking racial progress with Black people's increased professional opportunities, particularly for white audiences:

> I feel like there is a certain idea of social mobility embedded in the shows or some type of homage to the Black middle class and acknowledging that they exist. I think that's really the branding of these shows. We're not content with our position as a lower-status class and we're working towards that the best we know how. Like in *Moesha*, [her father, Frank] sold cars and [her stepmother, Dee] was the principal. "Oh, that's a nice Black middle-class family." *That's a decent life for a lot of white people. It just makes white audiences feel like that's good racial progress* [italics added]. Like Martin, he's the radio personality, you know Black people couldn't have those positions in the 1940s, so that's good for Black people.

Focusing on *Moesha*'s narrative, Taj explains how the show's cross-racial appeal is predicated on affirming, rather than challenging, the idea that the American Dream is accessible for all. *Moesha* and *Martin* reinforced the commonsense notion that by the mid-1990s race relations in the United States had progressed to the point where there were few substantive differences between the life chances of Blacks and whites. As a high school principal and a car salesman, *Moesha*'s Dee and Frank Mitchell represented a path to upward social mobility that could be achieved through higher education and an entrepreneurial spirit.

The increased opportunities for Black actors in the television industry during the 1990s also suggested that talent and a strong work ethic was all that was necessary for Black Americans to achieve social mobility. Herman Gray writes, "Successful blacks who populate primetime television are charming, unique, and attractive individuals who, we assume reached their stations in life through hard work, skill, talent, discipline, and determination," confirming "the American value of individual success and mobility."[14] For Black viewers, the higher number of Black bodies in 1990s television proved inspirational for those needing the cultural source material to imagine a better life for themselves:

> LORENZO: [The 1990s] was a time when Black folks had just gotten their foothold in the television industry. They had just begun to get their own television shows with their own names on [them]. I feel like it did play a big role in the Black community. It put out the image that you can obtain that as a Black person.

The presence of eponymous Black situation comedies in the 1990s like *Martin*, *The Fresh Prince of Bel-Air*, and *The Jamie Foxx Show* advanced a perception that Black actors wielded considerable creative control over the shows that boasted their names. For Black viewers, the actors' success in the white-dominated field of prime-time television is evidence that social mobility is possible for all Black people. In the next section, I explore how Black Millennial audiences watching reruns of 1990s Black sitcoms on syndication, streaming, or YouTube today produce a cultural rebooting that enacts imaginative strategies for visioning future versions of themselves, educationally, professionally, and socially.

Rebooting the Cultural Past to Imagine Educational Futures

Black television in the 1990s placed particular emphasis on featuring college-educated Black people, reinforcing a long-held belief in the African American community that obtaining a college degree is key to combating systemic racism en route to achieving the American Dream. Black scholars and cultural critics often point to the popularity of *The Cosby Show* and its university-based spin-off series, *A Different World*, as contributing to a spike in Black college enrollment during the 1980s and 1990s, particularly at Historically Black Colleges and Universities (HBCUs).[15] The shows were often recruited into a broader discourse in 1990s Black popular culture that constructed the university as one of the sites where Black youth could gain a deeper understanding of their racial identities while also acquiring the preparation necessary to embark on a well-paying job and ultimately leading to economic stability. The audiences I interviewed drew on the pro-college ethos of 1990s Black situation comedies not only to help imagine themselves as college students but also to gain some understanding of what was required to become college students.

For Tonya, a twenty-one-year-old senior, double majoring in psychology and molecular environmental biology, not only did the shows provide images of college life to which she could aspire to, but they also provided points of comparison as her life started to resemble the lives of the characters she admired:

> It really felt good to kind of be at the same level as some of the characters I liked. I remember *A Different World*, like "Oh, I'm in college like them now." I always thought that was really cool. And just remembering *Moesha* and *Sister, Sister* and all of them started going to college, like I was part of that process too. It was really real. I always knew I was going to college but it was like getting a glimpse of what that might be like for me from the shows. Even though I knew it wasn't real, it was like "Oh, this could still happen."

Like Tonya, others cited *A Different World* as a critical text for helping them see themselves in college.

As the only network television show to focus on the lives of students at a historically Black college, *A Different World* is a stark contrast to the predominantly white images of university life often seen in mainstream television, such as *Saved by the Bell: The College Years* (1993–1994, NBC), *Felicity* (1998–2002, The WB), and *Blue Mountain State* (2010–2011, Spike) and films like *Animal House* (1978, Universal), *Old School* (2003, DreamWorks), and *Neighbors* (2014, Universal). As one interviewee puts it, *A Different World* "showed a lot of elements of what Black colleges were like to television [audiences] and what they could be like. Everyone wanted to go to that college when they were young." While *A Different World* focuses on the experiences of Black students at an HBCU, the students I spoke with found the show useful source material for understanding their experiences at a PWI (predominantly white institution) because, as one participant puts it,

> Even though we don't go to a HBCU, we're still black students pursuing higher education in [a] context where we're not supposed to pursue higher education . . . Even though we're at a PWI and we're hella low in numbers, but that TV show just helps capture the world that we kind of exist in and the struggles we have.

As the above quote illustrates, the syndication of *A Different World* carries considerable resonance for Millennial Black college students trying to make sense of their new identity, seeking to understand the circumstances of the new economic world they are striving to join.

For example, while participating in a pre-college summer enrichment program, Taj turned to *A Different World* to help ease her transition into the university. In the TV show, Hillman students' attempts at balancing their social lives with their academic responsibilities served as cautionary tales for her while also offering cultural guidance on navigating campus life, information that Taj did not have access to from other sources like siblings or parents:

> I remember every day I would have to take an hour nap and I would watch *A Different World*. I would just go on YouTube and watch different episodes. And that was cool because this is the world I'm about to embark in and *it is a different world* [italics added]. My family can't really relate when I'm saying I have twenty-page papers due. "Oh, baby, you got it." I'm like, "No I don't." You don't understand. It was cool because on *A Different World*, niggas were really not going to graduate on that TV show. It was good to see what mistakes they made fooling around too much. That was a note to me, maybe you shouldn't do too much.

The meaning of *A Different World* for Taj confirms Louise Spence's observation that audiences turn to television for respite in "a world that does not always meet our needs; the flickering iridescence of the television can be an active site in which our dreams impinge on the isolation and fragmentation of our daily life."[16] For Taj, the digital rebooting of *A Different World* supplemented the encouragement she received from family members, who, while well-intentioned, were unable to relate to her on the challenges of academia.

Rebooting Normative Social Strategies for Black Millennial Students

One of the cultural promises inherent in 1990s Black television is the belief that a college degree leads to a well-paying career and the ability to enjoy the spoils associated with an upper-middle-class lifestyle. Bambi Haggins argues that shows like *Living Single*, which focus on the work and love lives of young Black urban professionals, function as "colorized fables of social instruction" that call for a "commitment to a decidedly middle-class pursuit of happiness."[17] *Living Single*, and to a lesser extent *Martin*, belongs in the category of 1990s film and television reflecting the sensibilities of a then-emerging segment of the Black middle class: college-educated, childless, never married, Black professionals who either lived alone or cohabited with their romantic partner, popularly termed BUPPIEs during the 1990s. Inspired by the 1997 film of the same name, Lynda Dickson and Kris Marsh dubbed this demographic the *Love Jones* cohort.[18] Cultural production highlighting the *Love Jones* cohort advanced a vision of Black excellence that was predicated on acquiring well-paying jobs and establishing romantic relationships with other Black professionals.[19] As some of the primary media focusing on the lives of Black young adults in their twenties, 1990s Black situation comedies were critical texts for audiences to imagine their post-college work and social lives.

Pursuing careers with high levels of occupational prestige was integral to my interviewees' visions of their post-college lives. Representations of Black women in such occupations as college professors, magazine publishers, or attorneys had particular resonance for female audiences in the study, contributing to a sense of optimism that they could follow in their favorite characters' footsteps. For example, Tonya declares that reruns of *Living Single* project "a picture of success" for her. While audiences were inspired by characters who were established in their careers, like *Living*

Figure 12.1. Kyle (T.C. Carson) defends his locks in *Living Single*. *Source*: Fox. Screen capture by the author.

Single's Khadijah James and Maxine Shaw, they had strong affinities for younger characters who aspired to similar success:

PJ: If you could think of a TV show character that you relate to, who would that be?

MARISA: I kind of like Moesha, Brandy's character. She's really driven and she cares about her friends and family . . . I also didn't feel like I got to see a lot of other Black women on TV that were around my own age when I was a lot younger, so when I first saw that show, that was refreshing to me.

In this example, Marisa's statement about television's lack of young ambitious Black female protagonists confirms Mia L. Mask's observation that "were it not for sitcoms like *Living Single* and *Moesha*—or films like *The Wood* and *The Best Man*—a large group of young Black folks are completely written out of the (sub)urban worlds depicted in *American Beauty, Dawson, Buffy, Friends*, and *Felicity*."[20] In programs like *Moesha* and *Living Single*, Black audiences found characters whose drives, work ethic, and professional ambitions matched their own:

> TAJ: I fucking loved *Moesha* because Moesha wanted to be a journalist and she wanted to work for *Vibe* [magazine]. I was like "Oh my god that's what I want to do." I wanted to be Moesha . . . [1990s Black TV] just did a really good job of setting up scenarios we could plug ourselves into.

Like Tonya and Marisa, Taj describes an intimacy with her favorite characters, which speaks to television's ability to "reduce the distance between itself and its viewers, weaving a space/time continuum" in which viewers and characters "share a common universe of experience."[21]

Along with respect for the professional careers of their favorite characters, audiences also coveted the autonomy and financial independence that characters enjoyed because of their professions. *Fresh Prince*'s Philip Banks inspired Caron to study law because

> [Philip] seemed to have a very easy lifestyle. You saw him in the house quite a lot. His kids were a bit spoiled but other than that he didn't seem to work too hard. And he had loads of money and he seemed to, sometimes, be connected to the Black community. He made it look easy.

Although he was an attorney at an esteemed law firm, most scenes and storylines involving Philip Banks took place in the family's Bel-Air mansion. Like his predecessors, *Cosby's* Dr. Cliff and Claire Huxtable, Banks is rarely seen practicing his profession. His professional success allows him to set his own schedule and be mostly housebound where he is able to attend to family issues. As a result, the pressure and stress associated with being an attorney were often invisible to young viewers like Caron, which leads to the romanticization of practicing law and only focuses on the pecuniary benefits of becoming a lawyer or the economic and prestige status associated with being an elite lawyer. As evident in Caron's reference to the Bankses' affluence, audiences used the characters as examples of the kinds of material success to which they aspired. The Banks family offer a cultural model from which audiences build their visions of the Dream.

The students I interviewed saw upward social mobility as tied to heteronormative coupling with partners who had similar educational backgrounds and career aspirations. Programs like *Living Single* and *Martin* offered some of the first television representations of urban, unmarried Black professionals. While this set of sitcom characters often referenced getting married and having children as eventual goals, they regularly celebrated the autonomy they enjoyed being unmarried and childless. Thus, students aspired to similar freedom in their romantic relationships.

> MONICA: On *Martin*, they both worked. So [it gave me an] understanding [of] a young couple working [with] no kids. They [were] always having fun, always going places, always doing something, always taking trips, buying things for themselves. So, me understanding, "Ok, that's the time in my life, I looked up to those shows and those characters, understanding that's what they did."

Here, Monica draws on *Martin* to envision a comfortable future wherein she has considerable disposable income. By partnering with someone of similar educational and socioeconomic status, Monica imagines reproducing a lifestyle where going on vacation or buying gifts does not produce financial strain.

Echoing Monica's sentiments, Randall aspires to a relationship similar to Martin and Gina's, comparing their financial freedom to that of *Good Times*' James and Florida Evans:

> Martin and Gina would actually go out places together. They would hang out in social environments together. They would hang out with friends together. They would invite people over. In *Good Times*, it was always some type of struggle. If they were hanging out it was always at home because they couldn't afford to go anyplace else.

The 1990s saw the rise of situation comedies focused on the lives of twenty-somethings, with the city, not suburbia, serving as the primary site where they pursued the Dream. With this shift emerged a new relationship between characters and their domestic spaces. Whereas Dennis and Caron identified Philip Banks's constant presence at home as signifying upper-middle-class success, for Monica and Randall, Martin and Gina's professional achievement was signified by their ability to live a vibrant life outside their apartments. *Martin*'s narratives often revolved around the couple going to nightclubs, attending concerts, and going on vacations with their friends. These two seemingly diametric tendencies work in concert with each other to create a contradictory, yet meaningful, narrative for Black Millennial audiences regarding their expectations as they grow older. Philip and Vivian Banks represent the desired destination for Martin and Gina, and other unmarried Black professionals, moving from heterosexual cohabitation to marriage, from an apartment to a mansion, and from being childless to becoming parents.

For these audiences, 1990s Black situation comedies reinforced the value of tight-knit friend groups by celebrating the "collective effort of those moving forward as a group, as family, striving together to seize a piece of the Dream."[22] The students I interviewed were particularly inspired by the relationships between *Living Single*'s lead characters, hoping to share similar intimacy with their friends:

> ROBIN: I used to wonder what would happen when I grew up and started living by myself. Would I have friends like this? Would it be like a community type of thing? Or is it going to be like a hi and bye type of thing?

Similarly, Tonya pointed to *Living Single* as providing the model for the kinds of relationships she hoped to enjoy as an adult:

> Watching *Living Single*, I tell some of my friends [that] we're going to move to New York and we're going to get a brownstone in Brooklyn. And that's going to be us. I tell them that all the time. I look forward to getting older and being a real grown adult woman, [a] Black woman and having grown adult Black woman friends.

Tonya and Robin's ability to imagine themselves having similar relationships with other Black women echoes some of the womanist resonances that Lisa Guerrero identifies in *Living Single*.[23]

Alice Walker describes womanist communities as consisting of women who "appreciate and prefer women's culture . . . and women's strength" and are "committed to survival and wholeness of entire people, male and female."[24] Tuning to the womanist frequencies in *Living Single* highlights the value of tight-knit communities that stand in "for the larger societal support that most black women lack in both literal and ideological terms."[25] The shows depict a "community of Black women friends" serving as "a surrogate family formation that assuages societal anxieties over the transgressive potential of the Black body."[26] Audiences draw direct comparisons with representations of Black women in dramatic programs featuring Black women in lead roles like *Scandal* (2012–2018, ABC) and *How to Get Away with Murder* (2014–2020, ABC), where the Black cisgender woman protagonists have little contact with other Black women despite living in cities with large Black populations. In contrast, Tonya prefers 1990s Black situation comedies because "You got to see Black women have Black women best friends." Recognizing that upwardly mobile Black people often inhabit spaces where they are the minority and are subject to various forms of microaggressions, audiences saw maintaining connections with other Black people as vital to their vision of "tasting the sweet life."[27]

Reading the Breaks

Critics often condemn 1990s Black situation comedies for depicting Black upward mobility absent of institutional and systemic obstacles or critiques of them.[28] Despite acknowledging 1990s Black situation comedies' immense popularity among her undergraduate students, Mary Beltrán finds the programs to be problematic texts for examining non-white media representations in her media courses. She writes,

> The 1990s programming that today's college students grew up on proves a complicated case in point. How to raise consciousness regarding patterns of representation that include the common invisibility and denigration of ethnic minorities, *as well as* the whitewashing of non-white histories and perspectives even while casting non-whites in more professional and "positive" roles?[29]

For Beltrán, the visibility of upper-middle-class African Americans in 1990s network television obfuscates the percentage of Black people who were living in poverty at the time. For this reason, Beltrán hesitates to label such programs as "Black," arguing that "a lack of contextual framework within the narratives themselves" leaves "these images mere positive caricatures, fantasies with fantasy storylines."[30]

As evident in the students' affinity for the programs' representations of Black professionals in my research, Beltrán's concerns are warranted. However, her contention does not account for the racial competences that Black audiences bring when they watch such programming.[31] Black audiences draw on their racialized experiences to fill in the gaps related to systemic racism that are often absent in the sitcom's overt narratives. As Tonya expresses, characters in 1990s Black sitcoms "didn't really have to say I'm Black." Instead, they were "just put in spaces and just let the Blackness be." As a result, for Tonya the programs "read as Black no matter how you put it." The shows' resonance with Black viewers like Tonya was not reliant on heavy-handed approaches to representing racial oppression. In fact, Tonya's statement reveals the pleasure that Black audiences derive from seemingly banal representations of Blackness, particularly those that reject framing one's Blackness solely as a problem. Yet for Black viewers, the material realities of Blackness are ever present, even when viewing episodes that are not explicitly about race. Thus, it would be difficult to dismiss Black young adults' ability to imagine their futures through the 1990s situation comedies as mere fantasy.

Instead, the programs engender what Lauren Berlant terms as a cruel optimism, "a relation of attachment to compromised conditions of possibility whose realization is discovered to be . . . *too* possible."[32] As a result, the Black Millennial audiences I interviewed sample 1990s Black television to foreshadow the potential challenges and dilemmas that await them as young Black professionals. They tune in to how the programs advance "a collective autobiographical narrative about the traumas of integration in a post-civil rights era."[33] Situation comedies like *Living Single* and *Martin* and films like *Strictly Business* (1991, Warner Bros.) and *Boomerang* (1992, Paramount) constructed corporate America as a space that offered Black people great opportunities for upward mobility. As Taj puts it, tongue in cheek, "We're like post-civil rights, post-1964. We got all of our rights. We can be in corporate America. We're fucking with it." Black professionals in these television programs and films were often warned to guard against compromising their integrity and sacrificing their racial sense of self in their attempts to advance within white corporate structures. Highlighting the forms of oppression and discrimination specific to their aspiration for upper-middle-class status, audiences develop tempered expectations for the future, reflecting their understanding of Black people's tenuous access to the Dream.

The students I worked with point to "very special episodes," or what one participant dubs as "PSA episodes," as explicitly addressing the racialized challenges associated with upward mobility. The very special episode breaks a situation comedy's narrative flow by confronting a social issue and using an unexpected dramatic tone. Rhonda Wilcox observes that television series often deploy the very special episode as a way to "claim redeeming social value by focusing episodes on unmediated presentations of social topics such as AIDS or alcoholism."[34] Hollis Griffin argues that very special episodes related to race disrupt the sitcom's often vacuous treatment of Blackness by emphasizing "the structural inequalities that are often occluded by racial difference's representation for profit: workplace inequality, unequal access to legal protection, unfair treatment in consumer settings."[35] Black millennial audiences work with these breaks in the programs' narratives to complicate their visions of the future and trouble the notion that Black people have unfettered access to the Dream. To this end, for Black audiences, very special episodes that explicitly deal with issues of race can briefly capture "what it feels like to live constantly exposed to racially organized and distributed vulnerability and risk."[36] Considering that the majority of sitcom episodes approach race relations in saccharine terms, the "very special episode" brings to the fore that which operates in the background of such representations—Black people are under the perpetual threat of harm, often inflicted by the very institutions that claim to support and protect them.

When referencing how 1990s Black situation comedies addressed the intersection of class and race, my interviewees pointed to an episode from *Fresh Prince*'s first season, "Mistaken Identity." The primary narrative for "Mistaken Identity," which first aired on October 15, 1990, focuses on racial profiling and "driving while Black." In the episode,

Figure 12.2. Will (Will Smith) and Carlton (Alfonso Ribeiro) behind bars in *The Fresh Prince of Bel-Air*. *Source*: NBC. Screen capture by the author.

Philip and Vivian plan to spend the weekend in Palm Springs with Philip's white law partner Henry Furth and his wife, Margaret. The Furths ask Carlton and Will to drive their Mercedes to Palm Springs. On the way, a police officer pulls over Will and Carlton, suspecting that they stole the car. While the boys are detained, Vivian storms into the precinct and angrily demands the boys' release. Rejecting Vivian's demands, the deputy also dismisses Philip's attempts to calmly explain the officer's error. Fed up with his family's mistreatment, Philip launches a legal salvo at the officer:

> When you got this alleged confession from these two young men did they have a lawyer present? No, because I'm their lawyer. Did you notify their parents? No, because we're their parents. So, officer don't tell us to wait. Don't tell us to sit down. Open that damn cell and let those two boys out of there or I'm going to tie this place up in so much litigation that your grandchildren are going to need lawyers.[37]

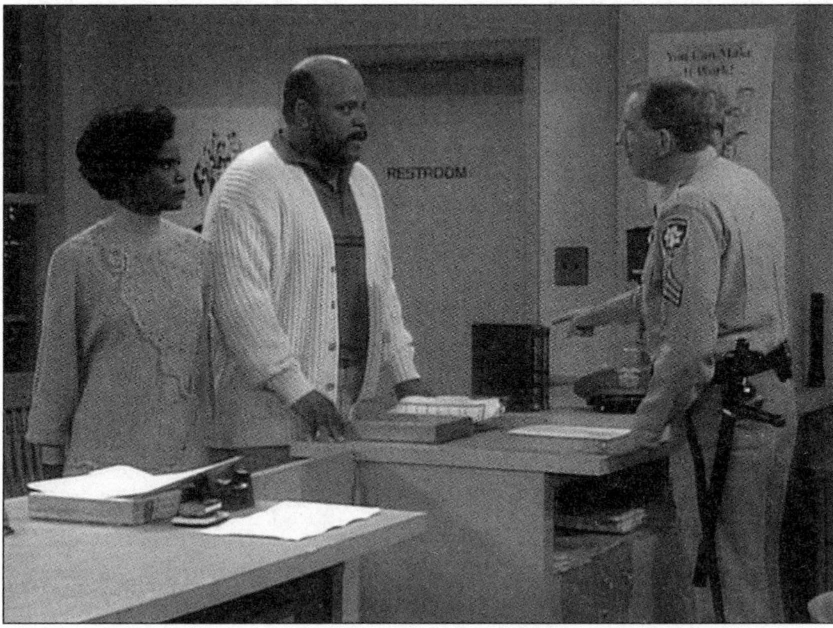

Figure 12.3. Uncle Phil (James Avery) and Aunt Viv (Janet Hubert-Whitten) talk to the police in *The Fresh Prince of Bel-Air*. *Source*: NBC. Screen capture by the author.

For Corey, a twenty-one-year-old dance and performance studies major, "Mistaken Identity" represented one of the "moments when we could see the reality of life." Corey was impressed by the Bankses' ability to speak back to law enforcement:

> Aunt Viv and Uncle Phil came up there and basically shut it down. It was like, yes, that's what I want to see. I want to see my Black people shutting it down. No, you will not wrongfully arrest my children. I know the law. I am a judge.

The Bankses' ability to "shut it down," in this case to voice their displeasure with their children's incarceration, is enabled by the considerable social capital they possess as an attorney and professor, respectively. Corey's move from third- to first-person perspective signals a form of embodiment where he imagines himself taking up a subject position where he could offer similar resistance if he or his family members were falsely accused.

However, the episode also demonstrates the limitations of class privilege when it is associated with Black bodies. Being the children of Black professionals does not protect Carlton and Will from police mistreatment. The access they have to white spaces makes them ironically and uniquely vulnerable to state-sanctioned violence. As Ann Ducille observes, "Blackness is so deeply inscribed as low-Other in the dominant consciousness that, in the wrong place at the wrong time, the trappings of wealth and privilege—a luxury automobile, let's say—can get you killed."[38] The officers' disbelief that Philip is Furth's law partner illustrates how Black professionals are excluded from the middle class through an explicit devaluing of their knowledge and perspectives.[39] Despite their accomplishments, Black professionals often wield little institutional power. For all of the Bankses' threats, Will and Carlton are only released after Furth arrives and confirms that the car was not stolen.

Whereas Corey felt emboldened by watching the Banks defend their children from law enforcement malfeasance, for Christopher, an eighteen-year-old media studies major, the scene revealed some of the traumas associated with assimilation and upward ascent:

> They were pulled over and Carlton was oblivious to the fact that they were pulled over because they were Black, driving a nice car at night in the wrong neighborhood. He didn't want to believe that. He asked his father towards the end of the episode, "If you saw a car driving slow wouldn't you stop it?" His father said, "I asked myself the same thing the first time I got pulled over." And [in] the jail scene, Carlton's father came in to get the kids out but it wasn't really [his father] that did it. It was the white friend who said "Let 'em go." [The officer] just let them all go because the white guy said it.

"Mistaken Identity" diverges from the situation comedy's penchant for resolution by closing with the exchange between Philip and Carlton described above. The episode does not treat racial profiling as an isolated occurrence but instead gestures to the quotidian nature of police harassment in the lives of Black people, including those with the financial means and social status of a successful attorney or college professor. In this sense, the episode serves as a commentary on the potential perils of upward mobility for Black people, suggesting that Carlton's affluence failed to protect him from the pervasive nature of racism in the lives of most Black people.

Conclusion

Throughout this chapter, I examined how Black Millennials return to Black situation comedies from the 1990s as pedagogical texts for imagining future versions of themselves. To this end, the perpetual recycling of 1990s Black situation comedies for my study's audiences highlights how "nostalgia is not simply a concept that suggests a longed-for past; it is a gateway to future experience."[40] Thus, the shows, as one student stated, provided futures that young Black viewers could "plug" themselves into. In returning to the media of the 1990s, Black Millennials read the era as one teeming with possibility for Black people, one where the mythical American Dream was within Black people's grasp. While my interviews and focus groups revealed that the 1990s Black situation comedies are clearly generative texts through which Black Millennials can envision the future, they are not without their limits and challenges.

As I have addressed in my previous work, Black Millennials' affinity for 1990s Black situation comedies should not be read as a wholesale embrace of the shows.[41] In inheriting television shows from the past, Black Millennials are able to reject or accept elements of the shows, assessing the relative utility of the themes and ideas advanced in them. As Jacques Derrida reminds us, "Inheritance implies decision, responsibility, response and, consequently, critical selection. There is always a choice, whether one likes it or not, whether it is or isn't conscious."[42] If, as my study evinces, we are to understand 1990s Black situation comedies as offering nostalgic prescriptions for upward mobility, we must also recognize that such prescriptions often come with an embrace of Black respectability politics. Sherronda J. Brown asserts that Black viewers who grew up watching the shows during their original network television runs did so without the knowledge of "how Black Respectability and elitism would never deliver us from the hellmouth of capitalism and the nation-state's racial violence."[43] Yet younger Black audiences may view the shows with a more critical eye, possessing language that allows them to identify the various forms of oppression that are present in the racial nostalgia produced by the shows. While there are some aspects of their nostalgia for the 1990s that is rose tinted, my study's audiences are clearly facile in reading the shows in nuanced and layered ways, taking what they need from the past as source material for dreaming a better future.

Discussion Questions

1. How has nostalgia for the 1990s shown up in other forms of Black media?
2. Can you think of any cultural object or style that makes you nostalgic for an era that you did not live through? This could be a television show, a movie, a style of clothing (like bell bottoms), or song. What does the object make you nostalgic for? What ideas do you associate with that particular object? What might be missing in your nostalgia for that era?

NOTES

1 Simon Reynolds, *Retromania: Pop Culture's Addiction to Its Own Past* (Faber & Faber, 2011), xii.

2 Simon Reynolds, "Perils of Loving Old Records Too Much," *New York Times*, December 5, 1993.

3 Nikki Ndukwe, "Top 5 Black TV Shows That Will Give You 90s Nostalgia," *www.top5.com*, February 24, 2018, www.top5.com.

4 Badia Ahad-Legardy, *Afro-Nostalgia: Feeling Good in Contemporary Black Culture* (University of Illinois Press, 2021).

5 JoEllen Fisherkeller, *Identity Work and Television: Young Adolescents Learning Within Local and Mediated Cultures* (University of California Press, 1995), 261.

6 Fisherkeller, *Identity Work and Television*, 251.

7 Tara J. Yosso, "Whose Culture Has Capital?: A Critical Race Theory Discussion of Community Cultural Wealth," *Race Ethnicity and Education* 8, no. 1 (2005): 77, https://doi.org/10.1080/1361332052000341006.

8 Jacqueline Bobo, *Black Women as Cultural Readers* (Columbia University Press, 1995); Stuart Hall, "Encoding/Decoding," in *Media Studies: A Reader*, 2nd ed., ed. Paul Marris and Sue Thornham (New York University Press, 2000), 51–61.

9 Leslie B. Inniss and Joe R. Feagin, "The Cosby Show: The View from the Black Middle Class," *Journal of Black Studies* 25, no. 6 (July 1995): 692–711, www.jstor.org/stable/2784760.

10 Bambi L. Haggins, "There's No Place like Home: The American Dream, African-American Identity, and the Situation Comedy," *Velvet Light Trap* 43 (1999): 30.

11 Haggins, "There's No Place like Home," 11.
12 Herman Gray, *Watching Race: Television and the Struggle for Blackness* (University of Minnesota Press, 1995).
13 Gray, *Watching Race*, 87; Darnell M. Hunt, "Making Sense of Blackness on Television," in *Channeling Blackness: Studies on Television and Race in America*, ed. Darnell M Hunt (Oxford University Press, 2005), 1–24.
14 Herman Gray, "Television, Black Americans and the American Dream," *Critical Studies in Media Communication* 6, no. 4 (1989): 382, https://doi.org/10.1080/15295038909366763.
15 Andrea Adelson, "How Television Is Cultivating New Ways of Looking at Blacks," *New York Times*, February 7, 1991; Eric Alterman, "Black Universities: In Demand and in Trouble," *New York Times*, November 5, 1989; Paula Whatley Matabane and Bishetta D. Merritt, "Media Use, Gender, and African American College Attendance: The Cosby Effect," *Howard Journal of Communications* 25, no. 4 (2014): 452–71, http://dx.doi.org/10.1080/10646175.2014.956549.
16 Louise Spence, *Watching Daytime Soap Operas: The Power of Pleasure* (Wesleyan University Press, 2005).
17 Haggins, "There's No Place Like Home," 34.
18 Lynda Dickson and Kris Marsh, "The Love Jones Cohort: A New Face of the Black Middle Class?," *Black Women, Gender, and Families* 2, no. 1 (Spring 2008): 84–105, www.jstor.org/stable/10.5406/blacwomegendfami.2.1.0084.
19 Mia L. Mask, "Buppy Love in an Urban World," *Cineaste* 25, no. 2 (2000): 41–45, www.jstor.org/stable/41689232.
20 Mask, "Buppy Love in an Urban World," 45.
21 Farrel Corcoran, "Television as Ideological Apparatus: The Power and the Pleasure," *Critical Studies in Media Communication* 1, no. 2 (1984): 137, https://doi.org/10.1080/15295038409360025.
22 Haggins, "There's No Place Like Home," 34.
23 Lisa A. Guerrero, "Single Black Female: Representing the Modern Black Woman in Living Single," in *African Americans on Television: Race-ing for Ratings*, ed. David Leonard and Lisa A Guerrero (Praeger, 2013), 177–90.
24 Alice Walker, *In Search of Our Mother's Gardens: Womanist Prose* (Harcourt, 1983), xi.
25 Walker, *In Search of Our Mother's Gardens*, 184.
26 Walker, *In Search of Our Mother's Gardens*, 185.
27 Mask, "Buppy Live in an Urban World," 41.
28 Christine Acham, "The Cosby Show: Representing Race," in *How to Watch Television*, ed. Ethan Thompson and Jason Mittell (New York University Press, 2013), 103–11; Mary Beltrán, "How Would Fresh Prince Do It? Teaching Diversity to Late '80s Babies," *Flow Journal* (February 23, 2007), http://flowtv.org; Inniss and Feagin, "The Cosby Show"; Zeus Leonardo, *Race Frameworks: A Multidimensional Theory of Racism and Education* (Teachers College Press, 2013); David Marriott, "15 Black Cultural Studies," *Year's Work in Critical and Cultural Theory* 15, no. 1

(2007): 277–86, https://doi.org/10.1093/ywcct/mbm015; Fredrick L. McKissack Jr., "The Problem with Black TV," *The Progressive* 61, no. 2 (February 1997): 38–40; Brennan Williams and Gazelle Emani, "How to Make It as a Black Sitcom: Be Careful How You Talk about Race," *Huffington Post*, October 21, 2014, www.huffingtonpost.com/.

29 Beltrán, "How Would *Fresh Prince* Do It?"

30 Beltrán, "How Would *Fresh Prince* Do It?"

31 Bobo, *Black Women as Cultural Readers*.

32 Lauren Berlant, "Cruel Optimism: On Marx, Loss, and the Senses," *new formations* 63 (Winter 2007): 33, https://doi.org/10.1215/9780822394716-002. Italics in original.

33 Kristal Brent Zook, *Color by Fox: The Fox Network and the Revolution in Black Television* (Oxford University Press, 1999), 15.

34 Rhonda V. Wilcox, "There Will Never Be a 'Very Special' *Buffy*: *Buffy* and the Monsters of Teen Life," *Journal of Popular Film and Television* 27, no. 2 (1999): 16, https://doi.org/10.1080/01956059909602800.

35 Hollis Griffin, "Never, Sometimes, Always: The Multiple Temporalities of 'Post-Race' Discourse in Convergence Television Narrative," *Popular Communication: The International Journal of Media and Culture* 9 (2011): 245, https://doi.org/10.1080/15405702.2011.605312.

36 Herman Gray, "The Feel of Life: Resonance, Race, and Representation," *International Journal of Communication* 9 (2015): 1110.

37 *The Fresh Prince of Bel-Air*, season 1, episode 6, "Mistaken Identity," written by Benny Medina, Jeff Pollack, and Andy Borowitz, directed by Jeff Melman, aired October 15, 1990, on NBC.

38 Ann Ducille, "The Colour of Class: Classifying Race in the Popular Imagination," *Social Identities* 7, no. 3 (2001): 414, https://doi.org/10.1080/13504630120087244.

39 Nicola Rollock et al., "The Public Identities of the Black Middle Classes: Managing Race in Public Spaces," *Sociology* 45, no. 6 (2011): 1078–93, https://doi.org/10.1177/0038038511416167.

40 Ahad-Legardy, *Afro-Nostalgia*, 145.

41 Patrick Johnson, "It's a Man Thing, Gina: Watching Gender in *Martin*," *Communication, Culture & Critique* 14, no. 3 (September 2021): 422–37, https://doi.org/10.1093/ccc/tcab005.

42 Jacques Derrida and Bernard Stiegler, *Echographies of Television: Filmed Interviews* (Polity, 2002), 69.

43 Sherronda J. Brown, "Beloved Black Sitcoms and What We Can Learn from Nostalgia," *The Black Youth Project*, October 13, 2020, http://blackyouthproject.com.

ACKNOWLEDGMENTS

Working together with Isabel Molina-Guzmán to put a volume together has been a dream and goal—now accomplished. I've said it before, and I'll say it again: I have had the privilege and fortune of this long-term collaborative, nurturing, and intellectually provoking relationship with another scholar with whom I do not have to explain or justify theoretical, conceptual, and intersectional approaches. That is a gift I acknowledge.

I also thank the Institute of Communications Research (ICR) and the Department of Latina/Latino Studies (LLS), where I remain on faculty. Students at ICR continue to inspire me and push me to stay abreast of the latest research. I want to single out ICR doctoral student Stephanie Pérez, who not only assisted me with this project but also with whom I have many generative discussions. Stephanie will be teaching the Latinx and the Media course at the Department of Latina/Latino Studies, thus rounding out a circle of influence from ICR to LLS.

My work and productivity are happily enabled and energized by my lovely and loving supportive family.

—Angharad N. Valdivia

When I first met Professor Angharad N. Valdivia as an undergraduate student at Penn State, I never in my wildest dreams imagined I would be co-editing a collection with her. When I first met Professor Valdivia, I did not know what graduate school was, much less what it meant to be a professor. Without her mentorship and friendship and our intellectual collaborations and shared experiences, this edited collection would never have come to be.

Luckily for us an international and interdisciplinary group of scholars were energized by our ideas and vision for this collection. And I am filled with gratitude for them, their intellectual curiosity, and their professional patience with the five-year process (yes, this project began during the pandemic) to get this book published. Thankfully Eric Zinner, Furqan Sayeed, and Jonathan Gray at NYU Press believed in the importance of this book from its inception, and they have also patiently waited for it to be completed. I am particularly grateful for the research assistance of Stephanie Perez, who literally helped us get this edited collection across the finish lin.

I also would like to express my gratitude to Dean Venetria Patton at Illinois's College of Liberal Arts & Science for allowing me as an academic administrator to go on sabbatical, which finally created the space for this collection to be completed. An extra note of thanks goes to the amazing leadership team and staff at LAS's Student Affairs Staff for providing me with the professional space to leave them for eight months and welcoming me back when I completed my sabbatical.

Finally, I am continually thankful for my close-knit family and chosen family. It is because of our shared dream for a more socially just future that I research, write, and teach.

— Isabel Molina-Guzmán

INDEX

ABOUT THE AUTHORS

SONYA M. ALEMÁN is Full Professor in the Race, Ethnicity, Gender, and Sexuality Studies Department and Mexican American Studies Program at the University of Texas, San Antonio. She is published in *Critical Studies in Media Communication*, *Frontiers: A Journal of Women's Studies*, *Review of Research in Education*, *Feminist Media Studies*, *Race Ethnicity and Education*, and *International Journal of Qualitative Studies in Education*.

JILLIAN BÁEZ is Full Professor in the department of Africana, Puerto Rican, and Latino Studies at Hunter College, City University of New York. She is the author of *In Search of Belonging: Latinas, Media, and Citizenship*, recipient of the National Communication Association's Bonnie Ritter Award for Outstanding Feminist Book. She has published in *Centro: Journal of the Center for Puerto Rican Studies*, *Chicana/Latina Studies*, *Feminist Media Studies*, *Critical Studies in Media Communication*, and *Communication, Culture & Critique*.

RHIANNON BETTIVIA is Assistant Professor of Library and Information Science at Simmons University. Her work has been published in journals such as the *International Journal of Digital Curation* and *Digital Humanities Quarterly* and the proceedings of ASIS&T, iConference, and the International Conference on Digital Preservation. Her recent chapter with Elizabeth Stainforth on dynamics of scale, mass heritage digitization, and (supra)nationalist culture recently appeared in *Politics of Scale: New Directions in Critical Heritage Studies*. She received her PhD from the University of Illinois.

ZHUI NING CHANG is a Malaysian doctoral student and CHASE scholar at Birkbeck, University of London. Their research examines race and decolonization in twenty-first-century speculative fiction from Southeast Asia and its diasporas. In the creative sphere, Zhui

Ning's translations, essays, and reviews have been published with PEN Malaysia, *This Is Southeast Asia, Pandan Weekly, Strange Horizons, The BSFA Review*, and more. They are the editor-in-chief at *khōréō*, a Hugo-nominated and Ignyte-winning magazine for diasporic and immigrant speculative fiction, and a coeditor of the anthology *Best of Malaysian Short Fiction in English 2010–2020*. Zhui Ning holds a MA in Text and Performance from Birkbeck and the Royal Academy of Dramatic Art, and a BA (Hons) in Liberal Arts with a major in Comparative Literature from King's College London.

Aymar Jean Christian is the Margaret Walker Alexander Professor of Communications Studies at Northwestern University and Director of the Media and Data Equity Lab. He is the author of *Open TV: Innovation Beyond Hollywood and the Rise of Web Television*.

Esteban del Río is Professor of Communication at the University of San Diego. He serves as Director of the Frances G. Harpst Center for Catholic Thought and Culture. His research appears in the *Journal of Communication Inquiry, Communication Culture Critique, Participations: International Journal of Audience Research, Communication Yearbook, Metropolitan Universities Journal*, and the *Routledge Companion to Latina/o Media*. His courses examine media, culture and conflict, and his research contributes primarily to US Latino media studies, problematizing the cultural, economic, and political formation of Latinidad.

Sophie Eeken studied issues on contemporary television in her Masters in Television and Cross-Media Culture at the University of Amsterdam and subsequently worked there as a research assistant.

Tina M. Harris (University of Kentucky, PhD) is the Manship-Maynard Endowed Chair of Race, Media, and Cultural Literacy in the Manship School of Mass Communication at Louisiana State University and incoming President of the National Communication Association. Her primary research interest is interracial communication, with specific foci on critical communication pedagogy, race and identity, diversity and media representations, racial social justice, mentoring, and racial reconciliation, among others. She is a well-published and very active senior scholar with many accolades and awards for her long history of making valuable contributions to the discipline, university, and department for her teaching, research, and service. She received her PhD from the University of Kentucky.

JOKE HERMES is Professor of Inclusion and the Creative Industries at the ARC Knowledge Centre of Inholland University of Applied Sciences. She is also affiliated with the Media Studies department of the University of Amsterdam and is one of the three founding editors of the *European Journal of Cultural Studies*. Her recent publications include *Cultural Citizenship and Popular Culture* and *The Pocketbook of Audience Research* (with Linda Kopitz).

PATRICK JOHNSON is Associate Professor of American Multicultural Studies at Sonoma State University. Dr. Johnson's research focuses on the residual circulation of past Black media and the connections between television and Black music cultures. He teaches courses on Black representations in television, music, and visual art. His scholarship has appeared in *Communication, Culture, and Critique* and *Women's Studies in Communication*. He has also coauthored chapters in the anthologies *Culturally Sustaining Pedagogy: Teaching and Learning for Justice in a Changing World* and *We Dare Say Love: Supporting African American Male Achievement*.

ISABEL MOLINA-GUZMÁN is a Professor of Communication and Latina/Latino Studies, Research Professor at the Institute of Communication Research at the University of Illinois Urbana-Champaign. She is an International Communication Association Fellow, coeditor of the journal *Feminist Media Studies*, and author of *Dangerous Curves: Latina Bodies in the Media* and *Latinas and Latinos on TV: Colorblind Comedy in the Post-Racial Network Era*.

KRISTIN C. MORAN is Professor of Communication at the University of San Diego and currently serves as the Associate Dean for Faculty in the College of Arts and Sciences. She is the author of *Listening to Latina/o Youth: Television Consumption Within Families*. She teaches courses in Media Studies and her current research focuses on the reception of Latino-themed and Spanish-language media in the United States.

Céline Morin is an Associate Professor of Media & Cultural Studies at the Paris Nanterre University specializing in media representations of gender relations and feminist movements.

Shyamala Parthasarathy is an Indian academic, with an MFA in Creative Writing from the University of British Columbia and an MA in English and Cultural Studies from McMaster University, Canada. Her primary research interests include writing studies, fan studies, children's literature, and performance studies. Currently freelancing as a content editor and provider, she writes primarily children's books and young adult fiction. Her current research project is the study of podfic—audio-fanfiction—involving the mapping of the genre, its technical production and distribution, and the fan-labor that goes into it. Her reviews of young adult fiction can be found on youngadulting.ca

Stephanie Melissa Pérez is a Guatemalan-American scholar of media studies in the Institute of Communications Research, University of Illinois. Her research encompasses spectral Latine/x girlhoods in popular media, affect and joy in quinceañeras, and the Latina ingenue as a transgressive trope in young adult fictional television. She has published in *Flow* journal, *Routledge Handbook of Ethnicity and Race in Communication*, and the *Smithsonian Voices* journal. She was a co-curator of the *Quinceañeras: Celebration, Joy, and Ethnic Pride* exhibit at the Spurlock Museum of World Cultures.

Meghan S. Sanders is a Professor in the Manship School of Mass Communication at Louisiana State University, and Associate Dean for Graduate Studies and Research. Her research examines the psychological effects of entertainment media as they pertain to cognition, emotion, and psychological and subjective well-being. She has presented her work at national and international conferences and has published in journals such as *Mass Communication and Society*, *Journal of Communication*, *Communication Theory*, and *Psychology of Popular Media Culture*, among others.

ANGHARAD N. VALDIVIA is Research Professor Emerita of Communications and Media at the Institute of Communications Research and of Latina/Latino Studies at the University of Illinois. In addition to other books on Latina/o Media Studies, her latest monograph is *The Gender of Latinidad: Uses and Abuses of Hybridity*. The seven-volume *Encyclopedia of International Media Studies* and *A Companion to Media Studies* illustrate Valdivia's engagement and mapping of the field of Media Studies. Valdivia is a Fellow of the International Communication Association and Distinguished Scholar of the National Communication Association. She is also a recipient of the Teresa Award for Feminist Studies in ICA.